software creativity 2.0

software creativity 2.0

by
Robert L. Glass

guest foreword by
Tom DeMarco

guest essay by
Dwayne Phillips

developer.* books
www.developerdotstar.com
atlanta, georgia

acknowledgments

I wish to thank...

- **Steve McConnell** (author of Code Complete and many other important contemporary books on software development) for his generous encouragement and feedback...
- **Dan Read** of developer.* for going above and beyond a publisher's traditional helpful role...
- **Linkoping University** in Sweden, where I was a visiting professor during much of the creation of the original version of this book, and Griffith University in Australia, where I was a visiting professor during much of its revision.

—*Robert L. Glass*

software creativity 2.0
©2006 developer.* Books,
Atlanta, Georgia.

This book was previously published in 1995 by Pearson Education, Inc. as *Software Creativity*.

New material has been added, but the material from the first edtion remains unchanged in *Software Creativity 2.0*.

This book can be made available to businesses and organizations at a special discount when ordered in large quantities. For more information, contact the publisher:

developer.* Books
150 Walker Street SW #10
Atlanta, GA 30313
books@developerdotstar.com

ISBN: 978-0-9772133-1-3
Library of Congress information available upon request.
Printed in the USA.

Quality is important to us. If you receive a defective or unsatisfactory book, please write to us at books@ developerdotstar.com.

To all the software people
trying to change the world.

"...because the people who are crazy enough to think they can change the world, are the ones who do...."

—Jack Kerouac

other Books By Robert L. Glass

Published by developer.* Books

Software Conflict 2.0: The Art and Science of Software Engineering, 2006

Published by Computing Trends

Software 2020, 1998

Software Folklore, 1991

Computing Shakeout, 1987

Computing Catastrophes, 1983

Software Soliloquies, 1981

The Second Coming: More Computing Projects Which Failed, with Sue DeNim, 1980

The Power of Peonage, 1979

Tales of Computing Folk: Hot Dogs and Mixed Nuts, 1978

The Universal Elixir, and other Computing Projects Which Failed, 1977

Published by Addison-Wesley/Prentice-Hall/Yourdon Press

Facts and Fallacies of Software Engineering, 2003

ComputingFailure.com, 2001

Computing Calamities, 1999

Software Runaways, 1998

An ISO 9000 Approach to Building Quality Software, with Osten Oskarsson, 1996

Software Creativity, 1995

Measuring and Motivating Maintenance Programmers, with Jerome B. Landsbaum, 1992

Building Quality Software, 1992

Software Conflict, 1991

Measuring Software Design Quality, with David N. Card, 1990

Software Communication Skills, 1988

Real-Time Software, 1984

Modern Programming Practice—a Report From Industry, 1982

Software Maintenance Guidebook, with Ronald A. Noiseux, 1981

Software Reliability Guidebook, 1979

Published by IEEE Computer Society Press

In the Beginning: Recollections of Software Pioneers, 1998

Table of contents

foreword

by TOM DEMARCO

The software industry has long harbored its own little Red State/Blue State divide, with authoritarians on one side and a kind of software libertarian on the other. One side makes a mantra of "discipline" and "control," while the other is chanting about "agility." This split personality has enormously complicated the subject of software process, with more people talking past each other than to each other. As with the blues and reds in politics, the loudest voices seem to gravitate to the extremes so that the middle ground is relatively unrepresented. Of course, it's in the middle ground between software authoritarian and software libertarian where all the good work gets done.

Bob Glass has done us all a great favor by becoming the champion of the middle ground. In *Software Creativity 2.0* he sets out a rational approach to combining the best of the two extremes and demonstrates an ethic in which the approach to development is made project-dependent rather than loudest-extremist-dependent.

Over dinner one night, my friend and colleague, Sheila Brady, who ran OS development projects at Apple during the 90s, offered a rather exasperated explanation of the hurdle that women have to leap in order to break into management: "The built-in model of management is Dad," she said. Our earliest experience of management is in the family where Dad is boss, she explained, so of course we tend to think of a manager as someone rather Dad-like. Such a manager is naturally authoritarian, since parent-kid dynamics tend to favor that tendency. The result can be an almost perfect example of alpha male. Women can make great managers, Sheila observed, but are never going look anything like alpha males.

Many of us who manage software organizations today have fathers who were themselves managers a generation ago. So our earliest idea of management is of Dad, the family head, while our more mature idea of management is at least somewhat shaped by Dad, the manager of whatever organization he led. The stories that Dad brought home from the office or the plant have stayed with us to this day and tend to suggest their lessons whenever they can in our work—whether they fit or not.

My own father, for example, was a foundry manager. His heroes were Taylor (Scientific Management) and Gilbreth (Motion Time Management). When he and I talk management, it's impossible to miss the red/blue divide right down the middle of our small family. For instance, he can become nearly apoplectic at the notion of an irreplaceable employee: "If I discovered I had an irreplace-able employee working for me, I'd fire him immediately." He earned his stripes in the Industrial Age, and I earned mine in the Information Age. And management in these two different eras has diverged into two largely incompatible directions.

But don't think for a minute that Information Age manage-ment has simply replaced Industrial Age management. There is a residue of industrial management thinking that resides deep in the firmware of the modern organization. It has caused us to seek after factory methods like a holy grail, to try to systematize the very systemization activities that we were using to transform our organizations. Most of all it has caused conflict. What should be a rational discussion of method is often lost in the pejoratives:

"You're a cowboy."
"And you're a control-freak."
"Hacker!"
"Fascist!"

To complicate things even further, the academic community has come down squarely on both sides. The empiricists and the cognitive psychology communities have made it increasingly clear that methods are trumped by talent: Some software developers are just incredibly good at what they do and others can't keep up no matter how they strive to by copy-catting the methods used by their more talented peers. At the same time, the formalists have been asserting that there is a single best way to develop software, one that is so systematic that it can be conclusively proved correct. It's so systematic, in fact, that you could build a factory around it.

Then there is the real world. And that's where Bob Glass is at his best. His exposition of *Software Creativity* is thoughtful, methodical, and persuasive. It is also very often creative, a demonstration in book invention of some of the very ideas he advocates for software invention. For example, keep your eye open for the first time he uses the word "trapezoidal"—there is about to be a lovely insight that comes at you from left field and leaves you charmed and richer for it.

Because the 21st century is one of globalization, radical change, and intense competition, we all know that creativity is more important than ever. The result has been a radical escalation of lip service paid to creativity. We talk a good game. It's hard to find a company today whose management isn't willing to give you a spiel about creativity and its huge importance. But that's often the end of it. I hope this book will help creativity in our industry to move at least a little beyond lip service.

—*Tom DeMarco*
Camden, Maine

preface to the
first edition

The title of this book is *Software Creativity*. It is written from a powerfully felt, personal perspective:

- That software construction is primarily a problem-solving activity
- That all problem-solving requires creativity
- That software problem-solving is deeply complex, perhaps more deeply complex than any other activity
- That, therefore, software problem-solving requires the ultimate in creativity

When I began the book, I had the wrong reasons for writing it. I was tired of, and angered by, the claims of many in the field that the solutions to the problems of software lay in discipline, formality, and quantitative reasoning. My 40 years of experience in constructing software problem solutions, and my 6 years in the academic world ruminating over the relationship between software's literature and that experience, suggested the opposite— that the solutions to the problems of software lay in flexibility, creativity, and qualitative reasoning. Oh, of course, for huge, many-person projects, discipline was a necessary evil; but still, brilliant people, not brilliant process, were the way to progress, I felt.

However, as I began work on the book, looking to other fields for material to bolster the creativity theme, I also began a personal odyssey, There was a reason, I began to see, for considering the possibility of discipline, formality, and quantitative reasoning. No matter how deep the need for creativity in a field, there was also always a need for a more formal framework to nurture and support that creativity.

That thought crept up in many sometimes-surprising places. In a book titled, meaningfully, *The Discipline of Curiosity* [Groen 1990], the author said "Science is not just curiosity and creativity; it is a disciplined form of it...It is the seemingly odd couple of discipline and curiosity that makes for scientific progress. The curiosity of creative minds, asking continuously How? And Why?, and the discipline to realize that science is part of the world, that it is shaping it."

Once again, from a book on problem-solving [Judson 1980] in which the author reports on a conversation with Murray "Gell-Mann," the discoverer of quarks: "Any art that's worth the name has some kind of discipline associated with it. Some kind of rule—maybe it's not the rule of a sonnet, or a symphony, or a classical painting—but even the most liberated contemporary art ... has some kind of rule. And the object is to get across what you're trying to get across, while sticking to the rules."

Yet again, in an interview with cellist Yo-Yo Ma [Shapiro 1991]: "Creativity ... is not a result of instinct. Rather it is an endless conflict between discipline and intuition. The discipline—the years of practice, the musical knowledge—informs the playing. But there is a point at which the musician must make a leap of faith..."

There it was, again and again. Science requires discipline as well as creativity. Art requires discipline as well as creativity. Music requires discipline as well as creativity. Obviously, and to my chagrin, software also requires both discipline and creativity!

My personal odyssey was nearly complete. I now understood why, in a world where creativity seemed essential to success, the notion of discipline kept being raised. But that brought about a new dilemma: Was there any point in writing this book at all?

I re-read the computing literature, seeking once again those portions that focused on discipline, formality, and quantitative reasoning. And once again, in spite of my odyssey, my anger rose. What I began to see is that the advocates of discipline and formality were making the same mistake that I had been making. They were assuming that formality was all that was needed, and that creativity was counterproductive, just as I had been assuming that creativity was all that was needed, and that formality was counterproductive.

Perhaps there was a reason for the book after all! Perhaps it would help those imbalanced as far to the right as I had been to the left to see that the truth in problem-solving must lie somewhere in between the extremes. Also, perhaps, for those not as biased as my "opponents" and I had been, it might help a little in structuring a vitally important topic in the field.

My powerfully felt personal perspective need not change. It did, however, need to expand—to include that "odd couple," that "endless conflict," the interaction between that essential component, creativity, and that other essential, discipline. My odyssey was, at last, complete.

My wish for you—my hope for you—is that you will share my odyssey through the pages of this book, and that you will be glad you made the trip.

—Robert L. Glass
Summer 1994

references

Groen 1990—*The Discipline of Curiosity,* Elsevier Science, 1990; Janny Groen; Eefke Smit; Juurd Eijsvoogel.

Judson 1980—*The Search for Solutions,* Holt, Reinhart and Winston, 1980; Horace Freeland Judson.

Shapiro 91—"Yo-Yo and Manny," *World Monitor,* Aug., 1991; Michael Shapiro.

preface to the second edition

A funny thing happened along the way in the history of this book.

When it was originally published, it was a dud in the market-place. There were few sales, there were few royalties, there was almost no response from the software book-buying public.

I was disappointed, but not disheartened. I had poured a lot of work into the research behind the writing of the book, and what I had learned in doing that was important to me. I am pleased with how much I grew intellectually as I put this book together. Among the several books I had written—and have written to this date— this is perhaps the one of which I am the most proud. It constitutes just the right blend, in my mind at least, of a readable writing style with an appropriate amount of scholarly research behind it.

So what's that funny thing I mentioned above, you may be asking? Gradually, in spite of that poor start, sales began to grow. People approached me at conferences, or via email, and told me how much they liked the book. More and more frequently. I began to sense that the book was growing a cult following. By the turn of the millennium, I realized that the rest of the software world was beginning to see in this book something like what I had seen.

The cult status grew. The few books the original publisher had in stock sold out. The price of used copies, now that the book was out of print and out of stock, began to grow. I sold my own spare copy, greedily, on Amazon.com for around $100! The price continued to escalate dramatically upwards. As I write this new preface, I pulled up the Amazon window, and saw that the price is now $1196! It's hard to believe that anything I've written could possibly be worth that amount! The drums were clearly beating for a new and enhanced version 2.0 of *Software Creativity*. So work began.

I brought the existing essays up to date (lots of things happen in the computing and software world in 10 years!). I added some new ones, to accommodate the changing of the times and tides.

I made sure I added material on the Agile approaches since they're so related to the notions of flexibility and creativity and qualitative reasoning that formed the beginning point of my odyssey (although I hasten to add that they may need to undergo some of the same odyssey I went through if they are ever to accommodate those notions of discipline and formality that marked the result of my odyssey).

I also added material on Open Source approaches, which may be one of the last bastions of the notion of fun as a motivator for building software.

The heart of this book, though, did not need updating. The odyssey I described in the Preface to the first edition remains as relevant as ever.

The funny thing that happened along the way to here was also a wonderful thing. It's time to thank all you cult followers for caring enough to take a downtrodden, out-of-print, and out-of-stock book, and making it into a high-demand book beyond my wildest dreams!

And to you new readers who are encountering Software Creativity for the first time, enjoy!

—Robert L. Glass
Summer 2006

why software creativity?

> "Creative thinking requires an attitude that allows you to search for ideas and manipulate your knowledge and experience. With this outlook, you try various approaches … often not getting anywhere. You use crazy, foolish, and impractical ideas as stepping stones to practical new ideas. You break the rules occasionally, and explore for ideas in unusual outside places."
>
> —*Roger von Oech*
> *A Whack on the Side of the Head,*
> Warner Books 1990

There's a fundamental conflict in the software world, sometimes taking on the attributes of a war.

On one side, managers search for ways to impose more discipline and control on software builders, and researchers advocate and sometimes seek to mandate formal methods for the same purpose.

On the other side, software builders quietly continue to build software pretty much the way they always have, with freewheeling methods and creative solutions.

"Breakthrough" methods come, linger awhile, and go away, having made little impact on our ability to build software.

Methodologies fragment into variants, programming languages come and go, CASE tools become shelfware, object orientation is forever "next year's goal." The attempts to simplify and routinize the construction of software largely fail, one by one.

What's wrong with this picture? Are we dealing with stubborn practitioners, so stuck in their ways that they are intolerant of all change? That seems to be the view of management and research.

Or are we dealing with ignorant managers and researchers, so caught up in the new that they fail to understand the old? That seems to be the view of practitioners.

The key issue underlying this conflict, I believe, is creativity. If there is little or no need for creativity in building software, then those managers and researchers are right in what they advocate—we can simplify and routinize the work of software. If, on the other hand, creativity is and always will be an essential part of software construction, then those practitioners are right—we will continue to need freewheeling methods and creative solutions. It is this whole collection of issues, standing on this foundation of software creativity, that I hope to address, and perhaps to resolve, in this book. That's why the book is called *Software Creativity*.

We'll explore these polar views, and what might be done about them, beginning in Part I of the book. The view will be a disaggregated one. Rather than tackle creativity as a whole, we'll look at it one facet at a time, examining the roles of such aspects as discipline, formal methods, optimizing solutions, quantitative reasoning, process, theory, and fun. Each of those topics, and a few more, will be addressed by a series of informal essays. Along the way, we'll see a definition or two of creativity, and even the results of a study of how many of software's tasks really are creative.

Then, in Part II, we'll move to a somewhat more formal, more how-to view of creativity. We'll take two areas of the computing field in which creativity is particularly important—creativity in the organization, and creativity in software technology—and examine the role of creativity in those areas in considerably more depth. And then, to give a more complete coverage of creativity in the computing field, we'll look at the subject from a historical point of view: Where and how did creativity come about? In each of those topics, we'll look at ways of making creativity happen. There are a baker's dozen techniques for doing that, and they will be described and discussed.

Lest we be blinded by a narrow and constrained view of creativity from only software's point of view, Part III will examine some things we've learned about creativity in other fields. We'll see some surprising answers to the question "Can computers and software help (non-computing) people become more creative?", for example.

Then Part IV will tat up the loose ends of the book.

That's the structured view of what lies ahead; but what about the emotional view? Where will the trip through this book take us?

My hope is that, as you read further into the book, you'll begin to see the role of creativity, and the conflict I spoke of at the beginning of this introduction, in an evolving light. I hope to drop an idea here, a clue there, that may prove useful to you as you move toward forming your own view of how important creativity is in software. My own travels through the source material for this book led me on an emotional and logical journey, one that left me in a far different place from where I started. Perhaps that will happen to you as well.

Along the way, I'll call on a few colleagues to help out. For example, we borrow from well-known software engineer P. J. Plauger his notion of "the falutin' index," a light-hearted way of measuring software projects far different from the more formal metrics we read about in the formal literature. Similarly, we rely on Bruce Blum of Johns Hopkins' Applied Physics Lab to help us explore the tension between fun and tedium on software projects, and Dwayne Phillips steers us toward exploring the fun inherent in a peculiar project. Dennis Galletta, a professor at Pitt, talks about creativity in strategic systems. The late Dan Couger of the University of Colorado (and director of its Center for Research in Creativity at Colorado Springs) contributes a host of ideas from his own books on software creativity. Penn State researcher Iris Vessey teams with me to conduct, and write about, studies of the nature of software tasks. It is something of a communal effort, this book.

software
creativity

of two minds: an exploration of software creativity

"The most creative human problem solvers have an unusual capacity to integrate the two modes of conscious functions of the two [brain] hemispheres, and move back and forth between the holistic and sequential, between intuition and logic, between the fuzzy field of a problem domain and a clear specific small segment of a field. Such people can be outstanding artists and scientists because they combine the strong attributes of both ... Leonardo da Vinci ... and Einstein."

—*Moshe F. Rubinstein*
Tools for Thinking and Problem-Solving,
Prentice-Hall 1986

contents of part I

introduction to part 1

There are several ways to approach the creation of a book on software creativity:

- You could take a frothy swipe at the topic, the "whack on the side of the head" view of creativity, with a lot of good advice about how to be more creative and lots of anecdotes about people who used the advice successfully.
- You could take a fairly serious, academic view of the topic, doing a lot of library research and spelling out everything we've ever learned in any discipline on the subject.
- You could take an informal view of the topic from the point of view of whether creativity is important to software.

This book makes a gesture at all three of these approaches, but really puts its heart into the latter one. In Part I we get to that heart of the matter. The essays that follow are largely an informal collection of thoughts about the importance of creativity in software.

Framing this issue, it seems to me, are several more well-known and already key issues in the software field:

- The role of discipline
- The role of formal methods
- The role of optimizing solutions
- The role of quantitative reasoning
- The role of process
- The role of theory
- The role of academe
- The role of fun

In my mind, every one of those issues is really an issue about creativity. To the extent that we are creative in building software, I believe:

- We break free of (at least some) discipline.
- We move from formal methods to less formal ones.
- We adapt to providing solutions that satisfy rather than optimize.
- We shift from quantitative to qualitative reasoning.
- We look at both process and product.
- We understand that sometimes good practice is ahead of good theory, and that industry knows some things that academe does not.
- And we have more fun in the doing!

It is in this spirit of dichotomy—that creativity means breaking free of traditional patterns—that I chose the words "of two minds" in the title for this Part of the book. Each of the titles that follow is expressed as a controversy: formal methods vs. heuristics, quantitative vs. qualitative reasoning, industry vs. academe. I believe we live in a world, as this book is written, that has placed heavy emphasis on the disciplined, formal approaches to building software. I want to say that there are not only alternatives to that contemporary conventional wisdom, but that there are good reasons for moving away from that wisdom and toward a more balanced view of the field.

There are as many questions as answers in this chapter. Is discipline always the right approach to use on software projects? Is computer science right in placing its emphasis so strongly on formal methods? Is it true that "you can't manage what you can't measure"? Is theory always ahead of practice? Must serious thinking replace fun in our field? While exploring answers to those questions, I encounter and raise others.

However, there are some definitive answers here as well. There are research findings from a study of the tasks of software: To what extent are they intellectual? Clerical? Creative? Some of these definitive answers may surprise you.

chapter 1
Discipline vs. Flexibility

Introduction to Chapter 1

"Science is not just curiosity and creativity; it is a disciplined form of it ... It is the seemingly odd couple of discipline and curiosity that makes for scientific progress. The curiosity of creative minds, asking continuously 'How?' and 'Why?' and the discipline to realize that science is part of the world, that it is shaping it."

—Janny Groen
The Discipline of Curiosity, Elsevier Science 1990;
Janny Groen, Eefke Smit, Juurd Eijsvoogel

I've struggled for some time during the writing of this book to find a good word to represent the opposite of "discipline." "Undisciplined" is the obvious candidate, but that word comes with a lot of negative baggage. And besides, I don't think anyone would advocate a total lack of discipline in building software. Each time I return to the subject, hoping to have gained some new insight, my well comes up dry yet again. What I want to do is distinguish between behavior that is channeled and controlled (disciplined behavior), and behavior that is freewheeling yet focused (creative behavior).

What I have come up with is the word "flexibility." Focusing on the obedience and control aspects of discipline, I have chosen flexibility as its opposite. My dictionary defines flexible as "able to bend easily without breaking; adaptable, able to be changed to suit circumstances."

I like the definition, but I'm less sure that it's an appropriate opposite to discipline. So I'm not happy with the choice, but I guess it will have to do. If you have come up with a better word, mentally insert it into the title of this section!

Anyhow, enough of word play. Why is a section about discipline and (...er...) flexibility in a book on software creativity? Because one of the oldest dichotomies of our profession has been precisely this difference: Should software be built by teams that are disciplined and factory-like, or by teams that are flexible and highly self-motivated?

In fact, of course, the dichotomy precedes software. As the world moved out of the cottage-industry era into the smokestack era, it became very clear—at least back then—that disciplined approaches were the way of the future, and flexible approaches were not. The age of the automobile would not have been possible, of course, without Henry Ford's notion of a de-skilled, disciplined work force.

But that was then, and this is now. The smokestack era, most would agree, has given way to the information era. The society that used to depend on what we could make out of expensive raw materials by forging them in huge factories now finds that it depends on information enabled by literally cheap-as-dirt silicon. Knowledge workers are the key to the future, not factory workers. The question is, what is the best way to organize and optimize teams of knowledge workers?

Surely software developers are the ultimate knowledge workers. If you even slightly believe the claims of David Parnas and Fred Brooks that "software is hard" to build, that it is "the most complex activity ever undertaken by human beings," then it is easy to imagine that old models for organizing factory people simply would not work in the information era.

9

It is interesting to note that today's successful software houses fund their software development activities under the financial heading "research and development." That is, these companies see the building of software not as some sort of manufacturing activity, but as something more analogous to the mental explorations of a researcher.

Now think for a moment about research and development. Is it about "obedience" and "controlled behavior"? Of course not. Discipline may play a role in research and development (we will explore this theme further in the essays to follow), but flexibility— or whatever your choice for that word is—is far more important.

The relative roles of discipline and flexibility in software, then, should be determined by a model right at the heart of our understanding of the field of software development. Is the correct model destined to be factory-like, where assembly-line workers stamp out and install software parts all day long, or is it craft- and research-and-development-like, where developers puzzle over intellectual challenges during their workday?

That is the issue we explore in this section. To illustrate that the question is not a new one, I include ("reuse" sounds like a far better word in our field!) an essay first published 30-something years ago, "Will the Real Henry Ford of Software Please Stand Up?", which still frames the issue nicely, I think. And the final essay, "The 'Odd Couple' of Discipline and Creativity," represents my personal choice for a resolution of the dichotomy.

Read on! And think about your own answer to the "Discipline versus Flexibility" dichotomy as you do.

1.1

will the Real Henry ford of software please stand up?

The corporate headquarters of Alchemy Chemical and Softli Paper are no more than a mile apart on the Straightarrow Turnpike in Silicon Commonwealth, Massachusetts.

But their computing shops might as well be on Mars and Mercury. They are light-years apart in organizational philosophy. And the extremes in which they find themselves are characteristic of the dilemmas of modern computing.

Over at Alchemy, Stan Sorcerer runs a tight ship. His employees have a dress code, fixed working hours, specified coffee breaks and a strict behavior program. The standards defined for his programmers are profuse and rigid. Both documentation and listings are subject to periodic inspection and surprise review. C# and Java are required languages for all applications, and static analysis tools are used to both encourage and enforce programming standards. Management of tasks is by schedule, and if a programmer gets behind in his work he is expected to put in voluntary overtime to make it up. The atmosphere in Alchemy is tense, businesslike and productive. Stan is fond of quoting data which shows his programmers produce at 3 times the national average. From all outside appearances, Stan Sorcerer has built himself a software factory, and he runs his shop like an assembly line.

But at Softli Paper, Herb Bond sees things differently. Herb's programmers' dress could best be described as neo-hippy. They come and go through the swinging doors of Softli at all hours of the day or night. Their programming standards manual would fit within the index of that used at Alchemy, and it uses words like "can" and occasionally "should" instead of "shall" and "will." Herb uses peer code reviews but never conducts management code inspections. C# and Java are the predominant languages, but one of his ace programmers is coding a report generator program in Python now, and loving it. Management of tasks is by progress reporting, with emphasis on product quality rather than schedule. The atmosphere at Softli is laid back, unbusinesslike, and resembles a graduate school seminar. Herb never quotes statistics about programmer productivity, but he has been heard to say that he doesn't believe anyone who does—he's seen how they got their numbers. From all outside appearances, Herb Bond is herding a group of untamed software craftsmen in the general direction of product completion.

Now it is patently obvious that Stan Sorcerer and Herb Bond can't both be right about how to run a computing shop. Either programmers should function like an assembly line, or as craftsmen, right? But which?

Well, the question just isn't that easy to answer. Ten years ago, the assembly line philosophy appeared to be the only way to go. Software was characteristically overly complex, too expensive, and behind schedule. Software modules were hand-fabricated and fitted together by craftsmen. It seemed obvious that software's characteristic problems were caused by its craft-based approach.

Acting on that presumption, management poured a great deal of money into finding ways of assembly-lining software construction. Visual Basic was the first hope—a drag-and-drop, wizard-driven language that even amateur and inexperienced programmers could use to build applications faster than ever.

It didn't work out that way, though. No matter how you sliced it, programs were still programs. They had a level of nitty-gritty detail and complexity that even dragging and dropping couldn't wave away. Visual Basic didn't change that (and neither did Java or C# in later years).

Management kept trying, though. Techniques which promised standardization were encouraged. Individuality was played down, and teamwork stressed. The term "ego-less programming" was invoked. Configuration control and quality assurance were formalized. And when automated lifecycle management came along promising miracles, management bought it with alacrity. The promised land of assembly-line programming seemed on the horizon at last.

But there was a giant irony in this quest for the ultimate automation. While researchers poured their energy into assembly line techniques, hardly anyone was paying attention to the technologist's state of the art. In spite of all the assembly line action, it was still craftsmen who were producing software. And no one was developing and promoting better tools for those craftsmen. Oh, actually, that's not quite true. There were technologists whose efforts were directed toward creating better tools. But hardly anyone cared. If a new technique didn't promise a dramatic shift toward the assembly line, few managers cared to look further into it. And without management support, new tools never made it into the production programmer's hands.

Let me make one thing perfectly clear. I don't mean to be saying that assembly line programming won't happen, some day. Like, the Henry Ford of software may be designing the ultimate fabrication method somewhere right now. But while researchers and funders continue that search, someone needs to be concentrating on the nearer term needs. It is foolish to move the field impetuously into an assembly line posture when no one knows how to design an assembly line. And it is foolish to suspend tool development and usage because someday we won't need them any more.

13

That's enough of a soapbox presentation, though. Perhaps I digress too far from the world of Straightarrow Turnpike, and Stan Sorcerer, and Herb Bond.

Or perhaps I don't. Stan Sorcerer's shop is the culmination of today's state of the art in assembly line techniques. Herb Bond's shop is the culmination of the craftsmen-at-work approach. And that soapbox oratory was an attempt to explain why no one can really say that Stan and his productivity figures are right, and Herb is wrong. Or vice versa.

But, to get back to the realm of Alchemy and Softli, the dichotomy between the two companies obviously did not go unnoticed by the programmers in the two shops. In fact, Friday evenings at the Straightarrow Tavern sometimes got fairly exciting if a few of the crew from Alchemy and Softli showed up at the same time. It was one of those Friday evenings which led to the point of this story.

Picture the scene. Promptly at 4:43, a couple of car pools of Alchemy programmers drop by the Straightarrow on their way home from work. Properly dressed in their code-compatible dark grey polo shirts and designer jeans, they look with some disdain on a couple of bearded Softli folk nursing drinks in a corner, clad as they are in baggy shorts and sandals. The look does not go unnoticed, and one of the Softli pair, who has been at the Straightarrow longer than is wise given his deadline tomorrow, makes a derogatory comment about the coding skills and ancestry of Alchemy programmers in general, and about this group in particular.

Now if the Straightarrow drew a factory crowd, shoving and fisticuffs might have erupted on the spot. But in the think-tank-type atmosphere of this particular tavern, skilled and polished verbal violence broke out instead. Fine phrases formed and flew forcefully about the room. Before the battle was half warmed-up, Alchemy's dress code had been characterized as Hitlerian, and Softli's standards as vacuous; Alchemy's working hours as bean-counter-inspired, and Softli's productivity as high but negative; and Alchemy's disciplined programming as proceduralized nits, with Softli's working habits as kindergartenish. And the verbal fireworks were still escalating.

I'm not sure who it was who first suggested the code-off. I'm not even sure it was a good idea, in the long term. But as a battle stopper, it was a winner. The idea clanged like a bell in the forensic uproar, and silence followed by enthusiastic negotiation over terms quickly subdued the crowd. The idea was amazingly simple—it was one of those "my father is bigger than your father" numbers. It was a put up or shut up topper to all the other verbiage. It was "if you think you're such a good group of programmers, let's see if you can beat us."

The idea spread like wildfire. By the time the assorted group left the Straightarrow in their various directions that night, the ground rules had been set.

The code-off was simple enough. Two programs were to be designed and coded by two teams, one from each company. The first program was a report generator, relatively straightforward and unsophisticated. The second was a small interpreter for a language with a couple of complex data types and tricky semantics. Entities to be measured in the study were time to complete the program, cost to complete the program, and quality of the finished program. Quality was subjective, of course, but the group negotiated a matrix of quality attributes to help introduce some objectivity into the scoring, and selected a team of scorers from each company. Four successive Saturday mornings at the Straightarrow were set aside for the competition.

The Rose Bowl had nothing on the Straightarrow that series of Saturdays. Crowds from both companies packed the place, as word spread rapidly through both computing departments. Some of the keypunch operators from Alchemy formed a somewhat impromptu cheerleading team, clad in matching and properly modest sweaters and pants; and a group of staff analysts from Softli used a blog and RSS feed to track the competition in real time. By the time the third Saturday had rolled around, the local ACM chapter had turned out en masse, and on the fourth Saturday reporters from the Silicon Commonwealth Clarion Call and the Straightarrow Post were there taking notes and pictures. It was the biggest thing to hit Silicon Commonwealth since Hurricane Giselda.

The results of the code-off, in case you're waiting with bated breath, were an anti-climax. Scoring anomalies aside, it was a standoff. The Alchemy Assembly Liners had an easier time with the report generator, and scored well in time and cost factors. But the Softli Craftsmen did better with the interpreter, and their quality scores were higher. Which was perhaps a best-of-all-possible-worlds resolution, given the nature of the competition—nobody lost, and nobody felt bad as the crowd filed out of the Straightarrow that last Saturday.

Sometimes, though, I wonder what would've happened if someone had really won. I mean, suppose you could really prove that assembly lining was better than a craft-based approach. Or vice versa.

Can you imagine Stan Sorcerer being wrong, and letting his programmers come to work in sandals? Or Herb Bond being wrong, and demanding that his programmers all work the same 8–4:30 shift? Somehow, I'm glad the Henry Ford of software hasn't come forth yet. But maybe he'll show up at the Straightarrow next year—just in time for the second annual Silicon Commonwealth code-off!

1.2

software
Automation:
fact or fraud?

"**A** no muss, no fuss software factory." That's the alluring picture painted in [Moad 1990] and a thousand other articles on the future of software development that continue to appear in the popular computing press to this day. But is it really achievable?

The claims are well-known. "We produced more than 400 new programs with no failures and helped reduce maintenance by 70–90%," claims one enthusiastic manager who employed some new technology. "We can deliver [an application] as fast as they [the users] can take it," he goes on to gush [Moad 1990].

However, there is an opposite side to that picture. A lot of software people are less than enthusiastic about the same kinds of new technology. Is it stubbornness, or is there something missing in those glowing reports of success? Will advanced technology—some call it "software automation"—be able to fulfill the claims now made for it?

In the same article with those positive reports comes a sober warning: "The reason so many are cautious is that we've had so many dead ends," says another software manager. And: "Right now, very few [IS] people can go on record as saying that the high-level analysis and design tools don't work. Who wants to be the bringer of bad news?" says yet another.

There is certainly plenty at stake. We all know those numbers that say the cost of building software in the world is very large. So, we've all been exposed to the data that says software productivity has increased comparatively little over the last few decades. Certainly we in software all wish there were some magic solution to that data and those numbers. But can wishing—coupled with a little perspiration—make it so?

Some say yes. They tend to be the people selling solutions and the people seeking research grants to find new solutions. There is no shortage of promised breakthroughs in our ability to build software.

Some say no. They tend to be the people who have built software for a living for a long time and have seen similar claims rise and fall. There is also no shortage of naysayers to those promised breakthroughs.

The battle lines are clearcut. But who is right here?

Unfortunately, there is no data to support either position. There is, of course, wonderful and profuse anecdotal evidence. The gentleman above who built software so fast that his customers couldn't use it all is one case in point. So are the managers who trained all their people in some new "breakthrough" methodology, forgot they did it, and then tried to impose a competing and incompatible methodology a few years later because of the claims made for it. One can attempt to prove any point of view with anecdotes.

Slowly but surely, however, there are an increasing number of key people who are dubious about these claims. Among the first to go on record was noted computer scientist David L. Parnas, who expressed his doubts about the potential for automated software development in his article, "Software Aspects of Strategic Defense Systems" [Parnas 1985]. Then came another software guru, Fred Brooks, who expressed similar doubts and many more [Brooks 1987]. Two specialists doing research in the field of software automation expressed their concerns over exaggerated claims (they went so far as to call them myths!) [Rich 1988].

Subsequently, the chorus grew. Carma McClure, known in the past for being in the super-enthusiast's camp, has since characterized the CASE movement as one in which "the emperor has no clothes"—CASE, she says, has yielded little in productivity gains [SD 1990]. In fact, in my own comprehensive study of the research that examines such " breakthrough" concepts [Glass 1999], there is simply no research evidence to support any such claims.

Could these (admittedly very personal) beliefs be valid? Is there, in fact, no breakthrough to be had here? Is the only thing "to be had" the people who believe that breakthroughs are possible?

What we need here is some good, old-fashioned, scientific-method research. Propose a hypothesis about some particular "breakthrough" in software productivity. Design some research to explore the truth or falsehood of that hypothesis. Perhaps set up an experimental study, conduct a survey, or do protocol analysis on people actively using the new idea and its older counterparts. There are many legitimate choices of research approach. What is lacking is not the knowledge of what ought to be done, but the commitment—and, unfortunately, the funding (this kind of research is not cheap)—to do it.

In short, what is needed here is to strip away the advocacy, the locked-in posturing, that characterizes much of what we know about "software automation" in 2006 (and, for that matter, in 1996, and 1986, and 1976, and 1966!) and replace it with some objectivity, some truth-for-truth's-sake exploration.

There are a few examples of this kind of work, fortunately. A lot of it has been done at NASA-Goddard's Software Engineering Laboratory and reported at its annual Software Engineering Workshops, over the years. Some was done in the community that explored programmers at work to evolve theory: the Empirical Studies of Programmers people, some of whom now publish a respected academic journal on that theme. Some of it is being done in various research institutes around the world, such as

Fraunhofer in the United States and Germany, NICTA in Australia, and Simula in Norway.

There is also a scattering of good work done by individual researchers who are more concerned with truth than with advocacy. As one tiny example, [Davis 1988] contains a particularly insightful and specific analysis of what is good—and what is not—about CASE tools.

If enough people—researchers in both the academic and industrial worlds, and at institutions like the Software Engineering Institute—get caught up in this kind of exploration, perhaps we will come to better understand the underlying issue here.

Some say that software production is or should be a science. Lots of rigor. Lots of theory. Some mathematics sprinkled on to facilitate the work. There is a feeling that with enough science, enough discipline, software automation is possible.

Some say that it is more like an art. Lots of creativity. Lots of free thinking. Some techniques sprinkled on to facilitate that work. There is a feeling that discipline and automation simply won't work.

Yet another manager quoted in [Moad 1990] expressed it best. "What we've been trying to do is make software development more of a science, but what we have found is that some people are scientists and some people are artists. Many of our most creative people come from the artists, so we don't want to lose that."

With appropriate research findings, perhaps we can learn how and when best to use those scientists and artists among us. As with most issues where the opposing sides have become entrenched, the truth probably lies in some middle ground.

References

Brooks 1987—"No Silver Bullet," *IEEE Computer*, April 1987; Fred Brooks.

Davis 1988—"Commentary," *Accounting Horizons*, June 1988; Gordon B. Davis.

Glass 1999— "The Realities of Software Technology Payoffs," *Communications of the ACM*, February 1999; Robert L. Glass.

Moad 1990—"The Software Revolution," *Datamation*, February 15, 1990; Jeff Moad.

Parnas 1985—"Software Aspects of Strategic Defense Systems," *American Scientist*, September 1985; David Parnas.

Rich 1988—"Automatic Programming: Myths and Prospects," *IEEE Computer*, August 1988; Charles Rich and Richard C. Waters.

SD 1990—"Report on the System Development Conference," *System Development*, April 1990.

1.3

Are programmers Really "out of control"?

A famous computer scientist often said that, when he first joined a software-producing group in industry, his observation was, "These programmers are out of control."

It is certainly possible to build a case for this control problem in software development. The traditional stereotype of a programmer is an unkempt person clad in torn jeans and sandals working strange hours and eating enormous quantities of unhealthy food. And that stereotype applies not just to the programmer of yesteryear, but to the hacker of today. With people such as that, anarchistic in appearance, is it any wonder that control leaps to a potential manager's mind as an issue to be dealt with?

The issue of control is, of course, intimately connected to the issue of programmer discipline. Control is the vehicle for instilling discipline. If discipline is vital to the ability to produce software, control is an essential part of the software manager's repertoire.

Certainly it is easy to find those who cry out for more control and more discipline. For example, we frequently see statements to this effect: "... the introduction of strict discipline and mechanization through the application of advanced software engineering ... offers a practical solution ... The time for such introduction is ripe ..." [Lehman 1989].

However, there is a vital underlying issue here. Does control really result in more effective software development? Are there any studies, any data, to support or refute the need for control? Is it really true in general that programmers are out of control?

The answer, unfortunately, is that there were few such studies then, and there are few of them now. However, there are some odd findings, clinging to the fringes of research directed at other issues, which suggest that control and discipline may not be the solutions to the problems of software that some claim them to be.

One such odd finding is presented in [DeMarco 1987]. The result comes from an earlier study [Jeffery 1983] of the relationship between software estimation practices and the ability to achieve those estimates. In that study, these situations were set up:

1. Software was built to a schedule established by management.
2. Software was built to a schedule established by the technologists.
3. Software was built with no schedule imposed at all.

The study evaluated the productivity of the people who did the building. The findings were in some ways predictable, but in some ways quite a surprise:

1. Software productivity was higher when the developers set their own schedule as opposed to when they tried to meet one set by management. (This, of course, is not a surprise.)
2. Software productivity was highest when there was no schedule for them to keep to at all. (This, of course, is quite a surprise.)

These findings can be interpreted in a variety of ways. One interpretation hard to ignore is that, when left to their own devices (and thus "out of control"), software people are at their most effective! It is as if software people have an innate sense of responsibility, perhaps coupled with love of doing a good job, that is a more effective motivator than any amount of management pressure and control!

There is another similar finding, from an even older source. In an article exploring management technique, Lehman the author found that the tighter the control imposed on programmers, the less they produced [Lehman 1979]!

Granting that two pieces of data do not a finding make, this information should still make one pause. The trend since the very origins of software as a profession has been to seek more effective ways of controlling and disciplining programmers. The assumption here has been that in this spectrum of choice:

> *Theory X Management*—Workers are unmotivated and must be coerced by management into doing a good job.
> *Theory Y Management*—Workers are heavily motivated, and management need only facilitate them to obtain a good job.
> *Theory Z Management*—A mix of facilitation and control is the best way to get workers to do a good job.

Somewhere between Theory X and Theory Z lay the proper method of managing software development. These findings suggest instead that proper management of software should be between Theory Y and Theory Z.

It is interesting to note that in more traditional scientific fields, the required mix is better understood. Both of the quotations below, for example, speak of the need for a combination of creativity and discipline; but notice that the discipline they discuss must be largely self-imposed rather than imposed from without:

> "Science is not just curiosity and creativity; it is a disciplined form of it ... self-discipline ... to follow up the brilliant new ideas with down-to-earth applications ... It

is this seemingly odd couple of discipline and curiosity
that makes for scientific progress. The curiosity of creative
minds, asking continuously How? and Why?, and the
discipline to realize that science is part of the world, that
it is shaping it" [Groen 1990].

"Any art that's worth its name has some kind of discipline
associated with it. Some kind of rule—maybe it's not the
rule of a sonnet, or a symphony, or a classical painting,
but even the most limited contemporary art ... has some
kind of rule. The object is to get across what you're trying
to get across, while sticking to the rules" [Judson 1980].

It is time to think more deeply about what we really mean when
we speak of the need for more discipline and control in software. If
it is self-discipline that we are discussing, control is not the way
to achieve it. If it is the more traditional form of discipline, that
imposed by control from without, we need to understand why
these strange findings from the world of research do not mesh
with that view.

   Such fundamental questions as these may seem out of place 50
years downstream in our field. But 50 years is a very short time,
after all, when compared to the history of other fields. It is not too
late for software management to reconsider the questions "How?"
and "Why?"

References

DeMarco 1987—*Peopleware*, Dorset House, 1987; Tom DeMarco and Tim Lister.

Groen 1990—*The Discipline of Curiosity*, Elsevier Science, 1990; Janny Groen, Eefke Smit, and Juurd Eisvoogel.

Jeffery 1985—"Managing Programmer Productivity," *Journal of Systems and Software*, January 1985; Ross Jeffery and M.J. Lawrence.

Judson 1980—quoting from a conversation with Murray Gell-Mann, the inventor of quarks, in *The Search for Solutions*, Holt, Rinehart and Winston, 1980; Horace Freeland Judson.

Lehman 1989—"Uncertainty in Computer Application and Its Control Through the Engineering of Software," *Journal of Software Maintenance*, September 1989; M.M. Lehman.

Lehman 1979—"How Software Projects Are Really Managed," *Datamation*, January 1979; M.M. Lehman.

1.4
Discipline is a Dirty word: A story About the software Life cycle

Once upon a time there was a neat and tidy software life cycle. We studied the requirements of the problem to be solved. We designed a solution to fulfill those requirements. We coded that design. We tested that code. And we released the resulting software solution to the user for use and to the maintainers for maintenance.

Management became so enthusiastic about the software life cycle that they decided to manage to it. Literally. First you analyze the requirements, they would say. Then—and only then—should you start the design. And only when the design was complete could you start writing code. Of course testing could not begin until the code was complete, and users could not get the product until the tests had all been run.

In the world of intangibles that is software construction, it was so nice to have an ordering, a sequence of events that you could count on. And, in fact, you could do even more.

You could invent a "document-driven" version of this life cycle. After each phase was completed, there would be a document produced that would serve as the basis for the next phase. The requirements specification was needed to start design. The design document was needed to start coding. The unit development folder was essential to testing. The test report was a precursor of production and maintenance.

And—beauty of all beauties—suddenly the intangible became tangible. Management could now check project progress by examining those documents. And they could almost understand them! Instead of a few scraps of paper and an incomprehensible listing, there were now artifacts produced as part of the software process that management could read—even if it couldn't (or wouldn't) read the final product, the code itself.

But slowly, people began to realize, some bad things were happening.

First, software developers began spending enormous amounts of time on those documents. That wasn't all bad, of course, because the documents were important in the handoff to the next life-cycle phase. But if you know that a particular facet of your work is being judged by management, of course you spend quite a bit of time getting that right. And getting it pretty. The documents, the programmers realized, were more important than the program itself. After all, management didn't ever look at CODE! Those documents produced at the end of each life-cycle phase became the most important products of the software development process!

Then something else went wrong. As standards emerged for the content of the various phase-ending documents, software developers began to see that some documents that they had thought were important in the past simply were not. Or at least they were not high on the management check list, or in the standards definitions. For example, the standards for producing a user manual were cursory at best. And the standards for building maintenance documentation were sometimes non-existent. In the U.S. Department of Defense's standards, for example, little was said about either of these documents. And the result was, of course, that work on the user manual and the maintenance manual—hard to motivate in the past because many software developers hate to write—became afterthoughts, worth little more than cursory attention. After all, the phase-ending documents were clearly more important.

Maintainers were especially troubled here. Software documentation, from their point of view, has a short shelf-life. As the inevitable changes are made to the software product, most of the documents become out of date and worthless quite quickly. And the most worthless, from the maintainer's point of view, were those phase-ending documents. Who cared about the original Unit Development Folder, for example, when there was little or no information on how the software product was supposed to be used, or how it could be maintained? Everything seemed topsy-turvy. The maintainer got beautiful and polished documents that were mostly put on a shelf to gather dust, and didn't get the documents they needed to do their job. Did anyone really believe the data that said maintenance was 80% of the cost of software? If so, where was the emphasis on documentation that the maintainer could use?

Time passed, and slowly so did the emphasis on this rigid, document-driven life cycle. There were several forces at work to change the status quo. Most of those forces sprang in various ways from people who knew that this was not the right way to build software. Some people began discussing "rapid prototyping" and noted that its early cycle of design/code/test simply didn't fit with rigid phase endings and big, polished phase-ending documents. Other people began exploring alternative life-cycle definitions, like spirals and circles. Still others—primarily those who built software for a living who wanted to do the best job they knew how—quietly ignored the management direction and went ahead to do what they knew was right.

Let us stop and ponder, for a moment, that last group of people. These were the folks who might be characterized as "out of control." These were the folks who were using far from "disciplined" approaches. And yet, these were the folks who were doing the job right. What was going on here? And how prevalent was this situation?

The answer to the second question came, interestingly enough, from a research study. Marvin Zelkowitz, of the University of Maryland, investigated the practices of a group of software developers, what they were doing and when they were doing it [Zelkowitz 1988]. He had them record what life-cycle phase they were nominally in (that is, what phase did management think they were in?) and what their activities actually were. He found that, in fact, almost no one was following the rigid life cycle. Developers nominally studying requirements may actually have been doing a little prototype coding and testing. Developers nominally doing design may have created design experiments, writing and testing sample code to check the feasibility of their design solution. Developers nominally doing coding might be going back over, and perhaps even revising, the requirements (occasionally) and the design (surprisingly often). And developers nominally doing testing were doing almost all of the above.

In fact, Zelkowitz found, the rigid software life cycle was (although he didn't put it that way) a developer's joke. They told management what management wanted to hear, and did what they needed to do.

The answer to the first question above ("What was going on here?") was, in fact, that these unruly, undisciplined, out-of-control software developers were doing a good job of work in spite of management.

More time has passed since then, and of course the rigid view of the software life cycle has long since gone out of favor. Perhaps, then, software developers and management are in synchronization at last, and discipline and control have again been imposed on the software workplace.

However, I suspect that's not really true. My suspicion is that there is some other management-caused insanity happening out there now (does today's notion of "automated lifecycle management" integrated toolsets come to mind?), and the programmers—as they have always done—are programming around it, doing things the right way, ignoring the foolish management direction, "out of control" as always.

Reference

Zelkowitz 1988—"Resource Utilization During Software Development," *Journal of Systems and Software*, September 1988; Marvin R. Zelkowitz.

1.4

Discipline is a dirty word: A story about the software life cycle

1.5
The Faking of software Design

It's not often that someone is brilliant enough to solve a problem before the rest of us can even see that there is one. But this is a story about just such an event.

Once upon a time, more than two decades ago, all of us in software learned that top-down, requirements-driven approaches were the best way to build software. We take the top-level requirements, and use hierarchic decomposition techniques to chop up a big, unsolvable problem into a bunch of smaller solvable ones in an orderly fashion, so that when we are done there is this nice tree-structure-like definition of our problem and our solution.

Then something strange happened. One of the best-known computer scientists, David Parnas (who gained perhaps his greatest fame via his paper on the decomposition of software into modules), wrote an odd paper that essentially told us how to fake top-down design when we wrote our design documentation—the words "fake it" were even in the title of the paper!

Fake top-down design? Why should we do that?

Time passed. Parnas's paper seemed an anomaly, something out of synch with the rest of the brilliant work he had done. Fake top-down design indeed!

And then, from another part of the computing forest, came another rather strange finding. Bill Curtis, leading a group of computing researchers at the Microelectronics and Computing Consortium (MCC), began to do empirical studies of the process of design as conducted by skilled designers. In Curtis' early papers, he contrasted two design approaches; "controlled" design and "opportunistic" design. Controlled design proceeded the way we all knew it should, top-down and at least somewhat hierarchically. Opportunistic design proceeded in ways totally dependent on the individual designer, sometimes appearing almost random. At this early stage in these findings, we all wondered at those disorganized, opportunistic designers. Why would they behave in such an obviously incorrect way?

However, as more time went by, the findings of the Curtis people changed. Controlled design, they began to see more and more often, was not what good designers really did. Opportunistic design became more and more what they observed in their studies. The designer's mind, engaged in solving one problem, would dart off to another, usually more complex, problem. If one thought of the overall and emerging design as the tree structure we all thought it should be, these opportunistic diversions went to places on the tree that were remote and relatively unconnected to the place where the mind was nominally functioning.

What was going on here? Whatever it was, the finding became so prevalent that Curtis began saying, publicly, things like "The undisturbed design process is opportunistic." People simply don't do what we were all sure they were doing.

Were we observing here a fundamental flaw in how practitioners design software? Or were we observing a fundamental flaw in our model of how they should design software?

It is time now to reintroduce Parnas' "fake it" into our story. Remember that, for some odd reason, he told us how to fake a top-down design in our documentation (that is, to pretend that we had done top-down design even when we hadn't)?

In Curtis's findings lies the explanation. Those opportunistic designs produced by good designers simply aren't going to be top-down. Yet it would be impossible for the non-designer to follow the opportunistic trail of the creative process of building such a design. So we "fake" a top-down description of the design, because that is the only way readers of the design will be capable of understanding it.

With the Parnas piece of the puzzle clicking into place with the Curtis pieces, we begin to see that the problem lies not with design practice, but with design theory. Theory was idealized and, as it turned out, inaccurate. Our fundamental flaw lay in the model of the design process, not in its practice.

So where does this leave us? With our theoretical model of design serving us well as a representation schema, even if we have to fake it; and with our empirical model of design, called "opportunistic" by Curtis, serving us well as the real way we perform our design activities.

Because "opportunistic" still has a strange, perhaps random, perhaps even negative connotation, I like to think of this process in another way. When the mind reaches off in its opportunistic way, most often what it is doing is making sure that it solves the hard problems before it solves the dependent easier ones. We could almost define a new kind of tree structure here, not driven from the top by its overall requirements, but by some ordering of difficulty blended with coupling.

However, there is a problem with that view. What is a hard problem to one person may not be to another; problems tend to be hard if we have not solved them before, and each of us brings a different set of experiences to the act of design. Therefore, each person's hard-problem tree structure will be different from each other person's. How can a sensible model of design be built from that?

I prefer to think that the act of design is and should be what I call "hard-part-first design." I believe that covers, at least to some extent, what Curtis's empirical studies have discovered; and "hard-part-first" has a more organized image (whether it should or not!) than "opportunistic."

Be that as it may, it is not the terminology that counts here, so much as the understanding. Design is and ought to be opportunistic. Design representation ought to be, and usually is, top-down. And David Parnas gave us the answer even before most of us understood the question!

1.6
Agile programming— flexibility comes of age

The first edition of this book was published in 1995, a year in which disciplined approaches were the dominant force in the thinking of software engineering professionals.

Ah, how much has changed since then! Where the first edition of this book was a kind of voice crying in the wilderness to reconsider those disciplined approaches, now the voices of flexibility are just about as loud (if still not as numerous!) as those advocating discipline. I am speaking primarily, of course, of the advocates of the Agile approaches to building software.

The Agile movement is a natural outgrowth, I would assert, of all those craft-oriented, "out of control," opportunistic software development approaches that this book spoke of in the preceding material. (Agile approaches are an umbrella term over such methodologies as eXtreme Programming (XP), Crystal Clear, Adaptive Software Development, Scrum, Dynamic Systems Development Method, and Feature-Driven Development. XP is said by many to be the most commonly used Agile approach).

Is Agile really the outgrowth of all those other flexible approaches to building software that you have just finished reading about? To answer that question, let's take a look at the values and principles of Agile programming, as expressed in the

"Agile Manifesto" and the accompanying "Principles Behind the

Agile Manifesto," which were composed at a 2001 gathering held in Snowbird, Utah, in the United States. That meeting included 17 advocates of the then so-called "lightweight" methodologies mentioned in the preceding paragraph.

First, here are the Agile values, a statement of the relative importance of certain factors on software projects (Agile advocates refer to this as the Agile Manifesto, http://agilemanifesto.org):

- Individuals and interactions over processes and tools
- Working software over comprehensive documentation
- Customer collaboration over contract negotiation
- Responding to change over following a plan

And these are the Agile principles (http://agilemanifesto.org/principles.html):

- Place the highest priority on customer satisfaction, achieved through early and continuous delivery
- Welcome changing requirements, even late in development
- Deliver working software frequently
- Provide daily interaction between business people and developers
- Use motivated developers, give them what they need, and trust them
- Communicate face to face, it is the most efficient and effective way of conveying information
- Make working software the primary measure of progress
- Promote sustainable development; avoid death marches
- Pay continuous attention to technical excellence and good design
- Promote simplicity—the art of maximizing the amount of work NOT done
- Use self-governing teams; they produce the best software
- Reflect on improvement at regular intervals

Comparing these values and principles to the earlier material on craftsmen/opportunists is an interesting exercise. A little thought quickly leads one to see the similarities (e.g., people and products over process and documentation). But a little more thought leads one to realize that the Agile movement has gone well beyond those earlier ideas. Such Agile aspects as "customer collaboration" and "responding to change" and "customer satisfaction" and "welcome changing requirements" are much more profound than the, by contrast, simpler thoughts of the flexibility approaches of 1995.

Much of what the Agile movement has added to those earlier thoughts has to do with the sociology of software projects. Many of those values and principles are focused on the relationship with the customer. Others are focused on the relationships within the software organization. This rich addition of sociology to the notion of technical software development flexibility is an interesting and worthwhile contribution of the Agile advocates.

One of the most fascinating questions that arises regarding the Agile approaches is their applicability. That is, on what kinds of projects should Agile approaches be used? When the Agile approaches were first described, there seemed little question of the correct answer to that question. Alistair Cockburn, in his pioneering book Agile Software Development [Cockburn 2002], speaks of the Agile "sweet spots." Agile should only be used, he said, for these kinds of projects:

- 2–8 people working in one room
- On-site usage experts
- One month development cycles
- Fully automated regression tests
- Experienced developers

Even such strong advocates of the disciplined approaches as Barry Boehm agreed with Cockburn. In his book *Balancing Agility and Discipline* [Boehm and Turner 2004], which tries to seek middle ground between the Agile and disciplined approaches, Boehm says that Agile should be used for small systems development teams, where the customers/users are readily available, and where there are volatile requirements. (By contrast, Boehm said that disciplined approaches (he called them "plan-driven") should be used for projects that are:

- large and complex with reasonably stable requirements,
- involve high safety/reliability requirements, and
- exist in a predictable environment).

But those early agreements about Agile applicability are beginning to fray around the edges. Agile advocates like [Williams and Cockburn 2003] (yes, that's the same Cockburn mentioned above!) upped the ante on project size, speaking of "collocated team of 50 or fewer programmers." Others took the size constraints even further—[Sutherland 2001] states "Agile can scale into programming in the large."

What was at stake, of course, was how broadly Agile might be utilized. If it is limited to use on small teams, then there are severe restrictions on its applicability (and, interestingly, its teachability—should software engineering or computer science academic programs teach the Agile approaches if they are only applicable on small projects, for example?)

It has not been unusual in the history of software engineering for new ideas, originally modestly and probably accurately proposed, to be hyped into positions of grandeur. The Ada programming language was originally conceived to support real-time systems work, for example, with a dose of systems programming thrown in so that Ada compilers could be written in the Ada language. But it was not too long before Ada advocates were recommending it for all application domains, including for example business systems, where it had never been intended to be used. (It is interesting to note that these hyped claims were, in the end,

39

death rattles. The Ada language eventually died (or at least became pretty moribund), and part of the cause may well have been attempts to use it where it was not intended).

Earlier I spoke of severe restrictions on applicability. You alert readers may have wondered, at least in passing, what those restrictions really amounted to. A nice answer to that question was presented in an interesting debate between an Agile advocate and a disciplined approaches advocate in [Beck and Boehm 2003]. Boehm (yes, the same Barry Boehm!) cited data that originally seemed to support the Agile position, that fully 60% of software projects are small, involving fewer than 10 people. But interpreting any such data, Boehm pointed out, should involve the actual time spent building software, where the number of people and the total lines of code built are also factored in. Using that approach, Boehm pointed out, only 17% of the world's software work is small. Thus Agile approaches are, at least according to Boehm, of minor importance in the overall scheme of software engineering.

Another applicability issue centers around the question "How much methodological purity should Agile users employ?" Agile advocates tend to recommend that Agile be swallowed whole (those subordinate Agile methodologies such as XP contain lots of specific Dos and Don'ts).

An interesting "lessons learned" answer to that question is found in [Lindvall, et al. 2004], a study of Agile (mostly XP) uses in large organizations. Four companies reported significant benefits of adopting Agile (especially high quality, but also easy learning, increased flexibility, higher morale, and reduced costs). But none of them could use Agile "out of the box." Why? Tailoring of Agile was "absolutely necessary," all four companies said, because of such factors as (a) in projects where several Agile teams are involved, inter-group communication demands more formality and documentation, and (b) such Agile notions as continuous refactoring and continuous integration are in natural conflict with most approaches to configuration management. Examples of this tailoring, in fact, were largely in areas where the new (Agile) had to interface with the old (traditional approaches) at these four large organizations.

Meanwhile, as the debates about applicability and adoption rage on, there is some interesting name calling happening, somewhat reminiscent of the fracas in the Straightarrow Tavern related earlier in this book. Agile advocates speak of "the thrill of chaos" (some see Agile projects as chaotic) and the "dregs of structure" (Agile folks tend to find structured approaches (where structured is taken to mean disciplined) dull and boring). Disciplined advocates have been known to refer to the Agile approaches as "structured anarchy."

Now another school of thought has been heard from. [Skowronski 2004] takes the position that all those sociological factors we mentioned earlier are incompatible with the lone problem-solver approach so key to creative problem-solving. He tries to imagine such brilliant creators as Isaac Newton and Thomas Aquinas, notorious loners, working in such Agile approaches as XP's pair programming, and finds such team play unimaginable. Of course, that raises a new issue, what is the role of lone brilliance on today's software projects? That question, although one of huge relevance to this book, is one we will defer to post-book-reading discussion sessions! (I personally believe that lone brilliance is highly desirable in certain life cycle tasks, such as design, but is largely unworkable in the other tasks of a project of any significant size).

But another interesting question, also very relevant to this book, arises as well. Do Agile approaches enhance creativity? Certainly [Skowronski 2004] votes "no" on this issue. The alternative to Agile approaches is not lone brilliance, no matter how much some of us might wish it were so; it is the disciplined approaches. And given that Agile's flexibility allows much more creative freedom than discipline's "dregs of structure," I for one see Agile as much more compatible with creativity than its traditional alternatives.

How will all of this come out in the end? Most software innovations tend to ramp up to a position of maximally hyped claims, then fade back into the software engineering woodwork, often still being useful but not nearly as useful as the hypers proclaimed. There is probably a great deal of reason to believe that that will happen to the Agile approaches, just as it happened to the structured approaches (and, arguably, the object-oriented approaches) and CASE tools and 4GLs before them.

But there is another possibility. Some are beginning to argue that the Agile approaches should take their position alongside the traditional disciplined approaches as an alternative development approach for the right kind of projects. That is what Boehm argues, for example, in the book cited above.

References

Boehm and Turner 2004—*Balancing Agility and Discipline*, Addison-Wesley, 2004; Barry Boehm and Richard Turner.

Cockburn 2002—*Agile Software Development*, Addison-Wesley, 2002; Alistair Cockburn.

Evans and Boehm 2003—"Agility Through Discipline: A Debate," *IEEE Software* special issue on Agile methods, June 2003; Kent Beck vs. Barry Boehm.

Lindvall et al 2004—"Agile Software Development in Large Organizations," *IEEE Computer,* December 2004; Mikael Lindvall, Dirk Muthig, Aldo Dagnino, Christina Wallin, Michael Stupperich, David Kiefer, John May, and Tuomo Kahkonen.

Skowronski 2004—"Do Agile Methods Marginalize Problem-Solvers?" *IEEE Computer,* October 2004; Victor Skowronski.

Sutherland 2001—"Agile Can Scale: Inventing and Reinventing SCRUM in Five Companies," *Cutter IT Journal* special issue on the Great Methodologies Debate: Part 1, November 2001; Jeff Sutherland.

Williams and Cockburn 2003—"Agile Software Development: It's About Feedback and Change," *IEEE Software* special issue on Agile methods, June 2003; Laurie Williams and Alistair Cockburn.

The strange case of the proofreader's pencil

Sometimes the battle between discipline and freedom narrows down to absurdly small details. The case of the pencil behind the ear is just such a story.

This story happened when I was in college, eking out a living—as do most college students—with a summer job unrelated to my eventual professional interests. I was a proofreader, one of those people who read the newspaper galley proofs before they become the newspaper delivered to your door, looking for errors (it was the first paid debugging experience of my career!). The newspaper was the Quincy Illinois Herald-Whig, a small-city, middle-America newspaper with all the conservative stability that the paper's name implies.

There were two of us proofreaders on the evening shift of the paper. Our job was to proof the galleys for the morning edition, which was delivered to the rural subscribers of the paper by overnight mail. The paper was, at heart, an evening paper, and that edition had been delivered to the residents of Quincy by delivery people before we evening shifters even showed up to go to work. The point of all of this is that the evening shift was not a prestige time to work—we summer temporaries, and our boss, were not on the Herald Whig's advancement fast track!

One evening, as I had almost every other evening, I was sitting at my proofreader's desk, a bright light shining down on proof copy spread out in front of me, looking alertly for the inevitable typos. The typesetters were pretty good at their job, so the error incidence was well under one per paragraph of copy. My proofreader's marking pencil rested, as it always did, behind my right ear, ready to be grabbed to mark an error whenever I found one.

My boss, who had a peculiar mix of management styles that included gruff command-barking and slouching around, was making the rounds of his tiny evening fiefdom. As he approached me, I could see a scowl on his face. That was not unusual; what was unusual was that this particular scowl seemed directed at me. I began to feel a bit apprehensive.

My apprehension was confirmed moments later when he fixed a direct gaze on me and barked, "Get that pencil out from behind your ear, and put it in your hand poised over the copy like it should be!"

My mind whirled. My first reaction was to tell him where he could place my pencil, but I quickly realized that such a suggestion would be no help in this particular confrontation. Next I thought about ignoring the command ... but that, of course, was totally impossible. Finally, I considered refusing to do as he bid. However, the absurdity of making a serious issue out of where my proofreader's pencil was during my job finally made me realize that doing what he commanded was the intelligent response.

The pencil moved from my ear to my hand; but, seething inwardly, I scowled outwardly back at him to make sure that he knew how I felt about his command. Even then, in those young college years so long ago, I knew that what he asked of me was an absurdity, and that it would simply compound the absurdity if I made it into a fight.

Over the years, I have thought a lot about that incident, and what I have thought goes something like this: There is a thin line between appropriate and inappropriate management styles.

Certainly, management must take responsibility for the product its employees produce, and therefore to some extent the process by which they produce it.

However, management must also take responsibility for the productivity of its employees in performing the processes and producing the product. Productivity stems from a lot of different things, but high among them is the employee's knowledge that he or she, and his or her opinion, is valued by management. That feeling of well-being and contribution goes a lot further toward raising productivity than large heaps of process improvement, particularly when the process improvement is mandated from above rather than grown from below.

That manager was simply wrong in micro-managing my pencil, but he was not the last manager in the world to make that kind of mistake. As the computing world has been overwhelmed by calls for discipline—more methodologies, more attempts at process automation, more structured whatevers—more and more often, the managers involved are trying to solve computing's problems by changing the location of the proofreader's pencil. And it just doesn't work that way.

Discipline is a necessary part of the process of large-scale software development, of course, but there is discipline, and then there is discipline. Discipline is not one of those areas where if a little is good, a lot more is better. Like seasoning, it must be applied with care. And the manager who micro-managed my pencil—like the manager who forces his employees to use dubious "silver bullet" software "solutions"—was really pouring an excess of salt onto a wound of his own creation.

1.8
The Falutin' Index

We've already seen, in this book, a lot of different ways of referring to the many different kinds of problems and solutions we face in the field of software engineering. And we've seen, in this section, a discussion of the two important but very different ways of addressing those problems and those solutions. They can be approached using disciplined approaches, or they can be approached using flexible ones. Or, we are beginning to see more clearly, we can approach them with some combination of those two.

All of that is kind of abstract and esoteric. And if there's one thing I like to avoid, it's dryly abstract or dryly esoteric discussions of things that, in fact, really aren't very dry, very abstract, or very esoteric. Because of all of that, I can't tell you how pleased I was to come across some writing by one of my favorite computing authors, P.J. Plauger, who discussed these nuanced differences using his own wonderful term in [Plauger 1992]. He referred to all of this by the very informal term "the falutin' index."

"Falutin'," as in "high falutin'" and "low falutin'," is a term he used for a variety of related things regarding the complexity of a problem and its solution. High falutin' things, as the common U.S. slang usage of the term implies, are of somewhat high complexity and sophistication. Low falutin' ones, by contrast, are rarely complex and fairly unsophisticated.

What did Plauger apply his "falutin' index" to? Quite a number of things:

1. Problems can be high falutin' or not. That is, they can be of enormous complexity, or quite simple.
2. Solutions can also be high falutin' or not.
3. People can also be high or low falutin'.
4. And, finally, software projects can be high falutin' or not.

Now all of this might have been nothing more than word play if Plauger hadn't had a more serious point to make in his discussion. The biggest software engineering debacles, Plauger goes on to say, come about because of a mismatch between high falutin' and low falutin' things. High falutin' problems approached via low falutin' solutions (or vice versa). High falutin' programmers who work on low falutin' projects (or vice versa).

He told several stories about such mismatches. "I once saw an embedded system that essentially ran a glorified vending machine," he says. "It did the moral equivalent of counting coins, dispensing goods, and making change." Plauger went on to describe the designer's high falutin' approach to this low falutin' problem. "The proposed design modeled the data transforms as half a dozen processes running under a commercial real-time operating system. I'm sure the designer enjoyed using what he had learned, but he overdid it."

In the end, the high falutin' design had to be scrapped. The final system used a simple polling loop, and much less hardware than the cumbersome high falutin' solution would have. In other words, a high falutin' programmer tried to address a low falutin' problem on a low falutin' project with a high falutin' solution. Not good. Very not good!

But problems can occur with the opposite mismatch as well. Plauger talks about a significant project which tried to use low falutin' solutions for high falutin' problems. He says "The disease is common in large programming shops that are managed 'top down,' [where] management embraces the comfortable notion that programmers are a commodity. They hire under-trained programmers ..., then train them only superficially, if at all."

"Management tries to control the process," he goes on to say, "by frequent progress reports, code reviews, and a form of quality assurance [where] QA usually consists of still more under-trained programmers writing low falutin' test cases to beat against the low falutin' deliverable code. You don't have to guess the outcome. You've either experienced this sort of fiasco personally, had a friend who did, or read about the financial fallout." Whether we're talking about high falutin solutions to low falutin' problems or the opposite, big trouble is just over the horizon when these kinds of mismatches occur. And most programmers can add their share of mismatched falutin' stories to the ones Plauger tells.

It's important to point out here that Plauger makes another important point to underlie all of this. There is no one proper falutin' approach. The world proffers both high falutin' and low falutin' problems. The literature of software engineering offers both low falutin' and high falutin' approaches (and it is important for programmers to know which are which). Some people love to work in low falutin' settings, and some prefer high falutin' ones. There is not a right or wrong here. There are just differences, differences that must be accommodated in using people on a project to provide a solution for a problem.

"The name of the game," Plauger says at one point is his discussion, "is congruence." The techniques you employ had better be consistent with the intrinsic complexity of the problem you're trying to solve, he says.

Inappropriately use low falutin' approaches and you won't meet your deadlines. In fact, you may not complete the project. And that's the classic disaster of the software field—a gross underestimate followed by inadequate management and technology ending with a frantic rush to project completion, a death march. "A large enough project," says Plauger, "is primarily an exercise in management. The programming technology has only a minor effect on the outcome."

And what happens if you inappropriately use high falutin' approaches? You waste money and time—lots of it. You end up so consumed with documenting and reporting that you fail to notice whether the job gets done properly.

OK, so there are lots of stops and steps along the way using the falutin' index. How does Plauger tidy all of this up? He concludes, "Given all these aspects, the number of falutin' profiles are practically endless. Think about the projects you have worked on. Were they successful? How consistent was the complexity profile? My experience is that these two answers tend to be highly correlated ... Successful projects are congruent, or they aren't successful."

Reference

Plauger 1992—"The Falutin' Index," *Embedded Systems Programming*, May 1992, pages 89–92; P.J. Plauger.

1.9

The "odd couple" of Discipline and creativity

Some have called discipline and creativity an odd couple. They call them that because each word conjures up a totally different image in our minds. How can we consider both of them together?

Discipline causes us to think of identical marchers, moving in lock-step toward a common goal in a common way.

Creativity causes us to think of colorful and individualistic seekers, moving to a different drummer, choosing their own path. What can these two have in common?

If we think about it for a moment, we might see that our lives are constantly made up of blendings of the two. If we play or enjoy music, we love both the disciplined playing of a carefully crafted musical work and the creative improvisations of a master performer. If we appreciate science, we understand that the discipline imposed by the scientific method forms a frame for the opportunistic, even serendipitous, and certainly creative discoveries that constitute an amazing portion of what science has given us.

If we dabble in the writing of poetry, we know that the cadence of a poetic form guides, rather than constrains, our creative choices. Certainly in the search for rhymes, for example, we intermix the discipline of rhyming search (i.e., in seeking a rhyme for a particular word, we may pass through the alphabet prefixing our rhyme ending with the letters of the alphabet in order, hoping to find an appropriate rhyming word) with the creative flair of idea presentation.

The construction of software is no different; it requires that same odd couple. The creativity of design, for example, is interspersed with the discipline of coding. Design methodologies attempt to convert design into a disciplined activity, but they will never completely succeed in doing that as long as there are new problems to be solved. There is creativity in the writing of code, in solving the detail-level problems left unsolved in an inevitably incomplete design, and in the midst of the enormous disciplinary requirement to write code that tells a dumb computer in infinitesimal detail how to provide a desired solution.

We especially find this odd couple in software maintenance. The existing software, the program undergoing maintenance, imposes enormous disciplinary constraints on the creative maintainer. The current functionality of the existing software must be kept intact in the midst of adding new capability. Probably, this heavily constrained creativity is the most difficult kind; and in that difficulty lies the real reason that most programmers try to avoid doing maintenance. In the complex world of software construction, probably nothing is more complex than trying to be creative within inviolable disciplinary constraints.

There is a temptation, especially in the world of software, to see discipline and creativity as enemies. Those in the discipline camp say that more of it will lead to more effective software development. Those in the creativity camp say that less discipline is the key to more effective software development! A battleground is established; people choose up sides; and advocates lose sight of the fact that neither camp can be right by itself.

Finding an effective way of blending the odd couple of discipline and creativity is essential to further progress in our field, and achieving that progress requires that both camps lay down their arms and find ways of working together.

chapter 2
formal methods versus heuristics

chapter contents

Introduction to chapter 2

> "There are still enormous amounts of trial and error ... You go back and forth from observation to theory. You don't know what to look for without a theory, and you can't check the theory without looking at the fact ... I believe that the movement back and forth occurs thousands, even millions of times in the course of a single investigation."
> —*Joshua Lederberg,* Nobel prize winner (for his work on genes)as quoted in *The Search for Solutions,* Holt Rinehart and Winston 1980; Horace Freeland Judson (Reprinted by permission of Henry Holt and Company, Inc.)

I hope you'll forgive my penchant for word play.

This section, as you can see from the title above, is about formal methods and heuristics. It is about the relative role in the construction of software of an approach advocated by most of the computer scientists of our day—formal methods—and about another, alternative, almost opposite approach.

So what do these words mean?

My dictionary defines "formal" to mean "conforming to accepted rules or customs; regular or geometrical in design," and it defines "heuristic" to mean "encouraging students to discover information themselves; proceeding by trial and error."

Now, the dictionary definition of "formal" doesn't get very close to the computer science term "formal methods," but it certainly gives a hint of the intent of those methods. The essence of formal approaches is that they are rule-based and regular. (Although computer science definitions of formal methods vary somewhat, they generally include as a nucleus two notions: "formal specification," the use of mathematically rigorous languages to express problem requirements, and "formal verification," the use of mathematical approaches to "prove" a program to be consistent with its specification.) Computer scientists see formal methods as mathematically-based, systematic approaches to problem solution.

The essence of heuristic approaches is that they are exploration-based and irregular. Unlike the dilemma I faced in the previous section, where I struggled to match "discipline" with an opposite, here I think we have a fairly nice case of an obvious opposite.

What makes this pair of words particularly important in a book on software creativity is that, as we saw in the previous section, there are factions backing each word—and its underlying concepts—as the best way to build software. Not only are there advocates for each word, but in fact major emotional explosions have occurred in the literature over the years as the backers of each faction jockeyed for position!

What explosions? There was the "social processes" explosion in the late 1970s. Three respected authors—Richard A. DeMillo, Richard J. Lipton, and Alan J. Perlis—wrote a paper and published it in a couple of key computer science journals that took the position that formal mathematical—and therefore computer science—proofs were not the absolute we have always taken them to be, but rather that proofs require elaborate social processes before they can be relied upon. The reactions and explosions were almost immediate. Noted computer scientist (and formalist) Edsger Dijkstra took up the cudgel, saying in a published response that the authors had written "A Political Pamphlet from the Middle Ages," referred to the paper as "very ugly," and said that the authors had "gone much further than the usual practitioners' backlash."

Supporters of the original paper soon rallied. In the November 1979 issue of Communications of the ACM, frustrated pragmatists hailed the anti-proof paper as "the best I have read in a computer publication," and "marvelous, marvelous." One even said "It was time somebody said it—loud and clear—the formal approach to software verification does not work and probably never will ..."

(A more complete account of these incidents, including references to the papers in question, may be found in [Glass 1981].)

There was another major explosion to come. About 10 years after the previous anti-proof, anti-formal-methods paper, another was published, this time by James H. Fetzer. Once again, the reaction was swift and forceful. Ten respected formal methods supporters accused Fetzer, in a letter to the editor of Communications of the ACM, of "distortion," "gross misunderstanding," and being "irresponsible and dangerous" Fetzer responded in kind: his detractors, he said, exhibited a "complete failure to understand the issues," "intellectual deficiencies," and called their behavior that of "religious zealots and ideological fanatics."

(A more complete account of these incidents, including references, may be found in [Glass 1991]).

Why is there such heavy emotional overload on formal methods? Because it is a radically different approach to building software. Because it is largely unevaluated and unproven. Because, over the years, it has not attracted much support or use in the practitioner community. Because it is unabashedly advocated, and sometimes even enforced, by those who believe in its powers. And because those who advocate formal approaches tend to put down those who oppose them.

Above, I mentioned jockeying for position over formal approaches. The clear winners in this position-jockeying, as the original version of this book was being written (and in spite of the fiery opposition mentioned above), were the supporters of formal methods. Elementary computer science textbooks were more and more often including material on formal methods as a basic part of the framework for novices. The force of government and law had been invoked to support formal methods, such as the action of the British government requiring the use of formal approaches to build certain kinds of software. Most computer science professors taught and advocated formal methods, and (as we will see later in this book) were unwilling to listen to arguments that the value of the methods was unevaluated and unproven. Most conferences on computing subjects, at least those catering to academic audiences, contained mainstream tracks on formal approaches.

There was little doubt, as the new millennium approached, that formal methods had achieved a significant level of positional power (as described above). And now that the millennium is upon us, that positional power remains largely intact.

Is there any support for the notion of heuristic approaches at all? Is the battle really over?

Off in another part of the computing forest, adjacent to a larger forest populated by more traditional disciplines, there is a subject area called "problem-solving." In problem-solving, we see that the belief is quite the opposite of that in computer science. Problem-solving academics believe that, as the complexity of a problem increases, formal approaches become less and less valuable. In spite of the fact that heuristic (i.e., trial and error) approaches are conceptually inferior, the fact of the matter is—according to these specialists—they are the only ones that work for problems of significance. Herbert Simon, he of the Nobel and Turing awards, is one of the chief advocates of this point of view.

That, of course, brings us to the question, "Are problems solved in computer software complex and significant?" The truthful answer is, of course, "It varies." But here, the findings documented in [Dekleva 1991] become significant. The problems solved by software maintainers in 1990, he discovered in a survey, were 50 times larger than those of 1980! From these findings, it is fair to say that even the not very complicated problems solved by software are far more complicated than they were a decade ago, be that decade the 1980s, or 1990s, or even the 2000s.

In this chapter, I search for a truth or two in this emotionally charged morass. Whether you agree with the truths I discover, I suppose, will depend on your initial position on the line between formal methods and heuristics (this issue has moved well beyond intellectual analysis into the realm of advocacy and warfare, I'm afraid). Nevertheless, as you read, try to think as openly as you can about this vitally important issue. The future of computer science may well depend on it.

References

Dekleva 1991—"Real Maintenance Statistics," *Software Maintenance News*, February 1991.

Glass 1981—"A Look at Other Upstream Paddlers," *Software Soliloquies, Computing Trends*, 1981; Robert L. Glass.

Glass 1991—Preface of *Software Conflict*, Yourdon Press, 1991; Robert L. Glass (republished by developer.* Books in 2006 as *Software Conflict 2.0*).

2.1
clarifying a controversy

There is a controversy smoldering in the computer science world at the intersection of two important topics: formal methods and heuristics. The controversy, though it may sound esoteric and theoretic, is actually at the heart of our understanding of the future practice of software engineering.

There are some who see no controversy here. Many in the computer science community strongly advocate formal approaches and tend to look at heuristic ones as inferior. This viewpoint was reflected in the orchestrated theme issues of three leading IEEE software journals [Computer 1990, Software 1990, Transactions 1990], which said that the result of using formal methods would be "virtuoso software."

In addition, formal methods often form the substance of recommendations by computer science advisory groups about how to proceed toward software's future. In a report of the Computer Science Technology Board of the National Research Council (CSTB 1990], under the heading "Strengthen the Foundations," this statement is made:

"In the absence of a stronger scientific and engineering foundation, complex software systems are often produced by brute force, with managers assigning more and more people to the development effort and taking more and more time. As software engineers begin to envision systems that require many thousands of person-years, current pragmatic or heuristic approaches begin to appear less adequate to meet application needs. In this environment, software engineering leaders are beginning to call for more systematic approaches: more mathematics, science, and engineering are needed."

It is hard to disagree with such a statement. Somehow we all know that subtle force is better than brute force, rifle shots are better than shotgun blasts, and systematic is better than heuristic.

But there is an opposing viewpoint. We see it articulated increasingly often in the literature. Typically, its expression is subtle, appearing in the midst of a paper on some other subject. Consider these examples:

In a paper on software design [Rombach 1990], H. Dieter Rombach says, "The creative nature of the design process means that many aspects cannot be formalized ... at all. While formalization ... is a solution for more mechanical processes ... it is not feasible for design processes."

In a book on the history of medical informatics [Blum 1990], Bruce Blum says it even more strongly: "For well understood domains ... formulas and statistical inference as the best knowledge representations; for other tasks, heuristics and cognitive models provide the greatest power."

Even in the IEEE journal special formal methods theme issues mentioned above, there are niggling doubts expressed:

"Most formal methods have not yet been applied to specifying large-scale software or hardware systems; most are still inadequate to specify many important behavioral constraints beyond functionality, for example fault tolerance and real-time performance" (Jeanette Wing, [Computer 1990]).

"... less formal methods apply better to the more upstream problems [systems analysis and design]" [Software 1990, Gerhart].

These contemporary expressions of the value of heuristics and the limitations of formal methods have firm theoretic, historic roots. In The Sciences of the Artificial [Simon 1981], Nobel prize and Turing award winner Herbert A. Simon focuses on this very issue in a chapter titled "The Architecture of Complexity":

"The more difficult and novel the problem, the greater is likely to be the amount of trial and error required to find a solution ... selectivity derives from various rules of thumb, or heuristics, that suggest which paths should be tried first and which leads are promising."

Perhaps surprisingly, then, there is an argument to be made for heuristic approaches. In fact, as problems become more complex, some suggest that only heuristic methods are capable of providing solutions.

examples

Because this discussion has been somewhat intellectual and abstract, an example may help clarify things. Let me recount a homespun anecdote from my own experience to illustrate what happens to formal, mathematical approaches when problems become complex. The problem is, in fact, a largely non-computing one—it is the problem of determining the feasibility of loading a large object into the back of a station wagon.

Considered at its simplest, the cross-sectional shape of the interior of a station wagon is largely trapezoidal, and the feasibility question can be settled simply by measuring the trapezoid, measuring the object, and checking the dimensions to see if fit is possible.

But the problem becomes complex when we discover that station wagon interiors are not simple trapezoids. For one thing, there is a narrowed and lowered tailgate mouth to the trapezoid that restricts entry. For another, most of the trapezoid surfaces are actually curved. For a third, there are things that protrude into the trapezoid—wheel wells, door openings, clothing hooks, etc. The result is that, if the object fit in the trapezoid is marginal, the mathematics become exceedingly complex. Surfaces must have curves fit to them. Exception conditions must be dealt with repeatedly. The problem of determining fit becomes one of intersecting complicated surfaces in three dimensions. Even for a former mathematician with professional experience in Master Dimensions (the use of mathematics to determine aircraft geometry), this was a problem too difficult for me to want to tackle.

Confronted with dimensions that suggested fit was marginal, I rejected the complicated mathematical approach, and resorted to heuristics. I took the object to the station wagon, inserted it lengthwise through the narrowed tailgate opening, twisted and pulled and tugged it to the front end of the space, and finally found that (only) by opening the back doors to provide additional temporary interior space could I rotate the object into a position that would work.

Here, then, we see an example of a heuristic approach to a complicated problem. Perhaps mathematics and formal approaches could have solved the problem eventually (although I am doubtful that, immersed in the mathematics of the problem, I would have noticed the wisdom of opening the doors to increase interior space!); however, those approaches would have

- Required complicated additional skills
- Required algorithms not immediately available
- Probably required a computer program implementing those algorithms
- Taken significantly longer to achieve
- Been error-prone

In the practical world, it is important to note, time to do a task may often be as important as the quality of the result, and reliability is probably the most important result characteristic. Given that, I would assert, in this (prototypical) complex situation, heuristic methods did work and formal methods simply would not.

Some of the problems in the above bulleted list can be illustrated in another example, this one out of the computing literature. The Naval Research Laboratory funded, several years ago, a project that has been known variously as the A-7 project and the Software Cost Reduction Project (there is irony to the latter name, as we will see). Its outcome has been a series of frequently-referenced papers on formal approaches to stating the requirements of complicated systems, and in that sense it has been a dramatic success.

But there is another sense in which the project was a failure. It was originally conceived as one in which a formal approach to software development would be contrasted with an ad hoc one by redeveloping software for the A-7 aircraft using formal approaches, then comparing the maintainability of the formally developed code with the maintainability of the original *(ad hoc)* code (by installing the same changes in both). This aspect of the project had to be aborted, because the formal approach simply took too long. With the schedule and budget more than consumed, it was not possible to conduct the experiment that would have evaluated the benefits of the formal approach.

The conclusion of one of the key players in this project was that "Software is hard." That is, developing complex software is far more difficult than those who have developed only simple software might ever imagine. (A more complete version of this story appears later in this book.)

"smoldering"

At the outset of this essay, the word "smoldering" was used to describe the state of the controversy. The word was deliberately chosen.

In a tumultuous time several decades ago, the subject of formal verification of programs ("proof of correctness") exploded into controversy in the literature [DeMillo 1979, Fetzer 1988]. Opponents published papers suggesting fundamental flaws in the concept, proponents lashed the opponents with emotional and personal arguments, and more opponents leaped into the fray, making a verbal free-for-all. Arguments took on the characteristics of religious wars.

At about the same time, Edsger Dijkstra [Dijkstra 1989] was encouraged to engage in a public debate on a variety of topics focusing on the wisdom of teaching formal methods to entry-level computer science students. This (planned) exchange was more temperate than the previous ones, but the result was the same: strong emotional and sometimes personal reaction among the debaters and those who followed up with letters to the editor.

These incidents show that the drive toward formal methods is currently immersed in zealous fervor and reactionary resistance. Neither side of the controversy seems able to see any value in the beliefs of the other. Clearly, the issue of solving complex problems is central to the future of software engineering. Just as clearly, any controversies that stand between us and the solution of that problem must be addressed and resolved.

conclusion

It is the position of this essay that there is conflict between those who advocate formal methods and those who advocate heuristic ones; that the controversy spawned by the conflict is legitimate, with "right thinking" on both sides; and that the controversy needs to be aired in a non-emotional setting. Because discussions of formalism have tended to be forceful "pro" advocacy presentations countered by "con" rebuttals, this paper has attempted to summarize the positive aspects of the opposing position by reference, example, and anecdote.

It should be noted that careful reading will disclose a potential middle ground. Formal methods, perhaps, are appropriate for solving mechanistic and well understood problems or parts of problems; heuristics are necessary for more complicated and creative ones. Perhaps formal methods could help to steer the

process of "selective trial and error" that Simon describes (by, for example, giving us rules and methods for seeking choices and making selections). As is true in most significant controversies, the eventual "true" position will probably amalgamate considerations from both extremes.

references

Blum 1990—"Medical Informatics in the United States, 1950–1975," *A History of Medical Informatics*, ACM Press, 1990; Bruce I. Blum.

Computer 1990—Special issue of *IEEE Computer*, on "Formal Methods—Prelude to Virtuoso Software," September 1990.

CSTB 1990—"Scaling Up: A Research Agenda for Software Engineering," a report of the Computer Science Technology Board of the National Research Council, *Communications of the ACM*, March 1990.

DeMillo 1979—"Social Processes and Proofs of Theorems and Programs," *Communications of the ACM*, May 1979; Richard A. DeMillo, Richard J. Lipton, and Alan J. Perlis.

Dijkstra 1989—"On the Cruelty of Really Teaching Computing Science," *Communications of the ACM*, December 1989; Edsger W. Dijkstra.

Fetzer 1988—"Program Verification: The Very Idea," *Communications of the ACM*, September 1988; James H. Fetzer.

Rombach 1990—"Design Measurement: Some Lessons Learned," *IEEE Software*, March 1990; H. Dieter Rombach.

Simon 1981—*The Sciences of the Artificial*, MIT Press, 1981; Herbert A. Simon.

Software 1990—Special issue of *IEEE Software*, on "Formal Methods—Developing Virtuoso Software," September 1990.

Transactions 1990—Special issue of *IEEE Transactions* on Software Engineering on "Formal Methods," September 1990.

2.2

A Guilt-Free Approach to software construction

Does your approach to building software involve a lot of trial and error? Does that feel like a poor way to go about things? Do you think you ought to be mastering all those computer science formal approaches that some people are talking about?

Well, one possible answer to all of those questions is "Yes." Yes, you do a lot of trial and error. Yes, it seems like a poor way to go. And yes, perhaps you ought to try formal methods.

However, that is only one possible answer. There is another possible answer, it may surprise you to know, that is largely the opposite of "yes." With this answer, it is all right to use trial and error. Successful people do it all the time. In fact, the more you try and fail, the more likely it is that you will succeed!

I like to think of this as the "guilt-free answer" to building software. That guilt you may have been feeling about trial-and-error approaches is largely unnecessary and, in fact, uncalled-for.

So let's take a look at trial-and-error approaches to building software for a minute, especially from the point of view of the importance of failure in achieving success.

One of the finest ironies I know is that people who are successful tend to fail more often that those who are not!

That peculiar finding shows up in a lot of different places in a lot of different ways. For example, in software we see it arising in analyzing the work of good people versus those who are not so good: in [Vitalari 1983] we see that good systems analysts try, and reject, more hypotheses than do bad analysts. In [Curtis 1987] we see that good designers use a trial-and-error process to create mental models of a design solution, running mental simulations on them to see if they are correct—and that poor designers tend to seize on a solution with fewer trials and errors than good designers. In [Soloway 1988] we see that good maintainers conduct repeated "inquiry episodes," in which they read a section of code with some particular question in mind, conjecture an answer, search the documentation and/or code for information about the answer, and then reject or accept the answer based on the information found—and if the answer is rejected, they begin the iterative process again.

Good systems analysts, designers, and maintainers may have several traits that distinguish them from their less-good colleagues, but we see here that one of those traits is the ability to fail and recover. That kind of trial and error is what we call a "heuristic" process, and we could express this finding in another way: good people in software are those who have mastered heuristic processes.

That is not, of course, just true for software people. In fact, there is a whole book about the importance of failure—[Petroski 1985] finds, over and over again, that one cannot succeed without failing first. In the book, he hammers home that thought with chapter after chapter:

"Falling Down Is Part of Growing Up"

"Success Is Foreseeing Failure"

"When Cracks Become Breakthroughs"

And with quote after quote:

"The engineer no less than the poet sees the faults in his creations, and he learns more from his mistakes and those of others than he does from all the masterpieces created by himself and his peers."

"There is the greatest practical benefit to making a few mistakes early in life." (quoting T. H. Huxley, On Medical Education)

And even with wonderful stories:

"Pencils tipped with erasers were originally condemned by some educators because 'the easier errors are to correct, the more errors will be made'" (this quote is from Petroski's *The Pencil*).

Not only is failure important, but it is frequent. Nobel prize winner Joshua Lederberg (famed for his work on genes), talking about the scientific method, says, "There are still enormous amounts of trial and error ... You go back and forth from observation to theory. You don't know what to look for without a theory, and you can't check the theory without looking at the fact ... I believe that that movement back and forth occurs thousands, even millions of times in the course of a single investigation" [Judson 1980].

It is even possible to point to some of the better successes of the last century—people like President Harry S. Truman, or phenomenal candy maker Milton Snavely Hershey, and see that they failed for years, even decades, even with failures as severe as bankruptcy, before eventually becoming the successes that made them famous.

There are a couple of risks in advocating these failure-based approaches to success, of course. One is that the material here verges on the sickeningly sweet. It would be all too easy to lapse into a chorus of "if at first you don't succeed, try, try again," with "The Bluebird of Happiness" playing softly in the background; and that, of course, falls into the category of "trite and true."

The other risk is that all of this should not be an excuse to allow creeping errorism into your work. There is a time to fail in pursuit of success, and there is a time to fail out of laziness. The former is fine; the latter is a cop-out.

Still, the next time you feel guilty about the amount of error that trial-and-error solutions require, remember that without that error—and sometimes plenty of it—there's hardly any success.

Welcome, then, to the guilt-free approach to software construction!

References

Curtis 1987—"Empirical Studies of the Design Process: Papers for the Second Workshop on Empirical Studies of Programmers," *MCC Technical Report Number STP-260–87*, September 1987; Bill Curtis, Raymonde Guindon, Herb Krasner, Diane Walz, Joyce Elam, and Neil Iscoe.

Judson 1980—*The Search for Solutions*, Holt, Rinehart, and Winston, 1980; Horace Freeland Judson.

Petroski 1985—*To Engineer Is Human—The Role of Failure in Successful Design*, St. Martin's Press, 1985; Henry Petroski.

Soloway 1988—"Designing Documentation to Compensate for Delocalized Plans," *Communications of the ACM*, November 1988; Elliot Soloway.

Vitalari 1983—"Problem Solving for Effective Systems Analysis: An Experimental Exploration," *Communications of the ACM*, November 1983; Vitalari and Dickson.

2.3

Formal Methods: A Dramatic (Success, Failure) Story

One of the best-known software projects of all time actually has the strangest history of any software project I know. This is the story of that project.

The strangeness of this project begins with the project name. It is called two different things, depending on how you look back on its history. (That is not so unusual ... The Civil War was known for years in the South as the "War Between the States," and the British fought over the "Falkland Islands" while Argentina was fighting over the "Malvinas.") Those who see the project as a success call it the "Software Cost Reduction project." Those who see it in a different light simply call it the "A-7 project."

But whatever it was called, the project started out with Noble Hopes that ended as either a Roaring Success or a Dramatic Failure, depending on what your expectations were about those Noble Hopes. Let me explain.

This was no ordinary project, whatever else you may say about it. As our story begins, the Navy has some real-time avionics software for one of their aircraft, the A-7. It is not very maintainable, poorly documented, and shoehorned into a computer too slow and too small to do the job for which it was intended. In short, it is a fairly typical embedded computer system!

What made the project extraordinary had nothing to do with the problem being solved. What made it extraordinary was that the Navy was willing to use this project as a guinea pig to see if there were better ways to build such software.

Enter noted computed scientist David Parnas and a group of supporting researchers. Enter some funding from the Naval Research Laboratory. Enter the idea that the A-7 software would be redone, from scratch, with new and modern software approaches. Enter the idea that this whole project would be a giant experiment, with the effectiveness of the new approaches versus the old being measured at the end. Here's the way it was to go:

Parnas and his team were to retrieve the requirements for the A-7 software and start it all over again, using none of what had been done before. As they proceeded to develop a new version of the software, the old version, of course, would continue to be used and undergo maintenance. A record would be kept of all the changes to the old software, as well as the schedule and time cost of making the changes. When the new version of the software was up to the capability of the old software at the beginning of the experiment, the changes made to the old version would be made to the new. Once again, resource costs would be tracked. A comparison would then be made of the resource cost of the changes to the two versions.

In short, this was to be the biggest and most comprehensive experimental software research project ever done. There was little doubt about what the findings would be—most people assumed that the new version would be enormously easier and cheaper to change than the old—the only real question in most people's minds was "how much cheaper?"

However, trouble arose almost immediately. That simple phrase in the previous paragraph, "retrieve the requirements," turned out to be an immensely difficult problem. The requirements were embedded in the as-built code, of course, but that did not mean they were easy to comprehend. The original sources of the requirements—the responsible engineers and the project documentation—were either missing or unavailable, or the understanding they did provide was obsolete due to changes in the software that had taken place since the original requirements. The A-7 software had, in fact, taken on a life of its own, beyond documentation and human knowledge.

(As time goes by, we in the software business are beginning to realize that this problem is not that unusual. Many in the information systems field, for example, have experienced the dilemma of starting over on old software, only to realize to their astonishment and perhaps even horror that it is effectively impossible to glean the underlying problem from its software solution. No matter how sensible that approach may seem at first thought, it is now all too often impossible to reconstruct existing software from scratch [Glass 1991]!)

Parnas and his people struggled on, however. They did the best job they could of retrieving the old requirements, using whatever means necessary. They also began inventing techniques to record and later be able to reference the requirements. Here, in fact, is where the success of the "Software Cost Reduction" project is found. The formal approaches for stating and referencing requirements have probably been mentioned as frequently as any other work in the requirements field in recent years [Heninger 1980].

But time was passing; and with the passage of time, the original goal of the project was fading. There was an assumption, it is important to remember, that the new software project would in some sense "catch up" with the old, allowing the maintenance-focused part of the experiment to begin. The old project was instead pulling away from the new one. No matter how spiffy the new formal methods for recording requirements were, the goals of the original experiment were slipping out of reach. If the new software couldn't catch up with the old, it was simply impossible to begin the experiment.

More time passed. The successes of the "Software Cost Reduction" phase began to pale. From an "A-7 project" point of view, the whole thing began to resemble a government boondoggle. Even David Parnas, in discussing the work, said he wasn't sure, at the end, whether this would be seen as a wonderful research effort or a candidate for a "Golden Fleece" award (a hypothetical award given by a U.S. congressman to someone who has wasted a large sum of government money in some foolish way).

Eventually, the financial plug was pulled on the project. The experiment, the original goal of the project, was never really begun.

The amazing part of this story is that two camps view this outcome in two very different ways. Some could "point with pride" at the work done in requirements analysis and representation. From a practical point of view, it was a truly impressive attempt to create and/or restore order in a project that in some sense had gotten out of control. From a research point of view, a foundation was laid for follow-up work in requirements-in-the-large analysis.

However, some found it easy to instead "view with alarm" the inability to achieve closure on the original goals of the project. There were no experimental findings whatsoever. Nothing quantitative was learned about maintainability. The old A-7 software continued to be used, and the new was not.

There was even disagreement about the usefulness of what was accomplished. David Parnas says things like "The Navy Quality Assurance people [used the new requirements statement] to go through their tests to see if they were checking every case ... The Air Force took our A-7 document and rewrote it so that it covered their software ... They now use it for contracting [to] give them a quick way of writing a watertight request to contract for changes" [Zvegintzov 1988].

However, one key player in the original A-7 work took me aside at a luncheon one day and said, "We couldn't use the Naval Research Lab approach in industry; we had to give up on it."

73

So there you have it. Two very different senses of the outcome. Either the formal approaches used on the Software Cost Reduction project did a wonderful, useful job of attempting to extract order from chaos. Or, from another point of view, those A-7 project approaches took so long to accomplish that the work surrounding them was scrapped, and the methods were simply unusable in future work.

Success or failure? The answer probably depends on whether you think like a researcher or a practitioner. But however you view the ending here, this story of a project with an ambiguous name and an unhappy ending does a nice job of characterizing the dilemma of using formal approaches or their pragmatic alternatives.

The rigor of formality, we can see here, is sometimes something you can't afford to do without, and at other times something you simply can't afford. The trick is in knowing which instance you are involved with!

References

Glass 1991—"The Re-Engineering Decision: Lessons from the Best of Practice," *The Software Practitioner*, May 1991; Robert L. Glass.

Heninger 1980—"Specifying Software Requirements for Complex Systems: New Techniques and Their Applications," IEEE *Transactions on Software Engineering*, January 1980; K.L. Heninger.

Zvegintzov 1988—"Parnas Interviewed at ESP-2," *Software Maintenance News*, March 1988; Nicholas Zvegintzov.

2.4
Beyond Formal Methods

Some years ago two books appeared on the computing scene. One was called *The Science of Programming.* The other was *The Art of Programming.* They came out within months of each other. And, probably accidentally, they each constituted a challenge to the other. Which one was right? Is programming science or art?

Years pass, and the scene is played out again. Same theme, different chorus. Two keynoters address the annual International Conference on Software Engineering. One stresses the need for formal approaches to building software. The other stresses the need for approaches based on the needs of the application. Once again, the question arises: Who is right here? Should software development proceed along formal mathematical lines, or along lines dictated by the application in question?

A few more months pass. Buried deeply in a paper on an apparently unrelated topic, the issue surfaces again. In [Grudin 1989], we find, "There is an easily overlooked conflict between the search for formal properties of [user] interfaces and the call for 'user-centered' design and task analysis ... the more closely one looks [for formal, consistent interfaces], the less substance one finds."

Meanwhile, the issue surfaces in other forms. Most often, someone sees formal methods as the solution to the software problems caused by "undisciplined, heuristic approaches."

75

"Heuristic," especially, begins to feel like evil incarnate ... or a straw man to attack on behalf of formalism.

Then a surprising new voice is heard from. Peter Denning, a long-time academic computer scientist and activist, in an editorial [Denning 1991], advocates some surprising heresy. "There is nothing wrong with formality," he begins, innocently enough. "It has demonstrated remarkable technological power." And then comes the surprise: "I am saying it limits what we can accomplish. We need to go beyond formality and learn about communication in our organizations and in our software designs ... The time has come to pay more attention to the murky, imprecise, unformalizable domains of everyday practice."

The roots of computer science, at many academic institutions, lie firmly wrapped around the roots of the disciplinary tree called "pure mathematics"; and in the world of pure mathematics, where something called "applied mathematics" has been treated as an unwanted stepchild, analytic and formal approaches have been at the heart of the discipline. That same focus has, for historic reasons, become a strong part of the flavor of computer science.

However, off in the wings is a new cousin to that stepchild, called "software engineering," having the same applied relationship to computer science as applied math has had to pure math. And for that new cousin, what is good is what works, whether it is formal or not. As the complexity of problems solved in software engineering has magnified over the years—some say by a factor of 50 in 10 years!—we find, for example, problems being solved by simulation techniques (and thus heuristic approaches) that are simply too complicated to be solved by analytic (and thus formal) approaches. It seems possible that, with the power of the computer to move us forward, we are beginning to bump into problems subject to the limitations of formal approaches.

Contrarily, with the increase in complexity of problems to be solved, we are beginning to run into problems where formality is the only solution, and only the powerful computers available make those formal methods applicable!

The debate is clear. Some say that complex problems can only be addressed by formal approaches. Others say that formal approaches simply fail to scale up to complex problems.

Yet a third group—the ones I suspect will be seen to be correct when the smoke clears—say that "beyond formal methods" lies the answer to complexity. It's now time to begin exploring what "beyond formal methods" really means.

References

Denning 1991—"Editorial," *Communications of the ACM*, March 1991; Peter J. Denning.

Grudin 1989—"The Case Against User Interface Consistency," *Communications of the ACM*, October 1989; Jonathan Grudin.

2.5

My Readers write: some Thoughts on Formal Methods

Once people know that you have a contrarian view of a popular topic, you tend to become a magnet for those who share your view. My opinion of formal approaches, expressed in various forums over the years, has attracted some interesting responses.

Several years ago I wrote to Jeff Offutt, then a professor at Clemson University (and more recently at George Mason University) regarding my concern that tight coupling (characterized by, among other things, the avoidance of the use of global or common data access) was advocated by most computer scientists but used by few of them when the time came for them to actually build software. I chose to write to Offutt because he had presented some material on coupling at a conference that year. It turned out, however, that I had gotten the subject wrong—coupling, as used in the testing community that Offutt had addressed, was about something very different from what I was concerned about.

In spite of my mistake, Offutt took up the challenge of the topic that I had presented, with some surprising thoughts:

"The question you raise about advocacy of tight coupling by people who actually use loose coupling is a very thought-provoking problem. This could even be raised to a higher arena to ask why we, as software engineers, constantly teach students and practitioners to develop software in carefully measured, structured ways, but then we go back to our laboratories, close the doors, and implement programs in C that multiply pointers and the like. I myself am guilty of not always following my own advice; as a graduate student I implemented large portions of the Mothra mutation [testing] system and never once wrote down a requirement or specification and my designs were largely scribblings on sheets of scratch paper. There is obviously something fundamentally wrong with our formal approaches to building software*—and I think this coupling contradiction is one symptom of this."

Another correspondent, this time practitioner Douglas King of Hughes, also chose to share some thoughts with me. He was primarily concerned about the relative importance of people and process in the construction of software. However, regarding formal approaches, he said:

"Some of Herbert Simon's works refer to 'Gresham's Law of Planning':

"'[Gresham's Law] states that programmed activity tends to drive out nonprogrammed activity. If an executive has a job that involves a mixture of programmed and nonprogrammed decision-making responsibility, the former will come to be emphasized at the expense of the latter' [Simon 1965].

"When Simon talks about 'programmed' activities, he's talking about solving well understood problems via some systematic, structured procedure such as a formal method. When he talks about 'unprogrammed' activities, he's talking about solving ill-understood problems, using a weakly structured approach such as a heuristic. To me, Gresham's Law of Planning suggests that the tension between formal and informal methods is rooted in human nature and will therefore never be permanently resolved. Having a method in our madness is always more attractive than madness by itself, but sometimes there is no alternative. Methods, after all, are just rational, postmortem generalizations of madness. The interesting thing is that even though systematic procedures enable

*The emphasized in quotations in this article are my own, not those of the quoted source.

us to solve more and more problems, we never seem to run out of new problems that defeat them. It's a bit like medicine: as soon as researchers devise a vaccine to cure a particular flu, a new strain appears ... The real fun of engineering is tackling the new strains!"

From Offutt we see that the tension between formal and informal approaches is very real, and that we do not always practice what we preach (which, of course, suggests that something is wrong with what we preach).

From King we can see that this tension is ages old, not only unresolved but perhaps irresolvable. (That thought probably can be applied, in fact, to any of the dichotomies presented in this book!) But we can also see that the choice may be dependent on the nature of the problem being solved—for well-understood problems, formality is apparently appropriate. For new problems (such as Offutt's work behind the closed doors of his office!), it is apparently not.

I thank both of them, and anyone else who chooses to write to me about these matters (that is a non-subtle hint!), for helping reshape my thoughts in some new and worthwhile directions.

Reference

Simon 1965—*The Shape of Automation for Men and Management,* Harper and Row, 1965; Herbert Simon.

chapter 3
optimizing versus satisficing

chapter contents

introduction to chapter 3

"Uncertainty is present in most situations we face. It is a part of the human condition. We must learn to accept this fact and deal with uncertainty in two fundamental ways: develop tools to reduce it when we can, and learn to tolerate it when we cannot ... the predisposition to tolerating uncertainty is a crucial attitude for creative human thinking and problem-solving."

—*Moshe F. Rubinstein*
Tools for Thinking and Problem-Solving,
Prentice-Hall 1986

In the title of this chapter, I stretch the English language a bit. Optimizing, of course, is a pretty legitimate word, derived from optimum: "best, most favorable."

Satisficing, however, is a bit more questionable. It's based on a perfectly legitimate word, satisfy: "to give a person what he wants or demands or needs; to demand no more than this, to consider that this is enough."

But satisficing itself, I suspect, you will have difficulty finding in any dictionary. Certainly it's not in mine.

It is, however, a perfectly legitimate word in some circles. In fact, to the best of my knowledge, it was invented in those circles.

What circles? In the previous chapter's introduction, I discussed the discipline of problem-solving and its belief that heuristics were the most appropriate solution to complex problems. It is the problem-solving community, I believe, that invented this word, probably because there was a serious problem it needed to solve.

The problem was this: If you use rigorous, formal methods to solve a problem, you can probably arrive at a correct, perhaps even optimal, solution. Remember, from above, that optimal solutions are ones that are "best and most favorable." Nice solutions to have, optimal ones.

However, the problem confronted by problem-solvers was that, in the nasty world of heuristic problem-solving, it was never quite so clear that a problem solution was indeed a best one. According to the definition, a satisficing solution might be "good enough," but it would be difficult to call it "best."

There's a figure (3.1) in one of the essays in this section which illustrates that dilemma fairly nicely. Suffice it to say, at this point, that complex problems often have multiple solutions, and because of the complexity of the problem it is often not possible to identify a clearly best solution.

What is a problem-solver to do? The invented answer, according to the best and brightest problem-solvers, is the invented word "satisfice." If you can't find an optimum solution, then find one that satisfices.

What does that mean? Find a solution that, from the best heuristic efforts you have employed, seems to be a best solution.

But that's not good enough, I hear you saying. And, of course, you are right. Here are all these formal approaches parading their optimal solutions, and there are those poor heuristics not having the faintest idea whether their solutions are really very good or not.

What, then, should a problem-solver do? The answer is that satisficing solutions must be "supportable." (To justify one invented word we have to invent another?!) A solution is said to be a satisficing one by problem-solvers if it is supportable; that is, if there is a solid rationale for why it could be optimal.

One of the nice things about complicated problems is that it is difficult for anyone to say that your satisficing solution is, in fact, non-optimal. The very fact that your problem is complex means that few, if any, will be prepared to challenge your "optimal" (really, "satisficing") answer. And if they do successfully challenge your answer, of course, you simply adopt their new answer as a satisficing one—it is unlikely that theirs is truly optimal either—and wait for another, better but still satisficing answer to come along!

What do optimizing and satisficing have to do with software creativity? In the realm of problems where software creativity is most needed, I say in this section, the software developer will quite likely have to give up on the goal of optimizing and (reluctantly) move on to the goal of satisficing. And, if that happens, the creative software developer must understand the role of supportability in the world of satisficing.

Under the guise of this title, we wander a bit. We define and explore one of those cutesy acronyms that we computer people love so much ("BIEGE"); we engage in a little word play, making the discovery along the way that computer scientists, for some bizarre reason, have been misusing the phrase ad hoc. In the midst of all that, we pay a visit to the old Soviet Union and come to understand a bit more about that respected but now deposed leader, Mikhail Gorbachev, in a psychological investigation of "ambiguity." Can all of this diversity really relate to optimizing and satisficing?

Obviously, I think the answer is yes. A clearer understanding of things ad hoc and things "ambiguous," I believe, leads us to a clearer understanding of when we must transition from optimizing to satisficing solutions. However, at best that's a satisficing, not an optimizing, call. Read on, and make your own decision!

3.1
The BIEGE principle of problem solution

How hard should we work to design the software solution to a problem?

That sounds like a fairly simple question, and you would think it would have a fairly simple answer. It's sort of like the old conundrum about the length of an essay or a speech: like a woman's skirt, it should be long enough to cover the subject but short enough to be interesting (is there a female equivalent of this very male chauvinist viewpoint?!)

So the design solution to a problem should be good enough to completely solve it, and no more. Sounds simple, right?

Except that it's not that simple. There are solutions, and then there are solutions. Some solutions are overly elaborate and sophisticated (practitioners know these by the name "goldplating"). Some solutions are simplistic and trivial (practitioners know these by the name "inadequate" or even "wrong"). And some solutions, the ones we all wish we could provide, are elegant and beautiful and creative because they are simple solutions to terribly complex problems. The trick is first to strive for that elegance, and then, if we can't achieve it with an appropriate expenditure of resources, to make sure that, if we are forced to a complex solution, it's because the problem is complex, not just our solution.

However, all of that discussion suggests that there are a lot of different solutions to a problem, and that it's hard to know when you've got a good one. Well, surprise! That describes the software world, and the difficulty of providing software solutions, in a nutshell. Even for fairly simple problems, there is not one clearly best solution approach (or one clearly best solution) when designing software solutions (or coding software solutions, for that matter). Most problems addressed by software fall into the category that problem-solvers call "unstructured"; and for that class of problem solution, knowing how hard to work to solve the problem is a serious (er) problem!

(I remember the speaker at a recent computing conference who postulated a reuse-finding mechanism that depended on today's designer posing a design solution in the same form as that of the designer of the reusable component being sought. That sort of thing is simply unlikely to happen in the real world of software design solutions.)

For most complex problems, in fact, there are a lot of different levels of possible design solution. There's the ultimate, best-of-all-possible-worlds, solution. There's the acceptable, it-works-but-wouldn't-it-have-been-nice-to-do-it-better solution. There's the totally inadequate, this-won't-do-at-all non-solution. And there are lots of stops in between. Figure 3.1 gives a nice example of how one might arrive at such a diversity of solutions from the problem of trying to find the maximum point on the curve in the figure.

Now this whole issue is getting complicated. If there are many different levels of solutions, then, once again, "How hard should we work to solve a problem?"

Fortunately, there are some answers in the literature on problem-solving. Interestingly, the field of problem-solving is, as you might imagine, as old as humankind, but it encountered a resurgence about a third of a century ago with the advent of the computer as a new problem-solving tool. And there's one book on problem-solving that, I would assert, rises head and shoulders above the rest.

figure 3.1: optimizing versus satisficing. Think about a trial-and-error non-visual search technique for finding the maximum y-coordinate on this curve. (Assume that there is no analytic approach; for such a curve, that is probably an accurate assumption.) Unless the granularity of the search is exceedingly fine (and thus expensive), a less-than-optimal solution is likely to be chosen.

That book is *The Sciences of the Artificial*, a masterpiece of a book by Nobel and Turing award winner Herbert Simon. There's so much in that book that it dwarfs this simple essay, but one of the more fascinating ideas in that book is the notion of "optimizing" and "satisficing." Optimizing is what we do when we try to find the best possible solution to a problem. However, Simon says, for difficult problems there often is no obvious way to find an optimizing solution. For that class of problem, Simon concludes, it is necessary for us to settle for a satisficing solution.

What does he mean, "satisficing"? He means a solution that works, one that is "good enough," one that stops short of being an optimizing solution but will do the job in question.

How do you know when you have one of those? The answer, according to Simon, is when you can provide an adequate rationale for your solution. That is, the satisficing solution is "supportable."

Is this just semantic arm-waving? Well, look back at that curve in Figure 3.1 and try to figure out an approach by means of which you could guarantee that you would discover the true maximum. Be realistic, now. You do not have infinite resources to find a solution. Assume there's a boss breathing down your neck for a solution a week ago yesterday, which is the situation that most software folks are in; and assume that he or she has put severe cost constraints on what you could spend along the way.

This notion of a satisficing solution is an important one, but it also adds a new complication to the problem-solving process. It's not enough to begin the search for a solution. It is necessary, beforehand, to know what an acceptable level of solution is. Is this one of those rare problems where nothing short of an optimizing solution will do? Or is it one that is time-constrained and cost-constrained, and what is needed is simply something that works? Both kinds of problems exist in the real world, and it is important to know which kind you have before you begin to try to find a solution.

There's a nice saying that fits the message here. It's called the BIEGE principle. BIEGE is an acronym, and the principle goes like this: the Better Is the Enemy of the Good Enough.

It means, simply, that if you have a problem for which a satisficing solution will do, don't keep working the problem trying to find the optimizing one.

88

3.2
good enough software

Now of all of that stuff in the previous section or two was kind of philosophic. Conceptually, I think, almost anyone could agree with it. Certainly "good enough" can be trumped by gold-plating approaches that waste time trying to make them "better," and I think only the most hardened perfectionist would see striving beyond "good enough" as a (er) good thing.

All of this left the realm of philosophy and became fairly concrete about a dozen years ago. Advocates of satisficing and the BIEGE principle embarked on the course of supporting something they called "Good Enough" software. Although at the time a lot of energy had to be poured in to defining "good enough,' in the context we find ourselves in here I think it is unnecessary. Good enough = satisficing, right?

Perhaps not surprisingly, a lot of people chose up sides over the issue. Supporters noted that, of course, one shouldn't strive for perfection in a field where getting something that works is difficult enough. Opponents, by contrast, said that we were lowering the standards of the software profession needlessly, encouraging people to build shoddy software in an era where it is difficult enough to get software in the commercial marketplace that works as well as we all would like. There was a standoff of probably uncorrectable proportions.

While all this was going on, publications like *Cutter IT Journal* were fanning the flames, publishing special issues on the subject and stimulating public discussion about it. To be honest, I think it was a good thing that the IT Journal fanned those flames. Topics like this have a way of smoldering and, at unlikely times in the future, erupting in some really serious flames if they are not vented early on.

In a way, of course, all of this became a tempest in a teapot. Some people may indeed have tried to define methodologies and techniques that could result in "good enough" software. And others continued to fight those approaches on the grounds mentioned above. But the fact of the matter is, "good enough" is what most of us do, like it or not, because going beyond good enough is both fiscally and mentally taxing. The BIEGE principle is alive and well in the software engineering word, and the controversy over "good enough" has pretty well died down.

In case all of this is still too philosophical for you, let me tell you a story that illustrates this whole issue rather nicely, I think. Once upon a time a brilliant computer scientist, working for an aerospace firm in industry, was asked to develop an application program. The program was to be an assembler for a one-off on-board computer for a space vehicle. The overall application was, of course, exotic—most space applications are—but the specific task was not. Anyone who understood system programming could write an assembler, and it was a task that could be dashed off fairly quickly.

It was not in the nature of this brilliant computer scientist to dash off anything fairly quickly, however. He got a workable version of his assembler on the air right away, as you might imagine. But what happened next was a surprise to all the rest of us on that project.

There was other software work waiting in the wings, work that had not yet been assigned to any members of this team. But our brilliant computer scientist continued to work on his assembler, which over time became more and more of a work of art. He strengthened the user interface; he embellished the outputs/displays; he refactored the code into more elegant forms of solution.

Weeks passed. The rest of us had completed our project assignments and gone on to successor tasks on the project. But that assembler kept on getting better. Needlessly better, of course. But definitely better.

By the time I first heard of the BIEGE principle I had absorbed this particular anecdote fairly thoroughly, and I knew precisely what BIEGE meant in practice. At the time of this story, however, we used a different term to describe what was happening: our old-friend-term "goldplating." And managers were seriously concerned about making sure that goldplating wasn't happening on their watch. (I suppose the brilliant computer scientist's manager simply never caught on that it was taking unreasonably long to build that assembler. Picture Dilbert's pointy-haired boss!)

When it comes to the BIEGE principle, as you might imagine, my mind immediately leaps to that time so long ago when the repercussions of not adhering to it were so blatantly bad. Put me down as solidly on the side of those who supported the "good enough" software notion.

3.3
In Defense of Ad-Hocracy

What is the worst dirty word in the computer scientist's vocabulary?

Based on what I've observed over the years, I'd say it's ad hoc. Computer scientists use it to refer to anything evil in the way people build software. They use it to mean "unrigorous" and "without planning" and even "chaotic." If your way of working has been branded ad hoc by a computer scientist, you know that he or she doesn't think much of how you do business.

Now let me make a confession. When I first heard computer scientists label something as ad hoc years ago, I didn't know what they meant. So I quietly looked it up in the dictionary, and what I found there didn't seem all that bad. That early dictionary of mine said this:

ad hoc: for a special purpose, as an *ad hoc* committee (Oxford American Dictionary)

I was puzzled. There was nothing in the dictionary that forced ad hoc to carry all the baggage that computer scientists had heaped on it. Certainly, just because I do something for a special purpose doesn't mean that I'm doing it badly. What was going on here?

Time passed. I continued to keep this puzzle on a low-priority burner in the back of my mind. As that time passed, computer scientists continued to use the word in the same way. If anything, the equating of *ad hoc* with "badness" intensified. Even reports to the federal government about the future of software said that we had to move from these old ad hoc and chaotic ways of doing business to some newer, and apparently better, ones.

Recently I found myself in the presence of one of those library wonders, the dictionary so heavy that it takes a crane to lift it! "Perhaps," I said to myself, rummaging around in the back of my mind to find that burner on which I had filed the definition of ad hoc, "perhaps this dictionary will solve the puzzle." With great physical strength, I opened the cover of this huge dictionary and found the definition of ad hoc once again:

ad hoc: for this (special purpose); with respect to this (subject or thing) (Webster's Encyclopedic Unabridged Dictionary)

The puzzle, far from being solved, was growing deeper. Computer scientists, it was now becoming clear, had been misusing the word!

Since replacing the cover on that second dictionary and recovering from the physical exertion it entailed (!), I have begun to think a little more about this semantic curiosity. What would cause a whole generation of computer scientists to follow each other, lemming-like, to the wrong use of a word?

Here's what I've come up with: I think there are two things going on here. The first is about the history of computing, and the second is about the origins of computer science. Let's do the first one first.

From the earliest days of commercial computing in the 1950s, weird and wonderful people have been struggling with the issue of how to build this artifact called software. In the beginning, it was difficult but not impossible to focus in on the particular problem at hand, devise a solution, and code it. The solution was typically some machine or assembler code that ran on a relatively bare machine, one with little or no operating system, and solved the problem at hand efficiently (inefficiency in those days was intolerable) and simply (machines were too small to allow complicated solutions).

The problem was that each problem solution got us only a little closer to being able to solve the next one. What we needed was to generalize the software problem-solving process. In those early days, a small but growing effort was put into producing generalized solution approaches. Generalized programming languages were invented, generalized computers were manufactured, generalized tools and parts were made available, and the beginnings of a repeatable process to be used from one project to the next were put in place.

Most software people in those early days were pleased to move from old technology to new. After all, you weren't involved in software in those days if you weren't an innovator, and besides, technology was changing so rapidly—every year or two, dramatically—that if you didn't change you were almost immediately out of date. Moving from specific to general solution approaches was clearly the way to stay even with the rapidly changing times.

Now let's return to that pseudo dirty word, *ad hoc*. Back in those early days, if you stayed with solutions only relevant to a specific problem and didn't stay abreast of the rapidly encroaching generalizing technologies, you truly were a "bad" software developer. There was a time, I am saying, when it may have made sense to equate *ad hoc* with all the worst ways of building software.

What about that second reason for the misuse of *ad hoc*, the one having to do with the origins of computer science? Most academic computer science programs have emerged from a mathematics heritage, and many computer scientists are still tightly tied to that heritage. There are lots of both good and bad facets to that heritage, but one of the bad ones is that mathematicians, over the years, have divided into two professional camps: those who deal in "pure" mathematics, and those who deal in "applied" mathematics. Neither camp thinks much of the other. There are turf wars in mathematics departments that you wouldn't believe unless you'd been there to see them yourself.

How does this heritage effect computer science? Well, most computer scientists, I would assert, are closer to the pure math camp than the applied math camp. What this means is that they would much rather work with intellectual challenges close to the computer, rather than those close to the application problem. It is easy for people caught in that trap to view application/specific things as beneath them. *Ad hoc* things, those concerned with the solution of a particular application problem, are of no interest. Carrying that a little further, those people who use problem-specific solution approaches, seen through this knothole, could be using inadequate, chaotic approaches.

This has been a lot of words to discuss the definition of just one term. Is there any point to what I'm saying here? Obviously, I think there is.

I think the computer science community, over the years, has done a relatively good job of defining and advocating generalized solutions to the problems tackled by software folks. The representations and devices and methods and tools which that approach has produced have been, in aggregate, remarkable. However, I think that these same computer scientists have gone about as far as they can go with these generalized approaches. Further progress in computer science, I would assert, must take into account the notion of application.

We are already beginning to see that happening. "Domain analysis" is a term computer scientists have invented for exploring application-focused reuse approaches. We have programming languages that focus on a particular application domain, methods that are better for some than for others, and we've even played with computer hardware that is problem-specific, such as the database machine.

In addition, over the years there have always been some parts of the software job that simply had to be *ad hoc,* focused on the problem at hand:

- Systems analysis, where the analyst defines the problem to be solved.
- Top-down design, where the design is focused on the problem as defined by the requirements.
- Top-down implementation, where a skeletal total solution is produced, focusing on the problem in overview, before the lower-level parts are screwed in.
- Various kinds of testing. For example, "boundary value testing" is about inventing test cases to check application-specific boundary situations, and "statistical testing," part of the Cleanroom methodology, is about focusing test cases on a "usage profile" specific to the problem of interest.

I think the use of such ad hoc approaches is increasing. And I think that is something to be viewed with applause, not with alarm.

There is an interesting distinction in the problem-solving literature between "strong approaches," those focused on the problem at hand, and "weak ones," those more general in nature. A strong method, like a specific size of wrench, is defined to fit and do an optimal job on one kind of problem; a weak method, like a monkey wrench, is designed to adjust to a multiplicity of problems, but solve none of them optimally.

The misuse of the term *ad hoc* by computer scientists has, for too long, steered us away from strong approaches and toward weak ones. It is time to turn that around. The first move in doing so is to remove the overload that burdens the perfectly respectable term, *ad hoc.*

3.4
Mikhail Gorbachev and software productivity (!?)

I read something quite awhile back that seemed to have nothing to do with software productivity; and yet buried within it was some insight that makes it worth sharing with you, I think.

It was a piece called "Psyching Out Gorbachev" from the "Insight" section of the *Washington Post*, December 17, 1989. It consisted of an analysis of Mikhail Gorbachev by three prominent psychologists who specialize in studying political leaders and their thoughts (as expressed in their speeches and writings). One of those psychologists, Philip E. Tetlock had developed a scheme that measures the complexity of thinking and the ability to deal with ambiguity that he believed characterizes a significant leader.

Gorbachev, Tetlock found, scored near the top of his seven-point scale. (Certain American politicians, he said, ranked at one, citing Senator Jesse Helms as an example.) A person getting a seven would be able to see alternative approaches, balance judgment about them, and either act to resolve the dichotomy or tolerate the ambiguity if action is not warranted. It is interesting to note, Tetlock points out, that some view those who deal well in complexity and ambiguity to be weak (in the former Soviet Union, he said, some perceived Gorbachev that way), while someone who sees things in more black-and-white terms is perceived as strong. That is, of course, the opposite of Tetlock's own position.

Now, what does all of this have to do with software creativity?

I want to take two positions here. The first position is that, in a field as complex and young as computing and data processing, there is massive ignorance and therefore massive ambiguity in doing our job. We really don't know a best way to build software; it is unlikely we are going to find such a way in the near future.

The second position I want to take is that, given our level of ignorance, the best thing we can do is to expose and explore differences of opinion as openly and as honestly and with as much tolerance as we can.

For example, I would assert that the general topic of software productivity is probably more open to ignorance and ambiguity than any other subject in the software business. It has only been a little over half a century since our profession began. How could we expect the state of the field to be anything else?

Now, in the face of that ignorance and ambiguity, we seem to have two schools of thought. On the one hand, we have those who proclaim each new idea that comes along as the solution to software productivity. First it was structured methods, then it was 4GLs, then it was CASE tools, and next it was object orientation. These people, I would assert, are the level one thinkers. Some perceive them as strong, because they see a solution clearly and move swiftly toward it. Others see them as simplistic, for they ignore the complexity in the problem and seem unable to accept the ambiguity.

On the other hand, we have people like Fred Brooks in his "No Silver Bullet" paper, and David Parnas in his "Star Wars" papers, who see no breakthroughs on the horizon and are willing to say things like "Constructing software is simply hard work."

Let us go back to Tetlock and Gorbachev for a moment. It is unusual, Tetlock says, to find tolerance of complexity in politicians. "Usually," he says, "stress pushes them toward simple, rigid dichotomies."

I would like to assert that it is also unusual to find that tolerance of complexity in software managers, software entrepreneurs, and software academics. The search for simple solutions, and the image of strength, is too strong a lure for many to resist.

However, we in the software field are the poorer for it. As each new productivity proposal dissolves into mild success rather than the break-through originally claimed for it, we move swiftly to the next one. It is as if we are saying, "Somewhere out there is a break-through, if we only believe hard enough."

And perhaps there is. But breakthroughs cannot be scheduled, and they arise when we least expect them. Believing and proclaiming will not make them come.

For those of us in software who see our business as making change as well as solving problems, we could do worse than study Mikhail Gorbachev, probably the most profound change-maker of our time.

Complexity and ambiguity. They certainly characterize a lot of what our software field is all about. It is time we began accepting them, rather than trying to wish them away.

Where are the level seven leaders of our field who will be courageous enough to take that position?

chapter 4
quantitative versus qualitative reasoning

chapter contents

Introduction to chapter 4

"One of the deepest traditions in science is that of according respectability to what is quantitative, precise, rigorous, and categorically true. It is a fact, however, that we live in a world which is pervasively imprecise, uncertain, and hard to be categorical about. It is also a fact that precision and certainty carry a cost. Driven by our quest for respectability, we tend to close our eyes to these facts and thereby lose sight of the steep price that we have to pay for high precision and low uncertainty. Another visible concomitant of the quest for respectability is that in much of the scientific literature elegance takes precedence over relevance."

—*Lotfi A. Zadeh*
"Soft Computing and Fuzzy Logic,"
IEEE Software, November 1994 (©1994 IEEE)

The Q-word part of the dictionary is pretty short, and populated almost entirely with words starting with "qu." However, lying among those few pages are two towers of intellectual strength—the words quantitative and qualitative.

Quantitative is about numbers: "an amount or number of things; ability to be measured through having size or weight or amount or number."

Qualitative is not: "of or concerned with quality," where quality is defined as "a degree or level of excellence."

As I mulled over these two definitions, a spurt of indecision ran through me. We have traditionally made a sharp distinction, in our society, between quantitative and qualitative methods. Some things can be discussed in terms of numbers, and some cannot. My assumption, based on this tradition, was that the two words held a nice, crisp distinction between them.

But what's this? Qualitative is about quality? Does that mean that, if quant and qual are two very different concepts, that we cannot talk about quality in terms of numbers? Note that if we can quantify quality, the two concepts are not all that separable.

Quality, of course, is an elusive concept. It drove the main character of Pirsig's *Zen and the Art of Motorcycle Maintenance* over the wall mentally. It is the subject of more contention among definitionists in the computing world than any other word I can think of. (To pursue that train of thought, take the track leading to my book *Building Quality Software*, Prentice-Hall, 1992.) If we have trouble defining it and the very search for its meaning drives people crazy, can it ever be quantified?

The answer is, "we do it all the time" or at least "we try to do it all the time." We measure the quality of racers by timing them as they run. We measure the quality of jumpers by measuring the distance they jump. And when all else fails, we measure the quality of divers and skaters by panels of judges who hold up numbers giving them a score for their performance. Either we have real quantitative measures of quality, or we invent them.

In software, too, we try to measure quality all the time. We track errors per something or other (lines of code or function points) and say we're measuring reliability. We count operators and operands (or lots of other things) and say we're measuring complexity. We clock running time and say we're measuring performance. We count instructions and data and say we're measuring space efficiency. All of those things that we say we're measuring are part of that elusive thing called quality.

But let us not go too far down this particular path. In spite of all the quantitative aspects of qualitative things we have just discussed, there is still a fundamental difference between the two things. Some things can be readily understood in terms of numbers. Some things cannot. It is that fundamental difference, and its importance in the software world, that I discuss in this section.

What do quantitative approaches, qualitative approaches, and creativity have in common? My belief is this: as we enter more and more into the world of flexible, heuristic, satisficing approaches to solving problems—that is, as we enter those portions of the world of software creativity that we have explored in previous sections— we are moving from a nicely measurable world toward one that is not dealt with so simply. Just as we wish the world were address-able with appropriate applications of discipline, formal methods, and optimizing approaches, we would like a world that is easily measurable.

However, our world, the complex cultural, intellectual, and, yes, creative world in which we live, is not that simple. For example, compare this book with some of the other software engineering essay books you might have read. How would you go about comparing it with the latest book by Weinberg, or Yourdon, or DeMarco? What we would like—what we would all like, even I who might be embarrassed by the findings—is to be able to give some kind of neat, quantitative score to each book and thus place an ordering on them. DeMarco gets a 9.723 on a scale of 10, due to his clever mind, contrarian views, and humor. Yourdon gets a 9.683 due to his comprehensive outlook, his enormous circle of contacts, and his world-girdling search for information. Weinberg gets a 9.706 due to his clever intertwining of psychological and technical concepts, his wonderful anecdotes, and his enormous productivity. Glass? He gets a 1.738 for trying.

But, of course, there's a problem with all of that (aside from the fact that I have come in dead last!). Few among us would have much confidence in any aspect of those numbers. For one thing, their authenticity lies in the eye of the beholder. (I would like to believe that my mother, for example, would score the authors Glass 9.999, DeMarco 1.111, Yourdon 1.111, and Weinberg 1.111). For another thing, it is difficult to support the meaning of any of the digits in those numbers, and certainly the value of the digits goes down drastically as we move in a general rightward direction through the decimal point. In other words, we have created a quantitative scheme here for something for which it is largely inappropriate. Something for which qualitative approaches would, in fact, have been better. Aha! There is a valid difference between the two Q-words.

Where do we go in this section? First we explore one of those dangerous things, a computing truism: "You can't manage what you can't measure." Like most old wives' (or husbands') tales, this one contains a lot less than meets the eye.

Then we explore a few more relationships between quantitative methods and computing, always ending up with the notion that qualitative methods, although probably less desirable than their alternative, may be all we have sometimes. And finally, like a carpenter finishing a cabinet he is particularly proud of, we hammer that point home with one last essay. On a scale of 1 to 10, what kind of score would you give a section like that?!

4.1
"You can't manage what you can't measure"— oh, really?

"You can't manage what you can't measure." That is one of the truisms of computing and software.

But is it really true? Is it really impossible to manage unmeasurable things?

My answer is, "Of course not. We do it all the time." Let me suggest a few fairly generic examples.

For openers, we have been managing software projects for several decades now, and we have had few if any metrics. Of course, some would say that we have been doing it rather badly, but it is unarguably true that, even with "bad" management, we are well into a successful "age of computing," one that will go down in history as one of the most significant transitions humankind has ever undertaken. Could that have happened if it were impossible to manage what we weren't measuring?

We manage research and development, a virtually unmeasurable activity; and the results of that work have changed the face of the world.

We manage managers. In the hierarchically driven world of enterprise management, the higher up you go the less measurable is the work of people under you. And yet, even though you may debate how successfully we do that, we nevertheless do it.

In fact, probably the most generic statement you can make on this subject is that whenever you manage knowledge workers, the chances are that you are managing in a world of diminished quantitative techniques.

So I think it is fair to say that the truism is untrue. We do, in fact, manage what we can't measure, and it is being done by thousands of managers around the world even as you read these words.

We would, of course, like to manage quantitatively and to have appropriate measures for doing it. However, even in the absence of appropriate metrics, we can still manage to manage.

That is, of course, fortunate. Software management has persisted for decades without any good measures to rely on. Those products that successfully implemented the age of computing emerged from a world where there were neither good measures nor good advice on how to use them.

That is not to say that no one tried. In the late 1950s, I worked for a supervisor who tried to implement some fairly potent, for the time, measuring techniques for evaluating software development. I was his staff person defining and implementing the metrics. It got fairly detailed and specific, as I recall, moving far beyond the simple defining and achieving of milestones, to include measuring such things as the extent to which the declaration of all data items in a program was done with commentary, including the units in which the item was measured (a metric about a metric, I suppose you might say).

It was an interesting, very early attempt to manage by measurement, but it died aborning. Most of this manager's peers had no interest in managing to that level of detail, so no one else adopted it. The technical people resented what appeared, at the time, to be management intrusion into the details of their work, and they avoided it. When that manager moved up the management ladder another rung, his metric approaches atrophied in his absence.

The academic community tried as well, about a decade later. Murray Halstead, famous for his work in compiler-writing, embarked on a noteworthy attempt to add science and measurement to the software discipline, inventing something he called "software science." (It is interesting to note that "software engineering" and something called "software physics" were invented about the same time. Some of those notions survived, and some did not.) Software science, as most of us know by now, was about measuring the complexity of software through its operators and operands.

Enormous controversy has surrounded the work of Halstead and the others who followed in his wake. Both academics and practitioners have criticized the validity of the software science measures, academics via the soundness of Halstead's research, and practitioners via the usefulness of his findings. Tempers have even been known to rise when the subject is brought up; at one computing conference, a well-known figure in the software engineering field accused another of presenting "astrology" (implying an invalid science) when discussing software science. Although most spokespeople in the field now find the subject of dubious value, there is still an enormous quantity of publication on the topic in the academic literature, and there are now (ironically!) fairly successful commercial tools that calculate those metrics.

Those who measure the state of the practice find that the use of metrics to manage software projects has not even reached a state of infancy. At "Applications of Software Metrics" conferences, Bill Hetzel of the sponsoring organization regularly reported on the spread of metrics in practice and found it abysmal.

However, interestingly enough, there is no shortage of candidate metrics. In fact, there is a bifurcation in the metrics field. Academic metrics, including those of Halstead and the many who have gone beyond (Zuse has produced a nearly encyclopedic compendium of this field), have progressed in one direction. Practitioner metrics, even though they are admittedly not being used, have progressed quite successfully in another (the work of Robert Grady of Hewlett-Packard in this area has been exemplary).

(There is irony, of course, in the use of the word "successful" in the previous paragraph. How can something be "successful" if it is little used in the field?! However, it is fair to say that if a software organization of this millennium is interested in beginning a metrics program, there are plenty of both practical and theoretic metrics to base it on.)

The problem in the use of "You can't manage what you can't measure" is one of zealotry. Those who deeply believe in the usefulness of metrics are frustrated at the lack of progress in the field. To get the attention of funding sources and implementers, they use catchy phrases; but it is important to think through those phrases before they are given too much credence.

Can we manage what we can't measure? Of course.

Given a choice, would we prefer to measure the things we manage? The answer, once again, is of course.

The world is far more complicated than most of the catch phrases we use to describe it would imply. And the absurdity of a catch phrase like "you can't manage what you can't measure," far from motivating change, may become an excuse for the current state of the practice—not measuring at all.

4.2
Mathematics and the computer scientist

Computer science grew up in the mathematics departments of the world. It cut its teeth there, it moved to prominence there, and it continues to have strong ties to its mathematical heritage. In many colleges and universities, mathematics and computer science continue to cohabit in the same organizational structure.

But is that mathematical heritage important to computer science? Especially its software part?

Many would take that question to be heresy. "Of course," such people would answer. "The logic and rigor that mathematics represents are a vital part of what computer science is, was, and will strive for." And it is hard to find fault with such an answer.

However, there is another point of view. It is a little more complex, a little more unusual, and therefore it needs careful articulating, but it goes something like this.

There was a time that computers did nothing but compute. Back in those days, in fact, computers had no capability for doing anything else. They could not represent any characters other than digits, and therefore it was unthinkable that these marvelous new devices could be useful for much else.

That was the era of computing as applied mathematics. Computers performed wonderful tricks with numbers that either humankind had previously thought undoable or required rooms full of arithmeticians to accomplish over staggeringly long periods of time. The original productivity improvement that computers provided, in fact, was to the mathematician of that time.

But that era passed over 50 years ago. From the moment that computers expanded their character sets to encompass more than the ten digits, I would assert, they became "information processors." From the limited early days, when the six-bit byte limited alphabetic characters to upper case, to the present day, when we strive to incorporate into the "computer" every character used in every language in the world, the predominant work of computers has ceased to be numbers and has become digitized information.

Other academic disciplines have arisen that have chosen to focus their look at computing and software on information rather than mathematics. However, for better or for worse, the disciplinary powerhouse of the field continues to be computer science; and computer science continues to see mathematics to be the heart of the field. Government reports that study the future of the software field, for example, frequently call for "more mathematics" as part of the still-fledgling software theory and practice.

Meanwhile, the nature of computing practices has shifted over the decades. In the beginning, math- and information-focused computing were split into two rather different and non-communicating disciplines. The computing people had grown up with mechanical calculators, and saw the computer as a marvelously faster and more reliable calculator. The information people had grown up with punch-card equipment, and saw the computer as a marvelously faster and more reliable punch-card processor. Mathematical computers spoke in binary words, each consisting of a fixed number of bits, and—in the beginning—rarely thought in terms of any kind of "character," even the digit. Information processors, on the other hand, spoke in digits and characters, and the notion of "word" was dynamic—executing programs set a "word mark" to indicate how many characters were in the present version of a particular information field.

Gradually, the hardware separation between computing people and information people eroded. It was discovered in the early 1960s that binary computers, with character and perhaps decimal as well as binary arithmetic capability, were faster and cheaper than the traditional character-digit-oriented information machines of the prior era. With the advent of the IBM 360, which appeared on the scene in the mid/late 1960s, the hardware separation between the fields essentially disappeared. The same computers could perform both functions economically, and there was no longer any need for a hardware separation between the disciplines. Oh, the information processor continued to have decimal arithmetic capability in addition to binary, but that was a minor difference compared to the rest of the computer, most of which dealt with more essential things than mere arithmetic.

Today's computers, even the most mathematical die-hard would have to admit, are used for many more things than arithmetic and mathematics. There are word processors and simulators and games and software tools of various kinds, such as compilers, all of which do virtually no mathematics whatsoever. Oh, there are spreadsheet programs that do considerable arithmetic, and there are still scientific/engineering application programs that focus strongly on mathematical services, but the fact of the matter is that math applications of all kinds have become relatively minor in terms of the practice of the computing field.

With that slice of history, let us return to the original question. Is the mathematical heritage of computer science important to it? We can see, emerging from a quick look at the history of the field, that its importance as a function to be performed has diminished enormously.

But what about its underlying value? That is, are the concepts and skills of mathematics important to the computer scientist, even if the application of its techniques is not? Many computer scientists take this point of view.

Interestingly, there appears to be a hardware/software dichotomy in the answer to this question. The answer to the hardware specialist seems to be a clear "Yes." But computer scientists broaden this importance to the world of software as well.

I call this the "Latin Syndrome." Years ago, as the teaching of the language Latin began to slowly atrophy in the school systems of the world, there was a powerful argument that the skills one learned in acquiring competency in Latin were important to all other learning experiences. Latin lingered as a pedagogical topic far longer than its importance in the world might have argued simply because of this line of reasoning. And mathematics, I am saying, may be to computer science as Latin was to the rest of the disciplinary world of its day.

Now this analogy to Latin can be badly misused, of course. Mathematics is not now, and never will be, a dying discipline. Its contributions to the sciences, and to our lives in general, are potent and significant; and the underlying skills of logic and rigor that are a necessary part of doing mathematics are, indeed, a vital part of software's work. Software systems, in fact, are almost the personification of logic and the essence of rigor. A non-logical or non-rigorous piece of software is worthless and even dangerous.

However, that begs a question. Is mathematics the best way of teaching the logic and rigor that software specialists need? The opening answer to that question is that, to my knowledge, no one has ever investigated it. Mathematicians-become-computer-scientists are not motivated to; and the rest of us, awed by the beauty and value of mathematics, are loathe to raise—or investigate—such a controversial question. As I said before, it feels a bit like heresy.

Let me make a confession here. I am an ancient mathematician. I took my advanced degree at one of the citadels of mathematical learning several decades ago. And although my degree is ancient and my knowledge terribly rusty, I think I have at least entry-level qualifications to criticize my mother discipline.

From the very beginning of my movement from the world of academe to the world of software practice, I found little relevance in what I had learned in school to what I did in practice. My mathematics background had been in "pure" mathematics, among a group of academics who, like many of their "pure" colleagues, looked down on any application of the field. And my job, now that I was wearing an industry hat, was applying mathematics. Almost nothing in the courses I had taken, except for the two computing courses, was useful to me in my new environment.

All of that, as I have already confessed, is ancient history. Of course, it is easy to see that the mathematics of several decades ago might have had little relevance to the software specialist of today. Which brings us to the next obvious question: Is today's mathematics more useful to software practice?

I have browsed most of the books recommended by my mathematician/computing colleagues to see what they contain, and to analyze the relevance of that material to what I have now been practicing for over five decades, and I find very little, if any. If these mathematics-based books that are required reading for computer scientists of today are truly important to the field, then it is in some branch or some application of software that I have not yet encountered. And I (unlike most of my academic colleagues) have encountered most of them!

That, I suppose, is why I have invented the notion of the "Latin Syndrome." I have come to believe that we continue to go through the motions of linking mathematics to software long past the point where it is truly necessary. I am not saying, it is important to note, that mathematics is unhelpful to the software specialist. I am simply saying that the help it provides, for the vast majority of software people, is marginal at best. Perhaps, in fact, Latin would be at least as useful in terms of the logic and rigor it offers.

It has become popular in recent years to link mathematical thinking with new software concepts. The whole idea of structured programming, for example, was founded on a mathematical theory that all language forms could be represented by a significant few. The idea of formal approaches, for another example, is founded on the notion that mathematical representations and mathematical proofs are—or should be—an essential part of the practice of computing. There is a "power by association" trip going on here, one almost the opposite of "guilt by association." We have heard so many times that computing ideas with a mathematical foundation are somehow superior to those without it that we have come to accept such statements uncritically. I tend to think of this as the "Virgin Birth Syndrome." Some religious folk, over the years, have taken the position that a virgin birth is somehow more satisfying than its other, perhaps less immaculate, alternative. Certainly, there is enormous satisfaction to believing that mathematical computing is somehow purer and better than its less immaculate alternative.

But is immaculateness really important? In the messy and complicated world of software reality, the ground rule is more closely akin to "pretty is as pretty does." An idea must stand on its own merits, not the mathematical foundation from which it was spawned. If structured programming is useful, it is because it results in good programming products, not because it is mathematical. If formal methods are to become useful—and to date they have not shown themselves to be—it must be because, once again, they lead us to good programming products, not because they are grounded in the purity and beauty of mathematics. Mathematics must not be allowed to become a crutch that props up unevaluated ideas.

Is this issue worth this much space? That is, is there really any harm to all this mathematical mischief in the computing world, or is it more like Latin—there is value there, why should we worry about what form it takes? I believe there is a problem.

Our mathematical brethren, in their research approaches and research thinking, have found that analysis and proof are the ultimate research tools. A proven theory is a correct theory. There is no more powerful statement that can be made, mathematically speaking.

Computer science research has emulated that same approach. Much of the research in the field, I would assert, consists of a strong analysis of a new idea, some sort of attempt to prove that the idea is correct, and then a conclusion in which the idea is advocated. Proofs, in this newer field, are of course more complicated than in the world of mathematics. The real world tends to intrude into computing ideas, and proofs cannot exist in an environment separated from the ugliness of that reality. As a result, most computing research proofs are, in fact, simply arguments favoring the findings of the analysis. What we have, then, is poor mathematical research masquerading as good computer science research.

I would assert here that mathematical research is simply not a good model for computer science. I think a better model to consider is that of science. The scientific method, we all know, consists of formulating a hypothesis, evaluating that hypothesis, and reporting on the evaluative findings. Any advocacy must be dependent on fairly strong findings.

Computer scientists rarely use the scientific method. There is a modicum of hypothesis formulation, very little evaluation, and far too much advocacy in computing research. The result is a computer science theory world that tends to believe things that may not be true and places value on ignoring the real world and concentrating on brilliant thinking. There is nothing wrong, of course, with brilliant thinking but there are many serious things wrong with ignoring the real world in a field whose products interact with, and in fact are rapidly changing, that world.

There is irony in where I believe we have come in our search for an answer to our original question. Is the mathematical heritage important to computer science? I would assert that this heritage has led computer science into research that is neither good mathematics nor good science. Given that, as I suggested in the beginning of this essay, computing is no longer about "computing"; if it is also bad mathematics and bad science, then the name of the field is a hollow shell, and the content that underlies the field is something of a sham.

It is time for computer science to begin to understand what it is really about. If it is to be true to its mathematical roots, it must find new ways to express that heritage. If it is to continue to call itself a science, it must behave like one. And if it is to say it is about "computing," it should at least acknowledge that the name is retained for historical purposes, not because it is descriptive of the field.

Meanwhile, back to the original issue. Is its mathematical heritage important to computer science? The correct answer, I am afraid, is "far too much so."

4.3
The Role of Intuition in Decision-Making

Our society tends to put down intuition as a decision-making method. Given our choice of decision-making techniques, most of us would use quantitative approaches first, rational ones second, and intuition would come at or near the bottom of the list.

Truth to tell, we don't understand intuition very well. We attribute it to women, and in our institutionally sexist way treat it derisively. We see it as wisdom that emerges from some unknown fount, a wisdom not necessarily to be trusted.

But the funny thing is, when it comes time for real decision-making in complex topic areas, the other methods tend to fail us. Quantitative methods desert us first. They are beautiful and pure for fairly clear or mathematically inclined problems, but in the rough-edged everyday world, they simply won't often work. Simplifications to the real world to enable their use tend to give us good-looking, untrustworthy results. Whether we call our quantitative decision-making mathematics, statistics, or management science, or simply base it on numeric results obtained in some other fashion, applications of these approaches are only occasionally useful.

Rational methods stay with us a lot longer. We gather together the underlying information, we abstract out of that our decision factors, we apply decision criteria to those factors, and we come up with a decision. It all sounds plausible, crisp, and clear. And, in fact, if we do it well enough, it can look very quantitative. Numbers derived rationally can look just like numbers derived quantitatively! (There is a danger in that, of course, which is why numbers should always be questioned just as regularly as other forms of answers.) But even rational methods fail us, more often than we would think—or like. We tend to move beyond rational methods when politics or extreme complexity enter into the picture.

For example, take the topic of software estimation. If you look in the textbooks or in most practitioner standards manuals, you'll find some very rational suggestions for how to do estimation. Whether that rationality is based on expert judgment or historical data or algorithm, there is a nice, procedural, intellectualized definition of how to produce a project estimate.

However, in the world of reality, that rational approach seldom survives. The real estimates, the ones that go to upper management and to customers and up on those schedule charts, are derived politically. There is a negotiation process, in which those who need the results of the project tell the producers when they need it, and the producers respond with rationality, whereupon (in the majority of cases) the schedule is somewhat adjusted and then edicted based on need. Not on rationality based on production time, but on need—independent of production time. This conclusion has been documented in a study by Lederer [Lederer 1990], reinforced by findings of a CASE tool survey [HCS 1990], and experienced by most practitioners over and over again.

Now, of course, those political, need-based schedules could be rational in their own way. That is, the marketing organization could be determined to release the software product at the next major corporate computer show such as yesteryear's COMDEX, for example, and that alone establishes the schedule delivery date.

But how does marketing conclude that the next COMDEX is the required date for product availability? After all, COMDEXes came along with great regularity for a while, two a year at its peak. What is it that tells the marketing people that the product must be out by COMDEX next?

The answer, I would assert, is intuition. Based on their experiences with the marketplace over a long period of time, marketing believes that a product announced at this very next premier computer show will have the maximum chance of penetrating its desired market. Oh, they may have numbers and rationale to support that position, but if really challenged they will have to fall back on, "I know that we must release by the next COMDEX."

The problem we have seen above in estimation is, in fact, ubiquitous. Most people who have done staff work in industry have had an experience similar to the following one:

Your boss asks you for an answer to a question, one requiring some amount of research and analysis. You go away, do the research and the analysis, and come back with an answer. "That's the wrong answer," says the boss. "Go away and do it again." You repeat the process a few times, until you begin to realize that what is happening is that the boss knows what he wants the answer to be; your job is not really to find an answer, but to find a rationale to support the boss's answer. (Of course, the boss doesn't put it that way because that sound contrived and suspicious.) At that point, you deal one way or another with the ethical issue you have stumbled into, and either (a) give the boss the answer he is obviously looking for, with a rationale to support it; or (b) find a way out of your awkward position, such as insisting the boss take a really rational answer (this approach seldom works!), withdrawing from the assignment, or finding another job.

Once again, where did the boss get his "correct" answer? Out of his intuition. All that time spent bossing in his business has convinced the boss that he knows his field better than the quant jocks and the analysts who are now his hirelings.

Now it's time for two key issues:

1. Is this approach a valid one?
2. What, really, is intuition?

It is easy for most of us to be suspicious of the boss's approach. It doesn't fall into any of the patterns that we have been taught. It violates both what we learned in textbooks and what we learned in ethics. In private, we joke about these assignments and marvel at our intransigent, old-fashioned boss. How can he ever have gotten to be boss with this kind of approach?

But the fact of the matter is, in a surprising number of cases, the boss turns out to be right. That off-the-wall, irrational decision-making he uses seems to lead to some kind of success: a clean process, a crisp product, or good financial results. What is going on here?

The answer to that question is also the answer to our second question, above. Intuition, I would assert, is a function of our mind that allows it to access a rich fund of historically gleaned information we are not necessarily aware we possess, by a method we do not understand.

Notice that this definition allows us to say some further, more interesting things. For example, since intuition is a function of the mind, perhaps we can say that it is, in fact, also a rational approach. The fact that we do not understand how it works simply means that we can't explain it, not that it isn't rational. The reason the boss feels so confident of his apparently irrational decision is that, at some strange level, it may be rational after all.

Actually, this kind of decision-making has been treated more positively. We invent other names for it, cloaking its apparent irrationality in socially acceptable terms. For example, we speak of "gut" decision-making—decisions coming from some deeply felt belief that goes against the grain of the environment surrounding the decisions. In all likelihood, the origin of these gut decisions is our old friend intuition. And given that, "gut" decision-making— usually attributed to men as a positive trait—is also little different from "women's intuition," the process that we have found faintly suspicious!

In fact, there is a whole book that has been recently written (2005) about "blink of an eye" decision-making, a book that is very convincing in taking the position (via both research results and anecdotes) that blink thinking can be just as effective as the more rational approaches (see [Gladwell 2005]). So there is a certain degree of newfound respectability to this concept!

This intuitive thinking phenomenon is well known in the world of practice, but less well in the world of theory. Quantitative and rational decision-making are teachable, testable topics; intuitive decision-making just doesn't fit into our academic scheme of things. So it was especially interesting to me when an academic presenter at the annual International Conference on Information Systems, a few years ago, suggested recognizing the existence of at least political (and non-rational) decision-making by building decision support systems that would not quantize and analyze and rationalize, but rather accept as input an answer, and produce as output the rationale to support the answer! Whether one could ever build such a system could be the basis for hours of intellectual debate and exploration. However, in the final analysis, given that it might have to involve computerizing intuition, a process that we don't even understand in human beings, it seems a dubious goal. But a fascinating one, nonetheless!

Where have we been in this essay? What is the point I am trying to make? There are several points, and they are these:

1. Quantitative decision-making, when it really works, is usually preferable to its alternatives, but it doesn't work as often as we would like.
2. Rational decision-making is a good second choice, but it often gets overridden in practice by something else.

3. That something else is intuition, and even though we don't understand it, it is an acceptable and commonly used decision-making approach.

Isn't it nice to know that, when all else fails us, we have an innate decision-making tool to fall back on?

References

Gladwell 2005—*Blink: The Power of Thinking Without Thinking*, Little, Brown, and Co., 2005; Malcolm Gladwell.

HCS 1990—*1990 CASE/CASM Survey*, HCS, Inc., Portland, OR.

Lederer 1990—"Information System Cost Estimating: A Management Perspective," *MIS Quarterly*, June 1990; Albert L. Lederer, et al.

4.4
plenty of pitfalls: There are numbers and Then There are numbers

There are two opposing views of the importance of numbers in decision-making.

There's the "you can't manage what you can't measure" school of thought, which says that quantitative decision-making is better than its opposite.

There's the "lies, damn lies, and statistics" school of thought, which says that quantitative decision-making is no better than its opposite, and in fact is sometimes worse.

Which is right?

Ironically, the correct answer is probably "both." Certainly, quantitative decision-making using honestly obtained, relevant numbers is better than not doing it. But just as certainly, quantitative decision-making using dishonestly or ignorantly obtained or irrelevant numbers is not only no better, it is probably worse.

The problem is, it is all too easy to use the wrong kind of numbers unknowingly. What makes bad quantitative decision-making really bad is that bad numbers look just as good as good numbers. If I see 25.623 as a measure of something, I figure that it must be a pretty accurate representation of whatever it is measuring (e.g., average lines of code per module). However, if I think a bit about what has been measured, I see several things:

1. Is it really worth having a measure of this entity? For example, does "average lines of code per module" really tell me anything?
2. Has the measure been done accurately? For example, how many modules were taken into account to obtain this number? How were lines of code counted? Were these good modules or bad? Should these be both good and bad?
3. Is the measure meaningful? For example, does the .623 in 25.623 tell us anything more than 25 alone? Or does it lend a note of credibility that the number doesn't deserve?

Looking at 25.623 in this light, and considering the example of average lines of code per module, it is possible to say these things:

1. Until we identify a goal for the measurement, the number 25.623 is at best simply a number.
2. Until we identify the validity of the measurement, the number 25.623 may be no better than a random number.
3. Until we identify the correctness and relevance of all of the digits, the number 25.623 may be no better than the number 25. In fact, in this example, 3/5 of the digits are worthless. (The ".623" adds only a confusion factor to the "25".)

In other words, there are numbers and then there are numbers. Somehow, it is important to be able to distinguish between good ones and bad ones.

To complicate matters, advocates of quantitative decision-making have opened up a barrage of sloganeering designed to pressure the unwary software manager into accepting the approach:

"To measure is to know," James Clark Maxwell.
"You cannot control what you can't measure," Tom DeMarco.
"Invisible targets are usually hard to hit," Tom Gilb.

But sloganeering cuts both ways. Consider these, excerpted from [Leveson 1993]:

4.4

plenty of
pitfalls: There
are numbers
then there
are numbers

> "Risk assessment data can be like the captured spy: if you torture it long enough, it will tell you anything you want to know," William Ruckelshaus, two-time head of the U.S. Environmental Protection Agency.

The numbers game in risk assessment "should only be played in private between consenting adults, as it is too easily misinterpreted," E. A. Ryder, of the British Health and Safety Executive.

"In our enthusiasm to provide measurements, we should not attempt to measure the unmeasurable," Nancy G. Leveson and Clark S. Turner.

As is usually true, sloganism and religious advocacy are poor bases for any kind of decision-making, quantitative or not.

None of this should be taken to discourage quantitative decision-making. There is a sufficient number of excellent books on software metrics now, by such authors as Robert Grady and Bill Hetzel and Norm Fenton, that there is no excuse for a software organization not beginning to seriously consider the question, "Should I develop a metrics approach to make my software decision-making more quantitative?"

But beware. There are plenty of pitfalls along the way.

Reference

Leveson 1993—"An Investigation of the Therac-25 Accidents," *IEEE Computer*, July 1993; Nancy G. Leveson and Clark S. Turner.

chapter 5
process vs. product

chapter contents

Introduction to chapter 5

"Process innovation merely streamlines an established system of belief ... and does not call for any radically different patterns. But revolutionary science starkly calls into question the established system of belief and eventually replaces it with a new one."

—*Noah Kennedy*
The Industrialization of Intelligence,
Unwin Hyman 1989

Ah, now, here's a hot topic!
When the final decade of the previous millennium got yanked off our calendars, and the digits "200X" came up for the first time, what was the biggest, most hot-button topic in software?

Software process. Thanks to the Software Engineering Institute's (SEI) Capability Maturity Model work, we have studied, evaluated, and rated software process like we never had before.

Companies have pursued strange slogans: "Capability 3 by '03," or "4 by '04." And what those companies meant by those slogans was, "We want to achieve process maturity level X by the year 200X." They cared a lot, those companies. There was talk that the level of process maturity might determine how many contracts those companies would get. Survival and process suddenly got linked in the minds of a lot of people at a lot of computing companies.

Well, hold on thar, folks! I have a feeling we've pushed a little too hard down this particular trail too fast. We're more than halfway through the 200X decade, we're deeply committed to process as a measure of software success, and yet we still haven't evaluated the fundamental, underlying consideration: "Does good process lead to good product?"

That question ought to raise a lot of thoughts in our minds, almost simultaneously. One question is, "Is process our goal, or is it product?" (Most practitioners would answer that question immediately and forcefully—product is certainly our goal, without doubt. Some academics are not so sure.)

Let's assume that product is in fact the goal. Then another immediate question is this: "What other ways besides process are there to good product?" Or, "How do we know that this particular SEI process is the one that gives the best results?" And, of course, there's the important question underlying the overriding question that ended the previous paragraph: "How can we tell whether good process leads to good product?"

With all those questions dangling, let's do one thing before tackling them. In all the previous section introductions of this chapter, we defined the two key terms that identified the material. Let's do it again.

Process is "a series of actions or operations used in making or manufacturing or achieving something; a series of changes, a natural operation; a course of events or time."

Product is "something produced by a natural process or by agriculture or by manufacture or as a result."

(As an aside, notice how often manufacturing gets into the act in our 21st century definitions. Our dictionaries, at least, do not seem to have absorbed the transition from smokestack America to knowledge-worker America.)

Be that as it may, how about those questions?

Does good process indeed lead to good product? Truth to tell, we really don't know. Our intuition suggests that it ought to. However, there are few studies that have tried to answer this question for the software world. The SEI has tried, with mixed results (that will be covered in upcoming section 5.3 of this book). We'll provide a variety of answers to this question in the sections to follow.

Is process our goal, or is it product? We've already seen the typical practitioner answer. Product is it; it is nearly all that matters. I suspect that answer goes for most of us. I have a friend who's into genealogy. He deeply enjoys the hours he spends in libraries, pouring over dusty old record books, trying to put the pieces of a family history together like a jigsaw puzzle. But no matter how much pleasure he gets from the act of pursuing those records, the thing he's really seeking out is product. He wants to trace that family back farther than anyone else has done. And when he hits a genealogical dead end, where he can't find the ancestor of a character at the head of his evolving family tree, the look on his face says it all. He'd trade all the good process in the world for one good product at that point.

What other ways besides process are there to good product? That was another of the questions we asked above. And here, there are plenty of answers.

Good people are a way to good product. (Many say that good people are, in fact, more important than good process. The cover of Barry Boehm's book Software Engineering Economics shows very clearly that people, far more than process, are the key to software productivity. Bill Curtis, who succeeded Watts Humphrey as the head of the SEI process work, added a People-focused maturity model to the SEI maturity arsenal.

Good technology is a way to good product. (The Capability Maturity Model is about management process rather than technical process.)

Good contracting and negotiating are a way to good product.

If product is a table, there are many legs that hold it up—and process is clearly only one of them.

How do we know that the SEI definition of good process is the one that gives the best results? That's another of our questions from above. The truthful answer is, "We don't." There have been no significant studies doing an evaluation of the SEI model against others. (Although in Capers Jones' latest book, he takes the position that he has done such studies, and they show his way is better than the SEI's!) But what we do know is this: The SEI's approach is probably the best scrubbed, most analyzed, best evolved process model around. Visiting researchers have been invited from all over the world to pour over the model. Suggestions from those visitors have been incorporated. Here, perhaps, is the time to employ one of the key thoughts of this book: There will probably never be an optimizing definition of software process, and therefore (as we saw a couple of sections back) it is necessary to employ a satisficing one. And remember the key test of a satisficing answer … Is the SEI model supportable? The answer here is certainly "yes."

Our final question above was something of a clone of our first one: how can we tell if good process leads to good product? That, of course, is the key to all of this chapter; and it is, in fact, the subject of many of the essays that follow.

Read on. You will find multiple, conflicting answers to that key question in this section; but maybe, out of that confusion, some clarifying thoughts will emerge as well. The final essay, for example, takes a fairly straightforward view of when process focus must (unfortunately, in my view) replace product focus.

Here's an interesting point for you to ponder. Is it the point of reading this book to enjoy the trip between its covers? (That's process.) Or is it to learn something? (That's product.) Either way, I hope you achieve your goal!

5.1

Does good process lead to improved product?

We live in an era where process (the approach by which we build product) is considered to be more important than product itself.

Academic computer scientists focus on better process, with the underlying—and sometimes overtly stated—assumption that improving process will certainly improve product. For example, the high-visibility SEI Capability Maturity Model is based on that assumption. Companies throughout the world are spending a great deal of money on studying and improving their software development processes. They may be doing it because a better rating on the SEI 5-level scale will result in more business and more income, or they may be doing it because they truly believe that better process leads to better product—but either way, they are doing it.

But does process really improve product? Are there any studies on the subject? It would be nice to say, at this point in this essay, that there is the following collection of definitive studies, all published in the literature, that give us the answer to the matter beyond a shadow of a doubt. However, the fact of the matter is that I am not aware of any such studies. There are studies that tell us something about fringe issues related to the central topic, but I know of none (in fact, it is difficult to envision how such a study would be conducted) that clarify the central issue once and for all.

Certainly the SEI, though aware that some kind of validation of the CMM is needed, has been unable to produce a definitive one to date.

Given that, let's focus on the studies that attack the periphery of the issue. My favorite, probably because its results are so wonderfully intuitive and counterintuitive all at the same time, is a paper by Sasa Dekleva [Dekleva 1992] based on a survey of information systems professionals. The issue Dekleva sought to address in his study was this: What is the effect on the maintainability of software if the developers use advanced, improved software engineering approaches? That comes fairly close to the central issue, after all—does better development process lead to a more maintainable product?

Intuition—mine, and I suspect yours as well—cries out that the answer is obvious. In spite of all the palaver up above about the relative importance of process vs. product, somehow we know that improved development approaches will lead to a better product. The feeling is so strong, I would assert, that you might even wonder—as I did—if it is worth the bother to conduct the study at all.

But what Dekleva learned from his study, conducted by surveying software managers, surprised even Dekleva. Let's set the stage for what he learned.

First, Dekleva surveyed the existing literature for studies about the effect of improved development processes on productivity. What he found there was his first surprise. There were very few evaluative studies at all (Vessey and Weber [Vessey 1984] had found the same thing a few years earlier when they sought to identify studies quantizing the benefits of structured programming). Lots of people are proposing and advocating new software development processes, but hardly anyone is evaluating them. (The same finding was stated more generally in a later paper [Fenton 1993].) The only things Dekleva did find suggested to him that the productivity benefits simply didn't show up. (One author [Banker 1991] said, "Many of the presumed benefits of using a detailed methodology that requires a lot of documentation are not observed until the follow-on projects, when enhancements or repairs need to be made to the system." On which Dekleva wryly commented, "In other words, if development productivity does not benefit from the use of modern IS development methods, perhaps maintenance will.")

With that input as stimulus, Dekleva surveyed 112 managers of information systems at Fortune 500 companies regarding what effect these development processes did have on maintenance. He defined the improved development processes fairly specifically, identifying them as (1) the use of software engineering concepts, (2) the use of information engineering, (3) the use of prototyping approaches, and (4) the use of CASE tools. He sent off the survey instrument and waited for the results to come in.

The results, when they did come in, were in general not surprising. In most cases, what those managers told Dekleva matches pretty well with what our intuition tells us. Software developed with better methods was more reliable, with fewer repairs needed.

However, there was, as I previously mentioned, a surprise. When Dekleva measured the total time spent on maintenance vs. the use of improved development approaches, he found that the better approaches led to an increase in total maintenance cost. The pattern was clear. The cost dropped during the first year or so of system usage, as he had imagined it would, but then it moved sharply upward. What could explain this counterintuitive trend? And did this in fact demonstrate, as it seemed to, that better process led to a less maintainable, and therefore poorer, product?

Dekleva massaged his data a bit more, and a clearer picture began to emerge. It was not error correction that caused the cost of maintenance to rise; it was the cost of enhancements. Apparently, the customers and users of the well-developed system, far from needing fewer changes, were flocking to take advantage of the increased modifiability of the systems and asking for more changes. And that, in turn, meant that the implication of the data

software
creativity
2.0

was that the product was in fact better, not worse, for the improved development efforts, even with this counterintuitive factor of total maintenance cost factored in.

So let's pause here and go back to the original issue. What does all of this say about process vs. product? Did better process in fact lead us to better product?

The answer, if you think about it a little bit, is in fact a resounding YES. With respect to error incidence, the yes answer was straightforward and obvious. With respect to enhancement, the yes answer was indirect and counterintuitive. And yet it was a YES answer. A system that is so maintainable that its customers and users wish to change it frequently is clearly a better product than one they are reluctant to change because, for example, the cost of doing so is too high.

This study, then, which aims—I would assert—at some point around the periphery of the central question of process vs. product, still presents us with a positive answer to the question at hand. The results may surprise us, as they did the researcher himself, but they nevertheless provide some support to the notion that good process leads to good product.

We will explore this issue further in the pages to come.

References

Banker 1991—"A Model to Evaluate Variables Impacting the Productivity of Software Maintenance Projects," *Management Science*, January 1991; R.D. Banker, S.M. Dater, and C.F. Kemerer.

Dekleva 1992—"The Influence of the Information Systems Development Approach on Maintenance," *MIS Quarterly*, September 1992; Sasa M. Dekleva.

Fenton 1993—"How Effective Are Software Engineering Methods?" *Journal of Systems and Software*, August 1993; Norman Fenton.

Vessey 1984—"Research on Structured Programming: An Empiricist's Evaluation," *IEEE Transactions of Software Engineering*, July 1984; I. Vessey and R. Weber.

5.2

Does Good Process Lead to Improved Product? A second opinion

In the previous essay (with roughly the same title as this one), we explored the title question and came up with a positive, yet surprising, answer.

But let's take another look at this question. As we said before, it would be nice to come up with a series of experimental findings that demonstrate the truth of the viewpoint that good process leads to good product, but there is little such evidence around. Note, once again, that asking the question does not imply that good process does not lead to good product; it simply suggests that here is an issue worth pursuing.

Given the lack of evidence on the matter, another alternative in pursuing the issue is to examine expert opinion; and there is plenty of strong expert opinion on both sides of this issue.

Since the previous essay cast a relatively positive view, let's take a look at the other side. In an almost angry essay in IEEE Spectrum many years ago [Frosch 1969], Robert A. Frosch, then Assistant Secretary of the Navy and administrator for one of the largest U.S. research and development branches, tore into the pro position with a vengeance.

He kicked off the essay with his view in a nutshell: "I believe that the fundamental difficulty is that we have all become so entranced with ... technique that we think entirely in terms of procedures, systems, milestones, charts, PERT diagrams, reliability systems, configuration management, maintainability groups, and the other minor paper tools of the 'systems engineer' and manager ... As a result, we have developments that follow all of the rules, but merely fail."

Strong words. Frosch has lined up most of the process methodologies that one might use, independent of discipline, and mowed them down in one fell swoop! Does he support this opening salvo with some deeper thinking?

The answer is yes. Five pages worth. In words predictive of the failure of concepts like the waterfall (unidirectional) life cycle, he went on to say, "The PERT diagram and the milestone chart are excellent examples. These both essentially assume that the progress of development and design consists of doing step A, then step B, then step C, etc. Anyone who has ever carried out a development or a design (as opposed to setting up a management system for doing it) is well aware of the fact that the real world proceeds by a kind of feedback iterative process that looks more like a helix than a line." (Shades of the spiral life cycle, circa 1969!)

Frosch goes on: "The ... procedures simply ignore the ... nature of the real world because the process has been degraded to clerical reporting. To a large extent, this tends to constrain project managers from doing work in the real way toward doing it in a way that fits with their management tools. This is clearly nonsense."

So Frosch demolishes the old-fashioned way of managing, a way that we finally discovered, some 20 years after his pronouncements, was doomed to failure. But does his criticism apply to today's management techniques as well?

I think so. Here's Frosch's next sally:

> We have come to a time when meeting certain targets
> seems to have become more important than producing
> a satisfactory system ... Looking at what is actually
> happening in the development has been replaced

by measuring it against a simplistic set of predicted milestones ...

The only thing I know that works is to obtain a competent man and his assistants, and make sure they understand the problem—not the specification of the problem, not the particular scenario written down, but what is really in the minds of those who have a requirement to be solved ...

Although Frosch is still specifically teeing off on milestone management approaches, the implication here is that too much focus on process detracts from our ability to build good product.

Is that a fair assessment of Frosch's viewpoint? I think it is. Here's the conclusion to his essay: "We have lost sight of the fact that engineering is an art ... We must bring the sense of art and excitement back into engineering. Talent, competence, and enthusiasm are qualities of people who can use tools; the lack of these characteristics usually results in people who cannot even be helped by techniques and tools."

There it is—a second opinion on the relative worth of good process in building good product. According to this essayist, at least, all too often good process gets in the way of good product. The force of the author's words overcomes at least my intuitive reaction. Process, I believe Frosch is saying, must be wielded with extreme care. And the focus on product—including the role of people in building product—must never be lost.

This article contains some strong opinions on other, related, issues:

- Frosch supports the belief that "requirements specifications are considered harmful" (because they tend to make rigid something that must remain inherently flexible—he says "the idea of a complete specification is an absurdity").

- He supports the belief that "hard-part-first," not "top-down," is the appropriate way to attack problems.
- He argues for "satisficing" (finding a solution that works and is supportable), not "optimizing" (finding the best possible solution)—"optimization may merely be the definition of which catastrophe you want to undergo."

Reference

Frosch 1969—"A New Look at Systems Engineering," *IEEE Spectrum*, September 1969; Robert A. Frosch.

5.2

DOES GOOD
PROCESS LEAD
TO IMPROVED
PRODUCT? A
SECOND OPINION

5.3

A close escape from Greatness

A while back, I reviewed a research paper that came within one turn of the author's mind of being of major significance. However, the author, bent on one research direction, failed to see that a turn in a different direction would have been profound. And something important was lost to our field.

Let met tell you about this paper, what the author wanted it to be, and what it might have been.

What the author wanted out of his paper was a study of the benefits of structured analysis and design during the maintenance phase. That is, if software was built using the structured approach, is it more maintainable, and if so, by how much? That's an important question, of course, one of vital significance to our field. It should have been asked nearly 30 years ago, back when structured approaches were first being introduced into academic curricula and into practice at an astonishing rate. Still, better late than never to correct flaws in our understandings of our field. The author's original intent for this paper was laudable and important.

The research approach was interesting. The authors, upon learning of a federally mandated change to the business rules that most enterprises build into their software (I've forgotten the exact issue, but it might have involved a basic change in the payroll tax laws, for example), contacted a bunch of enterprises with these questions:

1. What was the time/cost for making this change?
2. Was the software that needed to be changed built using the structured approaches?

If all had gone well, the author would have been able to define a nice, crisp relationship between whether the structured approaches made it easier to make this particular modification, across a lot of different software in a lot of different enterprises, and if so by how much. A finding like "software built with the structured approaches was 5% (or 35% or 150% or whatever) easier to modify than software that was not" would have been a unique and significant contribution to our field.

However, it didn't work out that way. First of all (and remember this point—we're going to return to it), the time to do the modification was all over the map. Some systems required only a few hours to change, and others required person-months. But more to the point of this research, there was no correlation between the time to do the modification and the use during development of the structured approaches.

Thus, the author's finding, the one that was highlighted in the paper, was this: The structured approaches make no discernable difference in our ability to make (this particular) modification to software systems.

Now that's an important finding, of course, albeit one that most of us would have some trouble with. I think most of us believe, deep down inside, that the structured approaches do make a difference in our ability to build and modify software. What most of us don't know, if we are honest about it, is how much of a difference. And this author has given us a finding that is memorable, in the sense that it's counterintuitive, yet forgettable, in the sense that we don't really believe it.

But remember back to the beginning of this essay; it is my belief that the author failed to see a major and even more important redirection for this research. I dropped a clue for you up above, when I said we'd come back to something that I discussed there. Do you see what I see here?

Here's where I believe the author failed. Remember that it took some enterprises only a few hours to make the government-required system change, but others took many person-months? Think about that a minute. Here are some software systems presumably doing rather similar things, yet the time to modify them for an identical change request was dramatically different. And the question the author failed to ask at that point was "Why?"

It is enough to say "the structured methods don't explain it." Something does explain it. But what?

At this point I'd like to say a few words about research approaches and goals, because I think it's very important in what's going on here.

The author in this particular study was using what some researchers call a "theory-based approach." It's an approach I think of as being like the scientific method, in which the researcher formulates one or more hypotheses based on some underlying theory, then conducts research to test the validity of the hypotheses (and thus of the underlying theory). It's a particularly admirable form of research, because it gets to the heart of our field (the validity of underlying theories) and addresses that heart in an orderly process (by evaluative research). Interestingly, it's an approach much more common in the information systems field than in the computer science field.

The goal in this research I would characterize as "process evaluation." That is, the author assumed that the structured approaches, which are about the process of building software, would have an impact on maintenance time/cost, and set about evaluating the hypothesis that that impact would be positive. So far, so good.

product, not process

I would assert that what the author learned (but probably failed to grasp) midway through the study was that the systems in question differed profoundly in what they looked like and how they did what they did. What other possible explanation is there for the wide disparity in modification times? What is significant about this thought is that it was not the process of building the system, but the product itself, which exhibited the major difference that became visible in the study.

Let me repeat that in another way, to make the point I'm trying to make here. The author set out to measure the effects of process. There were no discernable process effects, according to the study; but there were profound product differences. And I believe what the author should have done, after winding down the process research, was to embark on a whole new question: What was it about these software products that accounted for the big differences observed?

exploratory, not just theory-based

Perhaps I'll never know whether the author saw what was going on here and immediately began some new research directed toward this new issue. I suspect not. And the reason I suspect that goes back to the research approach issue I discussed earlier. Remember, this research study was "theory-based." But what the author learned midway through the study, I would assert, was that something was happening for which theory simply offered no answers. To investigate the product differences I mentioned above would have required an entirely different research approach, an empirical study of existing software products where the author probably had no idea of what they would learn during the course of the research. There are exploratory research approaches, of course, and that was what was needed here. But some tend to deride such approaches, calling them "fishing expeditions" because the author has not hypothesized a finding based on an underlying theory prior to conducting the research.

This has been a somewhat meandering essay, starting with a research study that learned some unexpected things but failed to transition that learning experience into something truly profound. So let me tidy up the ending by making a couple of points that summarize where I think I've been here:

1. It is popular now to focus on process and its effect on software product. However, there is reason to believe—and this particular research study nicely shows it—that the relationship between process and product is at best unclear, and at worst nonexistent. Although product-focused research is much more difficult to do, I suspect that we will never conduct successful process research until we first come to understand the role of product much better than we do now.

2. It is popular now to focus on theory-based research, and in general that is an important way for research to proceed. However, there are times, in a discipline as new as that of systems and software, when the gap between theory and practice is so large that there is not yet any theory to account for the realities of practice. Under those circum-stances, theory-based research simply will not work, and exploratory research—the goal of which is to build theory that later can be tested by theory-based research—is the only way to make progress.

3. There was a profound learning experience for all of us in what this research failed to explore. I, for one, have no idea what that turn in research direction might have shown, but my message to researchers is this: If your research approach takes you through an area where you simply can't account for what you are learning, stop and take stock. You may be

onto something much more important than what you set out to learn in the first place.

5.4

A Miscellany of Thoughts on Software Process

You never know where you're going to run across some interesting software insight.

You expect to find such insight, of course, in the learned papers in the technical journals of our field. But it is somehow a special pleasure, at least to me, when I run across some software insight in a more obscure source.

Take this quote, for example: "Focus on results rather than process." Does that sound like something out of a practical software engineering journal, perhaps one that has chosen to tee off on the SEI Capability Maturity Model work?

Well, it's not. That quote is from an article in, of all places, *The Wall Street Journal*. The title of the article is "Why Smart People Do Dumb Things" (December 21, 1992), and it's from a column called "Manager's Journal," by Mortimer R. Feinberg.

The gist of the article is this: Super-bright people need to be managed in a way different from run-of-the-mill people. But what way is that? The article presents some answers to that question.

The gist of the thought we quoted above is this: Super-bright people don't always do things the way the rest of the world does them. Don't try to force-fit their creative genius into the straightjacket of a formalized process. But make very sure, when they finally produce a product, that it has value; and review their progress along the way, using whatever process-checking makes sense under the circumstances.

Interesting, especially given the source.

Now, here's another instance of an interesting (and, as it turns out, similar) idea coming from an unusual source. The following quotes are from a letter to the editor—that's what makes the source unusual—from one of our own technical journals, *Communications of the ACM*. The letter was written by Edward S. Ruete, appeared in the August 1990 *CACM*, and was in response to an also very interesting article written by Jonathan Grudin with the fascinating title "The Case Against User Interface Consistency." (In the Grudin article, the author had argued that application needs, rather than consistency alone, should drive interface design, and Grudin further suggested that following application needs will likely result in interfaces that are not necessarily consistent.)

In his letter, Ruete fundamentally agreed with Grudin. Midway through his letter, he added some thoughts that link nicely to The Wall Street Journal quote above. Ruete made the analogy that developing software is similar to creative writing, and said, "It does not matter how you do it, just so it is good. Once that principle is accepted, it puts all the tools and techniques of program development in perspective ... The tools are good only insofar as their application results in good programs."

And, in a summing-up kind of paragraph, Ruete said, "In spite of the best efforts of software engineering theorists, including myself, to convince us otherwise, programming is essentially a creative activity. Standards can no more guarantee a good program than they can guarantee a good play, novel, or communications article."

Tools and standards are limited in their benefit to software people. An interesting additional thought.

Now there's a third piece of material from a strange source. This is from a paper submitted to the Journal of Systems and Software that, in a transmogrification, went on to be published. The draft

was called "Controllable Factors for Programmer Productivity ...,"
and was written by Ali Mili and several others. "By contrast with
all other industries, the productivity of the worker in the software
industry ... improves very little as a function of programming tools
usage. According to measures taken by Boehm [in his *Software
Engineering Economics,* 1981], the differences of productivity between
a programmer who uses no tools at all and one who uses the most
up-to-date, powerful tools ... is no larger than 50%. To put this
figure in perspective, one ought to compare it with the difference
in productivity that exists between a car builder that has only
screwdrivers and a car builder that has today's most sophisticated
robots."

Once again, we see the opinion that tools (and thus process) are
limited in their software benefit. However, the argument is placed
in a particularly interesting context.

Finally, here's a fourth piece of material. This time, it's in a
response in *IEEE Computer* to a Point/Counterpoint debate on the
value of software process standards.

The response (*IEEE Computer,* May 1993) was by Norman F.
Schneidewind, but most of the response consisted of quotations
from interested readers. Here's a particularly relevant one:

Bill Dietrich of Atlanta said, "It is a widely accepted engineering
principle that a good process produces a good product. Is it
similarly accepted that a good design process produces a good
design? Is the design process so well understood that it is ready to
be standardized?

"... I am concerned that the fundamental nature of developing
software is being misrepresented by those who would standardize
the process. I understand their desire to make software development a measurable, repeatable, dependable process. But software
development is mostly design ... Where is the evidence that design
activity is measurable or repeatable? What are the criteria for
judging the goodness of a design?"

There you have it, four interesting viewpoints from four disparate sources. But what is especially interesting is that, I would assert, they all are saying a similar thing. If I may paraphrase, I see it as this. Process is not a universal software problem-solver. More important, it is not a panacea. Those who see it as one are simply not recognizing the facts available.

5·5
process versus people: getting to good product

Good people are a way to good product. Many feel, in fact, that people are far more important than process in building software.

Is that just a philosophical disagreement of little consequence, or are there some real-world implications?

Twice now, when IBM set out to build an operating system (OS/360 and later OS/2), it employed hundreds of people to do the job. How well that approach worked out the first time was nicely documented in Fred Brooks' classic The Mythical Man-Month. It didn't work very well. And with respect to OS/2, the end result was even less satisfactory.

(It is interesting to note that the SEI Capability Maturity Model—the ultimate in process definition and focus—has its roots at IBM, where some of its key architects have a history dating back to OS/360.)

When that many people get into the act on a software project, good process is essential. Harnessing and steering hundreds of programmers toward a common goal becomes a major chore of its own. That's what process is all about. No wonder IBM and the Watts Humphreys of the world place heavy emphasis on process!

But is there another way? According to other, smaller software companies, there is. Those companies can't afford the Mongolian

Horde approach to building software. They have to find another way. These companies see that other way as good people.

Where IBM uses hundreds of invisible, process-driven people to build an operating system, the small software houses of the world are using a few dozen at most. How can they do that? By choosing those few dozen very carefully. Some companies use such techniques as screening their hiring candidates (they even have to submit the code for a program they're proud of as part of their job application!) and getting rid of underperformers (peer votes result in those who aren't doing the work being dismissed). From hiring to firing, choosing good people is the most important part of how a small software shop does business.

If we start with the premise that good people get to good product a whole lot more cheaply than good process does, what remains to be determined is whether quality suffers along the way. I'll bet on the quality of the product produced by those good people. It has always seemed to me that good product quality, for products of any kind, is most determined by the quality of the people building the product. Why shouldn't that be true for software as well?

5.6
evaluating the Results of using the CMM

I n several preceding sections, we have tap-danced around the issue of how much value the process-focused Capability Maturity Model has. We described the initial efforts the Software Engineering Institute made to overcome the problem that evaluative research on the CMM's benefits was going to be difficult.

At first the SEI used expert opinion to define the content of the CMM—Watts Humphrey and his colleagues, who had done the initial development of these approaches at IBM and elsewhere, were the gurus on whose beliefs and opinions and experiences the CMM was based. Soon thereafter, they began to use expert review, bringing to the SEI a lot of software engineering experts who could go through the proposed processes, scrub and modify them, and produce a new and improved version. If you couldn't do an honest-to-goodness piece of evaluative research on the CMM, this was the next best thing to do. And it was a whole lot better than what most methodologists and gurus were doing to find improvements to our ways of building software. A shortage of evaluative research, as you will see elsewhere in this book, is probably the biggest failing of the academic fields of computer science and software engineering.

Time passed, and eventually researchers began to overcome this lack. Larry Putnam studied [Putnam 1994] the effects of a software organization moving from level 1 to level 3 (from the chaotic stage to a mid-range stage), and found such benefits as 170% less schedule time required, 320% fewer peak staff, and 570% less effort. These were truly impressive numbers, certainly ones capable of being cited to demonstrate near-breakthrough value to the use of the CMM.

Fortunately, other researchers took up the flag and did further research. Jim Herblseb and several SEI colleagues studied 13 companies where the CMM had been introduced, and found 9-67% productivity gains, and 6-25% defect detection gains [Herbsleb et al 1994]. These are nice gains, of course, but they are not the break-through benefits that Putnam found, and they begin to make one raise questions as to why the results are so different.

Other studies began being published. Thomas Haley conducted a study at Raytheon [Haley 1996] and found such benefits as these:

- 190% productivity gains over 8 years (24%/year)
- 17 defects per 1000 lines of code, reduced to 4, over 8 years (53% improvement/year)

Once again, these are nice benefits, but they don't match either of the two prior findings.

A few years later, Clark published a study [Clark 2000] showing that an increase of one level in process maturity could reduce development effort by 4-11%. Breakthrough? Not even close. But, once again, a nice and tidy improvement.

And finally there is one other, somewhat peculiar, piece of research that's worth examining. In an information systems journal, [Harter, et al. 2000] found that a 1% increase in maturity level led to a .61% decrease in development effort, and a 1.6% increase in product quality (as measured in defects). What is peculiar about this study is that it is not clear exactly what a 1% increase in CMM level really means. The CMM consists, after all, of a discrete series of steps, one, two, three, four, five, with essen-

5.6
evaluating
the results of
using the CMM

tially no increments along the way. Oh, there are key processes that can be used to determine when an organization has moved from one discrete level to the next, but there is nothing in the CMM description that would allow one to talk about fractional level advancement in any meaningful way. It's not that it's so diffi-cult to accept the meaning of these findings; it's just that it's not at all clear how the author of the study could have done what he says he did.

It is important to step back and look at these findings. There are a couple of things that leap out at us when we do. The first is that there seems to be no doubt that the process approaches of the CMM lead to benefits in software production. Those benefits, we see here, can be measured in both productivity and quality (at least, quality as measured in defects).

The second thing that leaps out is that it is very difficult to pin down exactly what those benefits really are. Are they orders of magnitude, as Putnam would have us believe? Or are they small percentages, as the other studies tend to show, dropping down to as low as 4%?

The third thing that leaps out (actually, it sort of creeps out, and then only if you look at the list of references below!) is that when you check the names of the journals where these findings were published, they are all practitioner journals. Where are the evalua-tive studies of CMM benefits from the academic research journals?

Now, let's step back even further and look at these findings about these findings. What we are seeing here is often a typical result of doing evaluative research in the software engineering world. Not much of it has been done, to be sure, and what has been done is rarely published in the research literature. Further, what we often find is tremendous variation in those studies that have been done. Technology X is better than technology Y, these studies tell us, by something between -5% and +112%. Not very satis-fying. It's enough to cause some researchers to give up on evalua-tive studies, both because they don't seem to be able to get them published in the research journals that give them tenure benefits, and because they're both hard to do and relatively inconclusive!

But it's important that we not give up. Because if we don't do such studies, then all we have to fall back on is some expert/guru's opinion on the benefits of a technology that, often as not, they are selling. Oh, they've analyzed it to death, but they have never put it to the test in a rubber-meets-the-road kind of setting, one where an attempt to apply objective and at least somewhat rigorous research approaches has been made.

So let me end this section by lauding the researchers who have given us the above numbers, no matter that they differ so widely. I can envision a time when, in a more stable field in which research approaches are better known and utilized, we will begin to obtain convergent and consistent evaluative research findings. And when that happens, we can truly begin to made progress in the software field.

5.6
evaluating
the results of
using the cmm

references

Clark 2000—"Quantifying the Effects of Process Improvement on Effort," *IEEE Software*, November 2000; Bradford K. Clark.

Haley 1996—"Software Process Improvements at Raytheon," *IEEE Software*, November 1996; Thomas J. Haley.

Harter et al 2000—"Effects of Process Maturity on Quality, Cycle Time, and Effort in Product Development," *Management Science*, April 2000; Donald E. Harter, Maryuram S. Krishnan, and Sandra A. Slaughter.

Herbsleb et al 1994—"Software Process Improvement—State of the Payoff," *American Programmer*, September 1994; J. Herbsleb, D. Dubrow, J. Siegel, J. Ruzum, and A. Carleton.

Putnam 1994—"The Economic Value of Moving up the SEI Scale," *Managing System Development* 14 (7): 1–6, 1994; L.H. Putnam.

5.7

product versus process focus: which do we do when?

Some people are process people, and some people are product people. It just seems to be an innate human difference.

I once knew a man who loved kites. He loved to make them. Flying them didn't matter very much to him. It was the process, not the product, that he enjoyed. His kites were the most beautiful, best crafted kites I have ever seen. They were the kind that would win a "best looking kite" contest. Whether they'd win "best flying kite," however, was problematic—and more to the point, from this man's point of view it was largely irrelevant.

Most of us, in our vocations and professions, don't have the luxury this man had. Try telling your boss that your next program is going to win "best looking kite" but won't even place in "best flying kite," and he may tell you to go fly one! Process, in the world of work, is largely only a device for creating product.

So it is important to figure out when to focus on product and when on process. I would assert there are times for each; and I'd like to get somewhat specific about it. My overall going-in position is that we focus on product whenever we can, and we focus on process only when we can't see the product as clearly as we need to.

What do I mean by that? Well, take contracting for a piece of software, for example. I'm writing a contract with you that will be a vehicle for your building a software product for me. I want that product to have all the right quality attributes, and to meet my functional needs, and to give my users satisfaction, and to be built on time and within budget.

My job in writing the contract is to maximize the chance this is what will happen. Seems straightforward, but it's not. A lot of those things I want in my product are hard to specify in any legally binding way. For example, one of the quality attributes I'd like your product to have is that it be highly modularized, so that it will be easy for you—or the follow-on maintenance contractor—to understand and modify. But how do I specify that the code be modular? I must do it in such a way that, if we ever have to go to court, it is totally clear what I asked for, so that if you don't provide it the court will agree with me that I deserved it and didn't get it.

Think about that a little. It is a difficult issue. Modularity, a concept at the heart of what we know about good software engineering, is very hard to specify in a binding way. First of all, the contract is going to have to define module. Try doing that. Now try doing it with your hands bound so that you can't wave them! No matter whether you talk about functional cohesion, or low coupling, or single entrance single exit, or any of the usual things we use to describe good modularity, we keep running into the problem that one difficult-to-define term begets another.

Those who have tried to make a contractual definition of good modularity have, in desperation, sometimes ended up with a very bad one. They want a definition where it is obvious if it has been met or not, and as a result they often specify modularity by the number of lines of code clustered together. Something like "The program shall be divided into modules, such that each module satisfies one or a very few functional needs and is no more than 50 lines of code in length." A lot of software specifications have been written with that sort of contractual definition for module, especially in the U.S. Department of Defense world.

However, where is it written that 50 lines of code—or 100 or 200—makes a good module? In an effort to make a quantitative, checkable definition, we have resorted to absurdity. In fact, in [Card 1990], the author shows that quantitative definitions of module size tend to result in bad modules.

What is a contractual specifier to do? If you can't define the product, define the process. Invent and codify a series of checkpoints during product construction at which, among other things, conformance to a more vague yet more meaningful definition of module can be verified. It's the answer to the old conundrum, "I may not be able to describe good art, but I know it when I see it." Process is the way we get early visibility into seeing it.

And that's the role of process in a product-focused environment, I would assert. If you can't define the product as clearly as you would like, then make a clear definition of the process that will be used to achieve the product. Specify milestones. Specify intermediate products to be delivered or demonstrated at those milestones. Make sure that the intermediate products do indeed show progress being made toward the product. Evaluate the intermediate products with that goal as a yardstick.

Now, if over time we find a process that seems to make a lot of sense in building hard-to-specify products, think about formalizing it. When we build these sorts of products, we will use this kind of process. That formalization of process we can call a methodology. Notice that we have arrived at a definition of methodology in a sort of bottom-up fashion; that is, we have seen a problem (a product that is hard to specify), defined an approach to the problem (defining process to help us achieve product), evaluated the approach (by using it several times), and only then defined a methodology (by formalizing the process used).

(This left turn into a discussion of methodology may strike you as strange. But how many methodologies are developed top-down by gurus—or even graduate students—who haven't cut a line of code in 15 years [or a lifetime!]. Those who haven't built product to a process in order to evaluate the process should never invent methodologies.)

After we have used the process-cum-methodology for awhile, we may even begin to think about some formalization on top of this formalization, (e.g., statistical process control). When we use this process, the following kinds of things normally happen. If those things are not happening, then we have a warning signal. For this product development, the process isn't working the way it usually does. That may be a problem, or it may not. However, it is a signal that investigation is warranted. Statistical process control is a useful tool, then, for detecting deviations from a norm.

There's one more important point to be made before we end this excursion. Good process does not guarantee good product. That is not the same as saying "good process doesn't lead to good product"; our intuition suggests it does. However, it has been popular, ever since the first guru invented the first methodology (formalized process, right?!) to say that the use of "my" methodology will guarantee that a good job gets done. Not only is that not the case, but we have some evidence that it is not. Tom DeMarco, he of many wonderful computing books and articles, reported at an International Conference on Software Engineering several years ago that he had studied software products built by people trained in and using a common methodology, and he found little if any similarity in the products they produced. And, in a case straight out of computing ancient history, the claims that structured programming produced error-free code were refuted some years back by the *New York Times* customers of the first major structured programming project, who are reported to have said, "If structured programming resulted in only one error per thousand lines of code, then the contractor owes about a million more lines." In other words, the reliability claims made for the benefits of structured programming at that point in time were grossly exaggerated.

Now, let's return to ground zero. The point of this essay is that there is a time for product focus, and there is a time for process focus. Product focus, at least in the workaday world, should always come first. Process focus, when the shape of the product is unclear, is a means to product focus. When we need it, we need it a lot. And when we have defined a process that really seems to work, there are some interesting formalisms we can layer on top of it.

Reference

Card 1990—*Measuring Software Design Quality*, Prentice-Hall, 1990; David N. Card with Robert L. Glass.

chapter 6
Intellectual vs. clerical tasks

chapter contents

Introduction to chapter 6

"A productive symbiosis of human beings and computers will assign the nonprogrammable tasks to human beings and the programmable to computers. The nonprogrammable include the holistic, global activities involving heuristics, values, attitudes, emotions and humor, while the programmable include sequential step-by-step detailed algorithms."

—*Moshe F. Rubinstein*
Tools for Thinking and Problem-Solving,
Prentice-Hall 1986

L et me tell you a story. The story is about the evolution of a research paper. (Don't stop reading now, there's more to this than you think!) It's a story about research whose goal was to answer the question, "To what extent is software work intellectually challenging?"

Why ask that question? Isn't it obvious that software is complex, challenging work?

Unfortunately, the answer of a lot of people in our society is "No, it's not." All around us, we see evidence that people think this way. Managers wonder why their software maintainers take so long to make a "simple" change. Academic deans denigrate and sometimes eliminate computing courses and even programs from their curriculum on the grounds that they have "no intellectual content." (Don't laugh—it happened at several A-grade institutions only a decade ago, and there are threats of it happening even today!) Gurus announce that the latest computing fad or fancy will eliminate the need for programmers. Researchers seek funding for projects that will "automate" the process of constructing software. Governmental agencies seek contractors to produce "order of magnitude" improvements in our ability to build and/or maintain software. The list goes on. In one way or another, these people are expressing their belief that software is somehow easy to build and work with.

The mischief raised by those beliefs has done untold damage to the computing field. Outsourcing is a result. Closure of academic computing programs is a result. Failure to fund appropriate (as opposed to infeasible) software research is a result. Cost and schedule pressure to achieve the impossible is a result. Credibility loss is a result.

Now back to the story I want to tell. For some time, I puzzled over this strange disparity of beliefs. Not only did I wonder why people felt this way, I also—in the back of my mind—wondered what it would take to convince them otherwise. Perhaps an appropriately chosen research study on the subject could do the trick. But what kind of research?

Then I saw the tapes. What tapes? A couple of research colleagues were doing a protocol analysis study of software methodologies. To do that, they had videotaped some novice systems analysts in the act of studying a problem. For some reason that I can't recall, I put one of the tapes in the TV one day and, out of idle curiosity, watched it to see what happened.

What struck me as I watched the tape was the amount of time the analyst did absolutely nothing! It was an incredibly boring experience. And yet I knew, because the subject on the videotape knew that their work was being filmed and timed, that they were intently involved in problem solving.

And then it hit me. The time the subject spent boring me out of my wits, doing absolutely nothing visible, was thinking time. And the time the subject spent acting on that thought, jotting down a representation of what they had been thinking, was by contrast clerical time. Here, on this tape, was a real-live representation of the issue of whether software work was intellectually challenging or not. Why not measure the amount of time each subject spent thinking, and the amount of time they spent writing or drawing?

We (my research partners and I) did just that. We studied the intellectual vs. clerical time for a number of subjects, we devised another scheme to measure the same kind of things in a different way just to run a consistency check on our findings, we wrote the paper, and we sent it off to a good journal.

Then a disappointing thing happened. What we had, we knew all along, was an excellent research issue pursued by a somewhat mediocre research approach. That is, there were flaws in the basic idea of the research:

1. Was inactivity, for example, really the same as intellectual time?
2. Was activity really clerical time?
3. Were novices appropriate subjects?
4. Were simple tasks appropriate vehicles to measure what we wanted to measure?

All of those legitimate issues were raised, as we knew they would be, by the reviewers for the journal to which we sent the paper. We hoped that the importance of the issue being explored would override the concern over research methodology. Unfortunately, it did not. The paper was rejected.

We sent the paper off to another journal, and—to make a long story at least shorter—this time the news was better. The paper was accepted and, after an appropriate period, it was published.

Then a particularly interesting thing happened. *InformationWeek,* a popular-press computing news magazine, published a brief mention of the paper's findings. Immediately, emails began arriving and the phone began ringing. Over the next month or two, more than 100 such messages came in, each from someone who was interested in the research findings, wanting to know more about them. Only as I write this material many months later has the number of messages dropped to zero. Whatever the quality of the research, the issue treated by the paper touched a nerve in the computing world.

That paper, as you might imagine by now, is in this book following this chapter introduction. In spite of the questionable research approach, its findings are startlingly consistent. Intellectual aspects predominate over clerical by a large margin. (To find out how much, read on.) Although more research studies are needed, there is no question—at this point—that those who believe that software is an easy task are clearly wrong.

And there you have it. A story about the evolution of a research project. And, as it turned out, one with a happy ending!

(P.S. There's more. Once the "intellectual vs. clerical" findings became public, another researcher interested in creativity—the late professor Dan Couger of the University of Colorado—contacted us and suggested extending the work to explore the extent to which software work is not just intellectual, but creative. (What could be more relevant to a book on creativity?!) With his help—he provided us with a good definition of creativity—we conducted a follow-on study. Those findings, though less dramatic than those of the original paper, are also here in this chapter.)

In all the other introductory material in this chapter, I've defined the key terms involved. Let's not move on to the remainder of the material until we have defined intellectual, derived from intellect: "the mind's power of reasoning and acquiring knowledge (contrasted with feeling and instinct)"; and clerical: "of clerks, the activity of copying or writing something out."

Now, on with an investigation of the intellectual vs. clerical (vs. creative) aspects of software.

6.1

software: challenging or trivial to build?

Robert L. Glass and Iris Vessey

The world view of the complexity of creating software is schizo-phrenic. On the one hand, we have numerous professional journals and much college/university coursework devoted to various aspects of software engineering and we hear such noted computer scientists as David Parnas and Donald Knuth expressing their strongly-felt belief that "software is hard" to produce [Parnas 1986, Knuth 1989].

On the other hand, we have a popular view that developing software is easy: "It is easier to teach a business person about technology than it is to teach a techie how to manage. MIS should be managed by a business generalist rather than a technology specialist. I can teach my mother to code [MBA 1990]."

Further, the 1990s glamour of CASE workbenches was due largely to the notion that major portions of software development could be automated. For example, [McClure1988] said:

"A workbench has integrated tools that automate the entire development and maintenance of software systems and software project management. The output of one life-cycle phase is directly

167

and automatically passed on to the next life-cycle phase; the final product is an executable software system and its documentation."

This quotation conveys the message that humans can by replaced by tools in the software development process.

Clearly these opinions are poles apart. In one we see software as challenging even for finely-honed intellectual minds. In the other we see software as so easy that almost anyone can produce it. What is wrong with these pictures? Can they both be right? If not, which is wrong?

Of course, the complexity of software is intimately related to the complexity of the problem the software is to solve. So it is entirely possible that some software is trivially easy while some is exceedingly complex. But, in saying that, we have avoided coming to grips with the still-important question "How difficult is this software job, anyway?"

There are many possible ways to answer this question. Parnas' experience with the A-7 project shows that software construction is indeed a complicated task [see, for example, Parnas 1985]. With regard to automated methods for producing software, Rich and Waters [Rich 1988] refer to the "cocktail party" myth of automatic programming.

Empirical evidence is provided by [Fjelstad 1979] who shows that software maintainers spend 45 percent of their time seeking understanding of a change to be made and of the software to be changed, 35 percent of their time verifying the change once it is made, and only 20 percent of their time actually making the change. Effectively, they spend 80 percent of their time thinking about the problem and its solution. Further empirical evidence [Woodfield 1979] shows that for every 25 percent increase in the complexity of a problem to be solved, there is a 100 percent increase in the complexity of the software required to solve it. This data suggests that the complexity of software is a problem of scale: easy tasks are easy to solve, hard ones are very hard.

Yet there is little evidence beyond that. We find the question begged in statements like "... testing comprises a planning part and an operative part. While the latter can take great advantage from the support of automated tools, the planning part is mostly based on human ingenuity and competence" [Bertolino 1991]. There is little in the way of specific or quantitative answers.

It is important to find these answers. The current state of the art and practice of software shows that beliefs such as those stated above, that anyone can develop software and that anyone can manage software development, are prevalent, if not predominant.

If software is largely a clerical activity, then these beliefs are valid. If it is not, then these beliefs are a disservice to the field. Getting an answer to the intellectual vs. clerical question, then, is a high-leverage task.

In this paper we take an initial, exploratory step toward answering that question. We present the results of a two-pronged approach to examining the intellectual versus the clerical components of the software development process. In the next section, we examine the tasks involved in software development, and determine which of them require intellect and which are largely clerical. Then, after that, we present the findings of an empirical study in which, for a systems analysis task, a record was made of the amount of time subjects spent thinking as opposed to drawing diagrams. Finally, we presents the conclusions and implications of the study.

software task classification

In Tables 1 and 2 we present several taxonomies of the tasks of software. Table 1 shows tasks performed by CASE tools as documented in the CASE literature. Because those tasks have been automated, it is probably fair to say that they are somewhat more clerical than those that have not. Table 2 shows a more abstract view of tasks, independent of whether there is a CASE tool to support them.

In understanding how much of software work is intellectual and how much is clerical, it would be helpful to ascertain from these lists which tasks are intellectual and which are clerical. Then a simplistic analysis could be used to say something like "X percent of software's tasks are intellectual, and Y percent are clerical." This would still not tell us what percentage of overall software work falls into each category, but it would be a major step in understanding, if not quantifying.

There are several problems in doing this, however. First, as can be seen from the tables, there is little consistency, at least at the wording level, to the task lists. Second, to someone unfamiliar with software development it is not apparent which tasks are intellectual and which are clerical. Third, outside of a specific context, even knowledgeable software specialists may have some disagreement in categorizing the tasks.

To overcome these difficulties, we used a simple approach to create the desired categorization. We used two experienced software professionals to independently categorize the tasks based on their intellectual(i) or clerical(c) implications for software development. Tasks that shared characteristics of both intellectual and clerical tasks were classified as indeterminate(id). The two classifiers achieved 77 percent agreement. Differences were resolved by using a third independent classifier to establish a majority decision. The findings of that process are presented in the right hand columns of Tables 1 and 2.

table 1 tasks performed by case tools.[a]	
software task[b]	code
Functionalities of representation	
Represent a design	i
Construct models	i
Customize the language or conventions used for representation	i

Table 1 Tasks performed by CASE Tools.[a]	
Software Task[b]	Code
Represent relationships	i
Combine entities or processes	id
* Show an object's attributes	
Maintain descriptions	c
Provide naming conventions	i
Maintain single definition	c
* Move between models	
Redraw a diagram	c
Map onto functional description	id
Combine equivalent processes	id
* Simultaneously display several views	
Choose a model	i
Functionalities of analysis	
Test for model consistency	i
Check for structural equivalence	i
Check for unnecessary or redundant connections	id
Detect inconsistencies	id
Identify impact of design changes	i
Search the design for similar objects	i
Suggest resolutions	i
Estimate characteristics	i
Search design for specified characteristics	i
Simulate the production environment	i
Identify rules violations	c
Trace relationships	id
Identify differences	i
Recommend a general model	i
* Perform an operation on part of a design	

TABLE 1 TASKS PERFORMED BY CASE TOOLS.[a]	
SOFTWARE TASK[b]	CODE
Functionalities of transformation	
Generate executable code	i
Convert specification	i
Transform a representation	i
Provide documentation	id
Perform reverse engineering	i
Generate screen mockups	i
* Import/export data	
Create templates for tasks and deliverables	i
Propagate a change	c
Functionalities of control	
Specify who can review work	id
Provide management information	id
Maintain a record of responsibility	c
Maintain a record of changes	c
Provide management information on more than one project	id
Specify who can modify	i
* Freeze a portion of a design	
Manage quality assurance	i
Alter rules	i
Provide prioritizing assistance	i
Estimate tasks/projects	i
Remind team about deadlines	c
Merge versions	c
Produce metrics	i
Maintain list of requirements and how satisfied	c
* Temporarily ignore a problem so work can continue	

Table 1 Tasks performed by CASE tools.[a]	
software task[b]	code
Functionalities of cooperative functionality	
* Maintain a dialogue with other tools users	
* Allow a group to work simultaneously on a task	
* Send message to others who use the tools	
*Allow concurrent use of dictionary/diagram/etc.	
* Provide group interaction support (brainstorming)	
*Attach electronic notes	
* Allow anonymous feedback	
Notify designer of changes	c
Build a catalog of macros	c
Facilitate design alternatives	i
Functionalities of support	
Provide quick reference aids	i
Provide instructional materials	i
Identify external sources of information	i
Build templates/examples for tutorials/demos	i
Browse in other segments of the tool	i
Explain why part of a design is inconsistent	
Anticipate user errors from past patterns	i
Allow undoing a series of commands	i
Generate outputs in a variety of media	id
Incorporate command macros	i
Generate reports and documents	id
* Provide change pages	
* Magnify a model to see greater levels of detail	
Build a library of customized models	i
* Prepare, edit, store, send, and retrieve documents	
Store versions of a design	c

TABLE 1 TASKS PERFORMED BY CASE TOOLS.[a]	
SOFTWARE TASK[b]	CODE
* Link a design to a library for testing	
* Develop, run and store customized reports	

[a] Henderson, J.C., and Cooprider, J.G., "Dimensions of IS Planning and Design Technology," *Information Systems Research*, Vol. 1, No. 3, 1990, 227–254.

[b] technology-based tasks

* technology-based tasks not considered in this task analysis

TABLE 2(a) SOFTWARE TASKS PERFORMED.a	
SOFTWARE TASK	CODE
Software requirements tasks	
Requirements identification	
Context analysis	i
Elicitation from people	i
Deriving software requirements from system requirements	i
Task analysis to develop user interface requirements	i
Identification of constraints	i
Requirements analysis	
Assessment of potential problems	i
Classification of requirements	i
Evaluation of feasibility and risks	i
Requirements representation	
Use of models	i
Roles for prototyping	i
Requirements communication	i

table 2(a) software tasks performed.a	
software task	code
Preparation for validation (criteria, techniques)	i
Managing the requirements definition process	i

a Brackett, J. W., "Software Requirements," *Software Engineering Institute, SEI-CMU-19-1.1, 1989.*

table 2(b) software tasks performed.a	
software taskb	code
Overall software tasks	
Requirements analysis	i
Data flow analysis	i
Functional decomposition	i
Production of design and specification documents	i
Control of document updates	c
* Reusable design access	
New code development	i
* Reusable code access	
Analysis and modification of existing code	i
Restructuring of existing code	c
Removal of dead code	i
Design reviews	i
Code inspections	i
Personal debugging	i
Test case development	i
Test library control	c
Defect analysis	i
User documentation production	i
On-line help and tutorial production	i

table 2(b) software tasks performed.a	
software taskb	code
User training	i

a Jones, T. C., "Why Choose CASE?" *American Programmer*, Vol, 3, No. 1 (Jan 1990), 14–21.

b technology-based tasks

The summary of these categorizations is presented in Table 3: the percentage of intellectual, clerical, and indeterminate tasks in the set of CASE and non-CASE tasks. From Table 3, we see that even for CASE tools, intellectual tasks predominate over clerical ones, 62 percent to 21 percent. For non-CASE tasks the breakdown is especially dramatic, 83 percent vs. 17 percent. Overall, intellectual tasks predominate 71 percent to 18 percent.

We see clearly, using this rudimentary taxonomy, that the predominant number of tasks in software work is intellectual. Given the limitations of the approach, however, it is important to see this finding as only one piece of evidence in the development of an accurate picture.

experimental findings

One drawback of the above results is that the findings are about numbers of tasks rather than time spent on tasks. In this section, we report another approach to answering the intellectual vs. clerical question. We sought to observe how much time developers actually spend thinking and how much time they spend acting on that thought, while engaged in a software task.

Table 3 categorization of case and non-case tasks.			
task categories	clerical	indeterminate	intellectual
CASE tool tasks Henderson and Cooprider (1990)	14a (21)	11 (17)	40 (62)
Non-Case tasks Brackett (1989)	0	0	13 (100)
Jones (1990)	3 (17)	0	15 (83)
Overall	17 (18)	11 (11)	68 (71)

a The table entries are numbers of tasks in each category; the figures in brackets are percentages.

A group of subjects involved in a study of systems analysis conducted for another purpose [Vessey 1992] was videotaped while problem solving. The purpose of the original study was to observe systems analysts using various methodological approaches to specify the information requirements for either one of two case studies. Subjects studied a problem statement, thought about how to represent the problem in the specification graphic of choice, and then drew the graphic (in this case, manually). It was possible, from the video tapes, to record thinking time vs. drawing time for the study subjects.

Table 4 shows the result of that study. There is a fascinating consistency to the results. Most subjects spent roughly 21 percent of their time writing (drawing graphics), and the remaining 79 percent of their time thinking. The range in thinking time is from 72 to 85 percent, certainly a narrow range for a group of subjects thought to have nothing much in common except for the pool from which they were drawn.

It is important to note, in spite of the interesting consistency of findings here, several limitations of this study. First, the subject pool consists of graduate students with little or no practitioner experience in systems analysis. Second, the findings are from a study conducted for another purpose; the experiment was not designed specifically to control any relevant variables. Third, the task of specifying information requirements is by nature an unstructured and therefore intellectual task since it deals with formulating the initial model of the real world problem to be solved.

table 4 Thinking Time versus writing Time During systems Analysis.					
				% of total time	
subject	problem	Total time (mins.)	writing time (mins.)	writing	Thinking
S3	1	153	23.1	15	85
	2	106	20.5	19	81
S4	1	117	24.2	21	79
	2	26	6.8	26	74
S6	1	108	18.7	17	83
	2	60	12.4	21	79
S10	1	51	11.0	22	78
	2	41	10.0	24	76
S11	1	61	12.8	21	79
	2	87	15.3	18	82
S12	1	61	16.9	28	72
	2	67	14.3	21	79

Because of the consistency of the findings, however, it is possible to say that, at least for a student population, intellectual time spent doing systems analysis is roughly four times the amount of time spent on relatively clerical activities.

There are several questions that still need to be answered: (1) Do the numbers differ for practitioner subjects? (2) Are the numbers similar for activities other than systems analysis? (3) Do the numbers depend on the case studies used in this particular study? (Note, however, that across the two cases examined here, the numbers vary little.) Answers to these questions would help in formulating a better understanding of the relationship between intellectual and clerical activities in software.

conclusions and implications

The issue of intellectual vs. clerical effort spent in software activities is an important one, and one that is somewhat controversial. Information bearing on the issue would help us to answer such questions as:

1. How much benefit can we REALLY expect from software automation?
2. Can we use relatively unskilled people (for example, untrained end users?) to build and maintain software?
3. How important are technical skills to the task of managing software?

In this study, we provide some initial, though diverse, evidence to resolve these important issues. The findings are interestingly consistent. From an examination of tasks performed, we see by analysis that intellectual tasks predominate over clerical ones in software work by roughly 71 percent to 18 percent, or almost 4 to 1. From an experimental study of time spent performing systems analysis, we see by observation that intellectual activities predominate over clerical ones by 79 to 21 percent, or almost 4 to 1.

The figures for the number of intellectual versus clerical software tasks and the amount of time spent on intellectual versus clerical activities in systems analysis are surprisingly similar. This initial exploration shows the tasks of software are considerably more intellectual than clerical. Thus, an early conclusion is that even simple software tasks are more intellectual than the "anyone can build software" viewpoint expressed in the introduction to this paper. The findings of these preliminary steps are certainly not definitive, however. Further work is needed to better differentiate and explore these findings.

Acknowledgment

The authors are indebted to Umesh Bhatia and Sue Conger for research assistance on this project. A modified version of this material was published in the *Journal Information and Management,* November 1992.

References

Bertolino 1991—"An Overview of Automated Software Testing," *Journal of Systems and Software,* May 1991; A. Bertolino.

Fjelstad 1979—"Application Maintenance Study: Report to Our Respondents," *Proceedings of GUIDE 48,* The Guide Corporation, Philadelphia, 1979; R. K. Fjelstad and W. T. Hamlen.

Knuth 1989—Keynote address, World Computer Congress, 1989, as reported in *System Development,* Dec. 1989; Donald E. Knuth.

MBA 1990—"More on MBAs in MIS," letters to the editor in response to an article on whether the employment of MBAs in Information Systems positions helps or hurts organizations, *Information Week,* March 19, 1990.

McClure 1988—"The CASE for Structured Development," *PC Tech Journal,* August 1988, 51–67; Carma McClure.

Parnas 1985—"The Modular Structure of Complex Systems," *IEEE Transactions on Software Engineering,* March 1985; David L. Parnas, et al.

Parnas 1986—Presentation at Seattle University graduate program seminar, 1986; David Lorge Parnas.

Rich 1988—"Automatic Programming: Myths and Prospects," *Computer*, August 1988, 40–51; Charles Rich and Richard Waters.

Vessey 1992—"Specifying Information Requirements: Factors Influencing Problem Analysis," unpublished manuscript; Iris Vessey and Sue A. Conger.

Woodfield 1979 "An Experiment on Unit Increase in Program Complexity," *IEEE Transactions on Software Engineering*, March, 1979; Scott Woodfield.

6.2

software Tasks: intellectual, clerical ....or creative?

Robert L. Glass and Iris Vessey

There have been few studies of the nature of software work. That is, there is little research evidence to support one or all of the following points of view:

- Software's tasks are easy and automatable.
- Software's tasks are intellectually complex and challenging.
- Software's tasks require large amounts of creativity.

What makes the lack of studies of these issues surprising is that each of the above viewpoints has intellectual and political support among some members of the computing community, and yet it is largely impossible for all three of these points of view to be correct.

For example, consider these statements:

- Managers of companies with significant computing activities have made public statements to the effect that "I can teach my mother how to code" [MBA 1990], conveying their belief that software's tasks are trivial.

- Gurus active in predicting the future of computing have taken the position that the future will see "application development without programmers" [Martin 1982], implying that software skills can easily be acquired by end users, or even "automated."
- Leading software engineering academics see software as the most complicated activity ever undertaken by humanity [USNRC 1990], implying that the search for order-of-magnitude improvements for the tasks of software is probably doomed.
- Authors of popular books in the field decry the advocacy of formal and disciplined processes for software development on the grounds that such approaches leave little room for the creativity essential to software design and construction (see, for example, [DeGrace 1993]).

The breadth of these conflicting beliefs and the depth of the underlying conviction of their supports begs a study of software tasks. Is it possible that all of these divergent points of view can, somehow, coexist? If not, which point of view is closest to the truth?

The objective of this paper is to present findings from a previous exploration of these issues and to report additional findings from a new and, to some extent, troubling study.

The paper proceeds as follows: The following section describes our previous study, which assessed the intellectual vs. clerical nature of software tasks. This is followed by a description of the current study, which assessed the creative nature of the tasks. We then analyze the findings of the two studies, while the last section presents conclusions.

The prior study

One way of approaching the issues presented above is to study the nature of software tasks by addressing the extent to which they are clerical, intellectual, and creative in nature.

This approach reduces the complicated issues identified in the preceding section to three surrogates. If we could somehow classify software tasks into one or more of these three categories, we would have a crisp—if perhaps simplistic—basis for tasks differentiation, leading to broader answers to the issues of concern.

In the prior study [Glass 1992] (it formed the preceding section (6.1) of this book), the authors used two approaches to answering this question:

- Measuring the amount of time taken by novice systems analysts in thinking about (intellectual activity), and carrying out (largely clerical activity), the tasks of specifying the requirements for some relatively simple software projects
- Evaluating, through expert judgment, the intellectual or clerical nature of several lists of software tasks appearing in the software literature and representative of all phases of the software development life cycle

Note that these approaches addressed part of the issue of concern (intellectual vs. clerical activities) via both a timing analysis and a task analysis, but did not address the creative nature of software tasks. That omission is rectified in the current study.

The current study

To address the issue of creativity, two things were necessary: a good definition of creativity as applied to software development; and a mechanism for evaluating the need for creativity in software tasks analogous to that employed in the first study, so that comparisons could be made.

The definition of creativity used in this study is based on the work on problem-solving presented in [Newell 1962] and used in most studies of creativity in software (e.g., [Couger 1990]). This work takes the position that to be creative, a solution must satisfy one or more of the following conditions:

1. The product of the thinking has novelty or value.

2. The thinking is unconventional, in the sense that it requires modification or rejection of previously accepted ideas.
3. The thinking requires high motivation and persistence, taking place over a considerable span of time (continuously or intermittently) or at high intensity.
4. The problem as initially posed was vague and ill-defined, so that part of the task was to formulate the problem itself.

The key words here—novelty, value, unconventional, high motivation, persistence, vague, and ill-defined—appeared sufficient to support a determination as to which software tasks were creative.

To solve the second part of the research problem—that is, to make this study comparable to the prior one—we used the same lists of software tasks as the first study, evaluating the tasks for their creative nature. Unfortunately, although we would also have liked to perform a timing analysis analogous to the first study, there was no way to identify in that research approach (protocol analysis recorded on video tapes) the amount of time spent being creative. Thus, in this current study of creative vs. intellectual and clerical tasks, we have classified the tasks of software into one or more of each of those categories, but we have not timed subjects to see how much of their time was creative as opposed to intellectual or clerical.

As in the first study, then, we used the judgments of experts to decide which tasks were creative. In the prior study, we used two experts, and for those tasks where the experts differed, a third expert resolved the differences. In this study, because we anticipated that the judgments might prove to be more difficult, we employed four experts. One expert had both academic and practitioner information systems experience; one was largely an academic information systems specialist; one was a software engineering academic specialist; and one had both software engineering and practitioner experience. Thus, the backgrounds of those participating in the study were reasonably diverse.

Tables 1, 2(a) and 2(b), and 3 present the findings of the study. (Note that the findings of the prior study are included in these tables as well.) Tables 1 and 2 present the raw data, the codes assigned to each of the tasks by the expert judges, while Table 3 represents a summary of the findings shown in Tables 1 and 2. In Tables 1 and 2, the judgments of the experts on the creativity inherent in the tasks is added as a new column to the original intellectual vs. clerical coding of the prior study. For each expert who judged a task to be creative, a creativity score of .25 was assigned. If all four experts judged a task creative, the total score was 1.00.

TABLE 1 TASKS PERFORMED BY CASE TOOLS[a]		
software task	intellectual/ clerical code[b]	creativity score
Functionalities of representation		
Represent a design	I	.25
Construct models	I	.75
Customize the language or conventions used for representation	I	.50
Represent relationships	I	.25
Combine entities or processes	id	.25
* Show an object's attributes		
Maintain descriptions	C	
Provide naming conventions	I	
Maintain single definition	C	
* Move between models		
Redraw a diagram	C	
Map onto functional description	id	.25

Table 1 Tasks performed by case tools[a]		
software task	intellectual/ clerical code[b]	creativity score
Combine equivalent processes	id	.25
* Simultaneously display several views		
Choose a model	I	.25
Functionalities of analysis		
Test for model consistency	I	.25
Check for structural equivalence	I	
Check for unnecessary or redundant connections	id	
Detect inconsistencies	id	
Identify impact of design changes	I	.25
Search the design for similar objects	I	
Suggest resolutions	I	.50
Estimate characteristics	I	.25
Search design for speci- fied characteristics	I	
Simulate the production environment	I	.25
Identify rules violations	C	
Trace relationships	id	
Identify differences	I	
Recommend a general model	I	.75
* Perform an operation on part of a design		
Functionalities of transformation		
Generate executable code	I	
Convert specification	I	
Transform a representation	I	

table 1 tasks performed by case tools[a]		
software task	intellectual/ clerical code[b]	creativity score
Provide documentation	id	
Perform reverse engineering	I	.50
Generate screen mockups	I	.25
* Import/export data		
Create templates for tasks and deliverables	I	
Propagate a change	C	
Functionalities of control		
Specify who can review work	id	
Provide management information	id	
Maintain a record of responsibility	C	
Maintain a record of changes	C	
Provide management information on more than one project		
Specify who can modify		
* Freeze a portion of a design	I	
Manage quality assurance		
Alter rules	I	
Provide prioritizing assistance	I	.25
Estimate tasks/projects	I	.25
Remind team about deadlines	I	
Merge versions	C	
Produce metrics	C	
Maintain list of requirements and how satisfied	I	
* Temporarily ignore a problem so work can continue	C	

Table 1 Tasks Performed by CASE Tools[a]	intellectual/ clerical code[b]	creativity score
Functionalities of coopera-tive functionality		
* Maintain a dialogue with other tools users		
* Allow a group to work simul-taneously on a task		
* Send message to others who use the tools		
* Allow concurrent use of dictionary/diagram/etc.		
* Provide group interaction support (brainstorming)		
* Attach electronic notes		
* Allow anonymous feedback	C	
Notify designer of changes	C	
Build a catalog of macros	I	
Facilitate design alternatives	C	
Functionalities of support	C	
Provide quick reference aids	I	.50
Provide instructional materials		
Identify external sources of information	I	
Build templates/examples for tutorials/demos	I	
Browse in other segments of the tool	I	
Explain why part of a design is inconsistent	I	

software task	intellectual/ clerical code[b]	creativity score
Table 1 Tasks performed by CASE Tools[a]		
Anticipate user errors from past patterns	I	
Allow undoing a series of commands	I	
Generate outputs in a variety of media	I	
Incorporate command macros	I	.25
Generate reports and documents	id	
* Provide change pages		
* Magnify a model to see greater levels of detail		
Build a library of customized models		
* Prepare, edit, store, send, and retrieve documents		
Store versions of a design		.25
* Link a design to a library for testing		
* Develop, run and store customized reports	C	

a Henderson, J. C., and Cooprider, J. G., "Dimensions of IS Planning and Design Technology," *Information Systems Research*, 1 (3), 1990, 227–254

bi = intellectual task

C = clerical task

Id = indeterminate task

*Technology-based tasks not considered in this task analysis

software task	intellectual/ clerical code[b]	creativity score
Software requirements tasks		
Requirements identification		
Context analysis	I	.75
Elicitation from people	I	.50
Deriving software requirements from system requirements	I	.25
Task analysis to develop user interface requirements	I	.25
Identification of constraints	I	.50
Requirements analysis		
Assessment of potential problems	I	.75
Classification of requirements	I	.25
Evaluation of feasibility and risks	I	.75
Requirements representation		
Use of models	I	.50
Roles for prototyping	I	.25
Requirements communication	I	
Preparation for validation (criteria, techniques)	I	
Managing the requirements definition process	I	

Table 2(a) software tasks performed[a]

a Brackett, J. W., "Software Requirements," *Software Engineering Institute*, SEI-CMU-19-1.1, 1989.

bi = intellectual task

C = clerical task

Id = indeterminate task

In Table 3, the section labeled "creative tasks" represents the accumulation of the results shown in Tables 1 and 2. The first column represents the range of tasks judged to be creative by the four experts, from the lowest number of tasks identified by an expert as creative to the highest. The next two columns represent the numbers of tasks identified as creative by at least one expert ("some support"), and by two or more experts ("considerable support"). The final column represents a "weighted" average obtained by summing the creativity scores in Tables 1 and 2.

Table 3 tells us, for example, that for the CASE tool tasks of Table 1:

table 2(b) software tasks performed[a]		
software task	intellectual/ clerical code[b]	creativity score
Overall software tasks		
Requirements analysis	i	1.00
Data flow analysis	i	1.00
Functional decomposition	i	.50
Production of design and specification documents	i	
Control of document updates	c	
* Reusable design access		
New code development	i	
* Reusable code access		
Analysis and modification of existing code	i	.25
Restructuring of existing code	c	
Removal of dead code	i	
Design reviews	i	.25
Code inspections	i	

table 2(b) software tasks performed[a]		
software task	intellectual/ clerical code[b]	creativity score
Personal debugging	i	.25
Test case development	i	.50
Test library control	c	
Defect analysis	i	
User documentation production	i	
On-line help and tutorial production	i	
User training	i	

a Jones, T. C., "Why Choose CASE?" *American Programmer*, 3, 1
January 1990, 14–21.

b i = intellectual task

  C = clerical task

  Id = indeterminate task

*Technology-based tasks not considered further in this analysis

- The range among the experts of the number of tasks considered creative was between 0 (one expert did not assess these tasks since they could be performed by CASE tools) to 18 (of the 40 intellectual tasks).
- There was some support (at least one expert) for 21 of the tasks being creative.
- There was considerable support for six of the tasks being creative.
- The weighted average number of creative tasks in Table 1 was 7.25.

What do we see in these tables? Perhaps the most dominant finding is that the experts viewed the tasks and their creative aspects in diverse ways. As opposed to the consistency of the intellectual vs. clerical classification, there was only marginal

6.2

software tasks:
intellectual,
clerical....or
creative?

193

agreement among these four experts. Given individual tasks, for example, although there were some cases of strong agreement—all four experts agreed that "requirements analysis" and "data flow analysis" in Table 2(b) were creative—there were often significant differences in the expert judgments.

table 3 categorization of CASE and NON-CASE TASKS							
	intellectual/clerical tasks			creative tasks			
Task categories	clerical	indeterm-inate	intell-ectual	Range	some support[a]	consider-able support[b]	"weighted" averagec
CASE tool tasks Table 1	14d (21)	11 (17)	40 (62)	0–18	21	6	7.25
Non-CASE tasks Table 2(a)	0	0	13 (100)	3–7	10	6	4.75
Table 2(b)	3 (17)	0	15 (83)	2–5	7	4	3.75
Overall	17 (18)	11 (11)	68 (71)	6–28	38	16	15.75

a Number of tasks identified as creative by at least one expert

b Number of tasks identified as creative by two or more experts

c Sum of creativity scores

d The table entries are numbers of tasks in each category; the figures in brackets are percentages.

Whereas one expert saw some modeling tasks as creative, for example, others did not. Note the predominance of .25 scores in the table; these indicate instances where only one expert ("some support") perceived a task to be creative.

The overall view of software tasks, presented in Table 3, also reveals considerable diversity. Percentages for the creative tasks are not given, since the clerical-indeterminate-intellectual figures in the table are from the prior study and already sum to 100%. (Note that tasks scored as creative almost always were those originally classified as intellectual.) The percentage of creative tasks out of the whole, however, is roughly 16%, with a range of 6%–29%. The wide ranges indicate that the experts did not agree on the extent to which software tasks are creative.

Analysis of Findings

Why did the experts differ so widely in their perceptions? There are several possible contributors to the problem.

First of all, the task definitions require considerable interpretation from the viewpoint of creativity. In spite of the fact that they are quite specific and represent a hierarchic decomposition to a fairly low level, there is still a great deal of room for doubt as to what they involve. One expert, for example, marked many tasks with a "?" regarding whether they were creative or not, and another scored many tasks as yes/no, implying that they might or might not be creative, depending on how one interpreted them. (It is interesting to note that, in spite of the fact that these "yes/no" votes were scored as no's in the tables, the expert who saw this ambiguity was the one who also saw the highest percentage of software tasks as being creative. In other words, if the yes/no votes had been counted as yes's, this person's overall scoring would have been far higher than 29%.)

Not only did the task definitions require interpretation; so did the definition of creativity. In spite of the fact that the definition is commonly accepted, the experts found it difficult to apply in the context of specific tasks. What constitutes "novelty," for example, or when is thinking "unconventional"? One person's "vague and ill-defined" problem might be another's oft-solved favorite. Personal experience probably played an important role in making judgments of this kind.

Finally, personal bias may also have entered into the expert judgments. Most experts already have a preconceived view of whether the work is creative or not. (Imagine trying to impanel a jury of professional peers who are impartial on the subject!) Thus, when interpreting a particular task in the context of an ambiguous definition of creativity, an expert might tend to favor their inherent view of the subject, rather than one formed at the time of the study.

conclusions

This paper presents findings from a research study of an important issue; it sheds light on the issue, but does not resolve it. Clearly, some amount of the tasks of software require creativity. Just as clearly, there is little agreement—at least in this study—of what that amount is.

In spite of the lack of definitive results, some conclusions can, we believe, be drawn.

First, from the point of view of practice, the fact that creativity is an essential part of some software development tasks ought to refute the "I can teach my mother to code" and the "application development without programmers" viewpoints that perceive software work to be not very challenging. Clearly, these studies show that there are substantive intellectual tasks in the development of software, some (perhaps many) of which require creativity in their accomplishment. Given that we do not presently know how to automate creativity, and quite possibly never will, the fact that some creativity is involved in the work means that software tasks will probably never be completely automated or delegated to those with an absence of significant software skills.

Second, from the point of view of research, the fact that creativity is an essential part of the work of software development ought to motivate further studies into the subject. The issue of how creative software tasks are remains important but unresolved;

and techniques for increasing and managing creativity might form an important focus for both software pedagogy and research.

Third, from the point of view of research funding, the fact that creativity is important for certain software tasks could motivate granting institutions to support proposals aimed at automating automatable tasks, rather than the less feasible current approach of automating all of the work of software development. Certainly, attempts to automate tasks requiring creativity are less likely to be successful than attempts to automate less demanding tasks.

These findings do lend support to the views expressed earlier in the paper, that software tasks are complex (note the sheer number of tasks defined in the tables—96 in all!), and that creativity is and probably always will be a key component of providing software solutions. The evidence is not as solid as we would have liked, but nonetheless, the evidence is there.

Acknowledgments

The authors wish to acknowledge the support of Bruce I. Blum, Dennis F. Galletta, and N. S. Umanath in the accomplishment of this work.

references

Couger 1990—"Ensuring Creative Approaches in Information
System Design," *Managerial and Decision Economics,* Vol. 11, pp.
281–295, 1990; J. Daniel Couger.

DeGrace 1993—*The Olduvai Imperative: CASE and the State of Software
Engineering Practice,* Yourdon Press, 1993; P. Degrace and L.
Stahl.

Glass 1992—"Software Tasks: Intellectual or Clerical?" *Information
and Management,* Nov., 1992; Robert L. Glass, Iris Vessey, and
Sue A. Conger.

Martin 1982—*Application Development Without Programmers,*
Prentice-Hall, 1982; J. Martin.

MBA 1990—"More on MBAs in MIS," *Information Week,* Fax Forum,
p. 56. March 19, 1990.

Newell 1962—"The Processes of Creative Thinking," in
Contemporary Approaches to Creative Thinking, H. Gruber, G.
Terrell, and M. Wertheimer (eds.), Atherton Press, 1962; A.
Newell, J. Shaw, and H. Simon.

USNRC 1990—"Scaling Up: A Research Agenda for Software
Engineering," *Computer Science and Technology Board,* U.S.
National Research Council, 1990.

6.3

Buying Breakthrough concepts for all the wrong Reasons

Each new software engineering idea that flows down the pipe from the world of research and the world of the vendor is heralded as the solution to all the productivity and quality woes of software.

And each new idea, once it hits the software shop floor, dissolves into a puddle of mediocrity.

What is wrong with this picture? Are software practitioners incredibly stubborn? Or stupid? Are researchers and vendors incredibly naive? Or wrong?

Whatever the answers to these questions, they are certainly well worth asking. Large sums of money are spent by management on each of these new ideas. Where are those promised benefits?

Oddly, there are few carefully thought-through answers to these questions. There are, of course, some very subjective ones. Researchers and vendors privately and quietly (and, on occasion, publicly and loudly) agree that, in fact, practitioners are incredibly stubborn and stupid. The whole premise of the "software crisis," in fact, rests on this belief.

However, this view does not really make sense. For one thing, today's practitioners—and yesterday's—have solved unimaginable problems in this new discipline, sending people into space, controlling the world's economic processes, totally redefining the edutainment industry, and waging war in whole new ways. Furthermore, the software practitioners of today are the product of yesterday's academics. (That is, most practitioners by now have graduated from the same programs in which our researchers are the teachers.) How could the wiles of practice have subverted these students-cum-practitioners so quickly?

At the same time as researchers and vendors are wringing their hands about practitioners, practitioners are privately and quietly (less often publicly and loudly) agreeing that, in fact, their nemeses are incredibly naive and wrong. "Just leave us alone," they frequently tell the researchers and vendors; "we have enough troubles without your getting involved."

But this view also does not make sense. For one thing, today's researchers—and yesterday's—are incredibly bright people who have created concepts and defined approaches that are as mind-boggling in their own way as the applications built by the practitioners. To imply that they are naive and wrong about practice suggests that they have not even tried to understand it; certainly, it is inconceivable that they could have tried and failed.

So why is this phenomenon happening, again and again? Why are claims made for new technologies that dissolve into nothingness?

I think there's a fairly simple starting place to look for an answer. That starting place lies in an understanding of the intrinsic nature of software construction, and it attaches itself to the title of this section. It is important, in order to understand why software breakthroughs so frequently break down, to understand the distinction between intellectual and clerical activities, and the degree to which each is important.

First of all, consider this issue. Do we, at this point in time, know how to build software that dramatically improves the capability of human beings to think?

Then consider this issue: For those human tasks that are thought-intensive, do computers offer breakthrough support?

I would assert that, if we divorce those questions from the issue of software construction, the fairly clear answers are "no" and "no." Computers and software, for all the wonderful power they offer, are not tools that can broadly augment the human mind in pursuit of challenging intellectual tasks. Not yet, for sure (this point of view will be substantiated by the essay "Computer Support for Creativity" later in this book). Not ever, perhaps. Time alone will tell.

But what of all the CASE tools and 4GLs and other major technology changes for software, I hear you asking? We must consider these issues in the context of software. And there, you may be saying, the answers are somehow different.

Well, let's take CASE tools as a particularly interesting example of this phenomenon. There was an article partway through the hoopla of the CASE revolution [Bird 1991] that shed some light on this issue. It was a popular computing press article, I grant you, and the author didn't quite understand the significance of what he was saying, but nevertheless there's some fascinating insight in what he said.

"Many companies using the most popular CASE tools do all of the early work on whiteboards," the article said. "Only when everything is correct (or nearly correct) on the whiteboard do users employ the CASE tools. Is this what management bought into when spending $10,000 to $15,000 for the CASE software?" the author asks. "Surely management has a right to expect better tools for the creative phases."

"For the creative phases." There's the nub of it all. The software was purchased, the author of this article is clearly implying, as a tool to help human thought processes. And he's right, of course. The manager who spent those large sums of money expected, probably based on vendor promises, perhaps in turn based on researcher claims, that these tools would support the essential, intellectual, perhaps even creative work of software development.

6.3

Buying
Breakthrough
Products for
All the Wrong
Reasons

And they don't. That's where the problem, and the truth, lies. Most CASE tools—especially the upper CASE ones that help the systems analysis and design process (arguably the most intellectual and creative of the life cycle phases)—do not, and were never intended to, replace the intellectual processes involved. They help the systems analysts and the software designers create and modify and keep representations of the result of the systems analysis and design process.

Let's say that again, because it's important. Most of these upper CASE tools are about supporting the representation process, not the intellectual process of creating those representations. They are two very different activities. The first, the one in which a problem comes to be understood and a design comes to be created, are deeply intellectual processes. The second, the one in which the drawings are made and the specifications and design are saved, is by contrast relatively clerical.

Seen in that light, a couple of things become clear. First, the expectations of the managers who bought the CASE tools were simply wrong. They may have thought they were buying intellect-augmenting capability, but they were not.

Second, the workers using the whiteboard before they used the CASE tool may very well have gotten it right. That is, they augmented their intellectual processes with a medium that (a) facilitated group work, and (b) permitted quick revision and rework. Most of today's CASE tools are not very good at either of those things. Yet group and heuristic processes, most would agree, are at the heart of the intellectually challenging parts of the software process.

What is the point of all this? We have done poorly, in our field of software, distinguishing between those parts of the job that are intellectually challenging/and those that are largely clerical. In the confusion resulting from that, we mistake capabilities that support one aspect of software work with capabilities that might help us with another.

Worse yet, we make that same mistake over and over again. We expect 4GLs to do away with the need for programmers, and we wonder why the need for programmers is even greater than it was in pre-4GL days. We expect CASE tools to automate the task of programming, especially systems analysis and design, and then we wonder why many of them end up as shelfware. We expect object orientation to be the next software panacea, once again reducing the work of software to something simple, and then we hear to our growing astonishment that object-oriented software developers probably need more skill and ability than their predecessors.

We spend a lot of money for breakthrough concepts, in short, that bring us small improvements—many say they average around 5–30%—but never the major change in productivity that we thought we were paying for. We end up angry and disappointed and suspicious. Upper management, wondering when the promised abolishment of programmers can finally happen, becomes impatient, then angry, and then loses all trust in computing organizations.

This cycle of breakthrough to bust is a vicious one, and it happens over and over again. This is because, I would assert, we understand our field so poorly that we have failed to distinguish between the software tasks that are intellectually complex and those that are not. Until software practitioners understand what they are buying; until vendors are honest enough to describe what they are selling accurately; and until researchers are thorough enough to evaluate what they are advocating, we will continue iterating through this cycle of promised breakthrough followed by bust. And we will avoid making the incremental progress that is possible in our field.

6.3
Buying
Breakthrough
Products for
All the Wrong
Reasons

Reference

Bird 1991—"CASE Crop a Flop," *Software Magazine*, November 8, 1991; Chris Bird.

chapter 7
Theory vs. Practice

chapter contents

introduction to chapter 7

"Nobody knows how the Arab architect designed [the dome of the Masjid-I-Jami in Isfahan] but centuries before the necessary mathematics were developed he managed to create a dome of almost perfect proportion."

—*Horace Freeland Judson*
The Search for Solutions,
Holt, Rinehart and Winston 1980
(Reprinted by permission of Henry
Holt and Company, Inc.)

"The Greek notion of science held it above vulgar pragmatics, leading to a pedantic tendency that tolerated intellectual laxity, sometimes with tragic consequences."

—*Noah Kennedy*
The Industrialization of Intelligence,
Unwin Hyman 1989

When it comes to choosing up sides on the issue of software approaches, we find some strange bedfellows. If the two predominant approaches are:

- Disciplined/Formal/Optimizing/Quantitative/Process/Clerical and
- Flexible/Heuristic/Satisficing/Qualitative/Product/ Intellectual

(and how's that for a nifty reprise of all the chapter titles in Part I of this book?!) what we find is that theory people, for the most part, have chosen the first collection, and practice people, again for the most part, have chosen the second.

But isn't that a bit strange? Think of the nature of the work that theory people do. Theorists, in their work, do all of the things that they do not choose for practitioners, and they avoid all of the things that they do choose for them.

Imagine, for example, a disciplined, formal theorist who expected to produce, in his or her research, optimal, quantitative findings using highly clerical approaches. It just doesn't wash.

So why, then, is it the theorists of computing who advocate all those things for software practitioners that are just the opposite of their own behavior? I've thought about that a lot over the years, but I've never come up with a very satisfactory answer.

Could it be that they genuinely believe that the task of building software is so easy that these disciplined, formal, even clerical approaches will work?

Could it be that, in spite of not wanting to use the approaches themselves, they don't really see the weaknesses inherent in disciplined, formal, clerical approaches?

Could it be that they don't want to believe, as Parnas and Brooks would have us believe, that software work is the most complex that humanity has ever undertaken, because it would belittle their own work?

Or could it be that the quest for formal, disciplined approaches is such an interesting assignment that they pursue it in the absence of any knowledge or philosophy on whether it is the right thing to do on behalf of software practice?

I tend to side with the latter answer. After all, the chief motivator for a theorist is the pursuit of interesting (as opposed to useful) work (a later essay in another chapter will reprise that theme). What could be more interesting than inventing languages and formalisms, and defining discipline and methodologies, to be used by others? And if there is a slight suspicion that these approaches, although interesting, are the wrong thing to do on behalf of practice, that can quickly be overcome by reading the writings of other theorists—there are plenty of them—who belittle practice and make it sound easy and automatable. Plus, as the capper on the problem, most theorists have never experienced the world of practice, and have little or no basis on which to pass judgments upon it.

However, to give the devil its due, as we move more and more in the direction of domain-specific software approaches and increase our knowledge of how to solve very specific problems in very specific domains, there is a chance that we will identify some problems in some domains which can be solved by disciplined, formal, even clerical approaches. What are 4GLs, after all, if not problem-oriented languages for the report generation cum database access application domain? And don't 4GLs come about as close as we know how, at this point, to reducing software work to an automatable task? Thus, there is some justification for the collection of concepts that these theorists support, and that justification could very well increase over time.

But that will be then, and this is now. In the world of today, I would suggest that this is the appropriate status of the choosing up sides issues ... a theory, you might say, about practice:

- Discipline vs. flexibility: Discipline is essential for programming in the large projects and useful for medium-sized ones, but can be a terrible burden on smaller ones. Flexibility? It is essential in all of those project categories. The "odd couple" must continue to live on!

- Formal methods vs. heuristics: Formal methods simply have not been shown to work in large projects or even medium-sized ones, and although they can be used on smaller ones, there is little or no evidence that the approach is very beneficial. (Bear in mind that this is after over 35 years of research in the area!) Heuristic approaches, on the contrary, are used on all sizes of projects.

- Optimizing vs. satisficing: Optimizing solutions, though eagerly sought, are usually impossible for complex and significant problems. Settling for satisficing is the state of the practice. (Of course, these statements are problem-dependent. Some problems, such as those in the information systems area, are solved optimally if they are solved at all. The same is not true for, say, weather forecasting.)

- Quantitative vs. qualitative: The search for quantitative answers always takes precedence in practice over the search for qualitative ones ... even when it shouldn't! But, of course, the search for valid quantitative answers frequently fails, because many things in life cannot be meaningfully quantified. Oddly and dangerously, qualitative answers masquerading as quantitative ones are often misused.

- Process vs. product: Process has always been a focus of software practice, from the earliest days when it was called "techniques" or "methods." (Early issues of Communications of the ACM, for example, had a "Pracniques" column). The Software Engineering Institute's process modeling work has brought the issue into sharper focus in recent years and directed it more toward management process. However, the focus of practice, then and now and always, is on product.

- Intellectual vs. clerical tasks: Intellectual activities predominate in practice, at around the 80% level, as we saw in the previous section. Clerical tasks do exist—configuration management, change tracking, test case execution, and others—and they are very important to the field, but there are far fewer of them.

There, for what it's worth, is my own theory about software practice. I'd be interested to know how it compares with yours.

In the essays to follow in this chapter, I will explore further this theory vs. practice issue; but here, we will have a different focus. I want to look at the state of the theory and the state of the practice, and how they relate to each other. I think you may find some surprises here.

7.1

The Temporal Relationship Between Theory and Practice

"Theory: a statement of the principles on which a subject is based."

"Practice: action as opposed to theory; to be actively engaged in professional work."

—*Oxford American Dictionary* 1980

The meanings of the words "theory" and "practice" are clear enough and accepted enough that we have little doubt about what someone means when they use them. But what about the temporal relationship between the two notions; that is, which comes first, theory or practice?

For most of us who have spent a decade or more in a school system, the answer is probably automatic; theory precedes and frames practice. But that automatic answer may be severely flawed, and in that automatic answer may be some profound misunderstandings.

Take, for example, this quotation from Christopher Alexander's *Notes on the Synthesis of Form* (Harvard University Press 1964):

> The airfoil wing section which allows airplanes to fly was invented at a time when it had just been 'proved' that no machine heavier than air could fly. Its aerodynamic

properties were not understood until some time after
it had been in use. Indeed the invention and use of the
airfoil made a substantial contribution to the development
of aerodynamic theory, rather than vice versa.

According to Alexander, then, practice here preceded theory. Are
there more examples of that perhaps surprising idea?

Another such quotation, astounding in its similarity to
Alexander's, comes from D. D. Price's "Sealing Wax and String: A
Philosophy of the Experimenter's Craft and Its Role in the Genesis
of High Technology" (*Proceedings of the American Association for the
Advancement of Science Annual Meeting*, 1983):

> Thermodynamics owes much more to the steam engine
> than the steam engine owes to thermodynamics. ... If we
> look at the usual course of events in the historical record
> ... there are very few examples where technology is applied
> science. Rather it is much more often the case that science
> is applied technology.

Two instances of practice preceding theory do not prove a case or
even establish a trend, of course; but Price suggests that in fact
there may be a trend here. Are there more examples?

Herbert A. Simon, in *The Sciences of the Artificial* (The MIT Press,
2nd Edition 1981), says:

> ... the main route to the development and improvement
> of time-sharing systems was to build them and see how
> they behaved. And this is what was done. They were built,
> modified, and improved in successive stages. Perhaps
> theory could have anticipated these experiments and
> made them unnecessary. In fact it didn't, and I don't know
> anyone intimately acquainted with these exceedingly
> complex systems who has very specific ideas as to how it

might have done so. To understand them, the systems had
to be constructed, and their behavior observed.

In accordance with Simon, the notion that practice precedes
theory is beginning to hit closer to home, in our own computing
and software worlds. Let us look more at theory and practice in
software.

I grew up in the practice of computing and software, and I recall
many of the formative events in the field. This notion of practice
preceding theory rings true to me. The origins of the computer, of
course, go back to the early research labs in institutions scattered
across North America and Europe. Yet by the mid-1950s, computing
and software were beginning to thrive as professional fields.
Practice, if not ahead of theory at the outset, in fact outstripped
it as the field evolved. It was not until the 1960s that the academic
field of Computer Science began to emerge. And the theory that
came with these early academic pursuits probably did not begin to
surface until the late 1960s or early 1970s.

Based on the personal recollections of an old timer in the field,
then, the notion that practice precedes theory certainly seems
credible. But experience, of course, can be a deceptive teacher.
What one person experiences can be far different from what
another experiences. Is there some other way to examine this
issue?

Thus far I have discussed computing and software as if it were a
single discipline, examinable as a whole. But what if, instead, we
were to look at some of the constituent elements of that whole? Can
we see a pattern of practice and theory emerge from that kind of
examination?

How about programming style? Which came first here, practice
or theory? Certainly, there were a lot of programs written before
there were books on programming style. I recall vividly that some
of those programs had excellent style, and some did not. I would
suggest that style in practice was fairly well-developed before a

theory of style evolved. (It is interesting to note that an early series of books on style, Ledgard's "Proverbs...," were essentially a codification of good practice.)

How about compiler writing? The practice of compiler writing produced compilers for such languages as Fortran, Commercial Translator, FACT, and later Cobol well before there was a well-documented theory of compiler writing. Once again, I would suggest that compiler writing, now a topic at the heart of computer science academically, was fairly well-developed in practice before a theory began to emerge.

There are examples of practice leading theory even today. Simulation is a frequently used tool at the system level to help define requirements and extract a design for complex problems. The topic of simulation, on the other hand, rarely comes up in the computing research world. (Note that simulation, as used in practice, is the creation of a tentative practical solution in order to establish a theory of the problem. Even here, practice leads theory!)

User-interface design, although firmly rooted in theory in its Xerox PARC origins, by now has moved forward more rapidly in computer practice than the theory that supports it.

Design itself is still poorly understood as the theory level. Courses in design frequently focus on methodology and representation, and yet most designers are aware that design is much more complex than simply having a framework for doing it and a way of writing it down. Once again, the practice of design is far ahead of its theory.

And in fact, the general notion of problem solving, which is what software engineering is really all about, is still in the early stages of theory building (see, for example, Simon's The Sciences of the Artificial, referenced earlier) even though the practice of problem solving (like that of design) is centuries old.

In other words, there is example after example of practice preceding theory. Does this surprise you? In spite of my historical perspective, it still surprises me. All of my academic background cries out for the notion that theory builds a framework upon which practice may construct things. If that notion is not true, then perhaps we should examine the implications.

Let us construct a diagram to show the relationship between theory and practice implied by this notion. What follows is my attempt at such a diagram. I believe, in essence, that given a particular discipline, practice comes first and evolves fairly rapidly at the outset; theory starts after there is a practice to formalize, and also evolves rapidly; and then there is a crossover point at which theory moves past practice. (See Figure 7.1.)

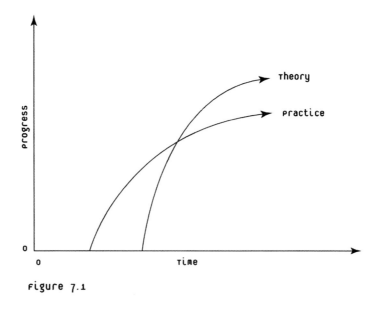

figure 7.1

Let us assume for the moment that this relationship holds true. What are its implications? For one thing, the diagram suggests that in the early stages of a discipline, theory can best progress by examining practice. True, theorists must also be free to formulate new ideas unfettered by past ways of doing things; but, nevertheless, there is much to be learned by examining what practice is doing, particularly the best of practice. This is an important thought. For the most part, the development of computing and software theory has not followed the implications of this thought.

Few computing theorists are former practitioners. There is little experimental, practice-simulating research in our field. And, except for some of the empirical studies of programmers' research, very little study is made of practitioners at work in evolving theory.

This thought suggests that at least the early approach to theory must change. The lore of practical knowledge may be far too rich for theory to ignore it.

Another conclusion that can be drawn from the diagram is that there comes a point at which practice, having been surpassed by theory, must listen to it. The framework that theory can provide in such areas as data bases and data structures, for example, far surpasses the knowledge of most practitioners in those discipline areas. Once again, the state of the practice has not reached this point. Just as theory fails to study practice when it is appropriate, practice fails to listen to theory when that becomes appropriate.

In other words, there are some fundamental problems in the interactions between theory and practice that the above diagram can clarify; and the failure to understand the implications of the diagram is fundamental to the state of the art and practice of computing and software.

Probably the diagram is an oversimplification. In the most accurate of pictures, the progress of practice and theory is more likely an intertwining series of steps, where practice and theory alternately take the lead. But even with that more complex picture, there will be places on this new diagram (zoom-lens snapshots, perhaps) within which the simpler diagram is still valid.

Does practice precede theory? At some levels, and at some points in time, yes it does. Now it is time for both practice and theory to absorb the implications of that fact.

acknowledgement

I wish to thank Iris Vessey and Dale Dowsing for their help in the evolution of these ideas.

7.2

Theory vs. Practice— Revisited

Imagine that anyone who comes out of our school system and begins to practice a profession forms some interesting opinions about what they learned, as opposed to what they wished they had learned.

My own personal trip from education to practice was through the field of pure mathematics. When I began working in industry, I was appalled to find that nothing I had learned in graduate school bore the slightest relationship to what I was asked to do on the job.

That began my career-long interest in the relationship between theory and practice. I see a massive "communication chasm" between the two and profound misunderstandings resulting from that chasm. And I see severe problems in both the products of theory and the products of practice resulting from that chasm and those misunderstandings. On occasion, in fact, my own job performance has been severely impacted by the chasm.

Out of this concern, I wrote an article entitled "The Temporal Relationship Between Theory and Practice" (it's the previous one in this book). In it, I identified a relationship between theory and practice as shown in its Figure 7.1—that is, initially practice leads theory, but later theory catches up with and passes it.

Subsequently, I had an opportunity to rethink what was in that essay. I think the essential truth it presented—that practice often precedes and helps form theory—is still true. But, like many things in life, I think it is more complicated than Figure 7.1 makes it appear.

Let me share with you the opportunity that caused me to rethink Figure 7.1. It was at World Computer Congress in San Francisco, and I was in the presence of greatness. Two speakers addressed this issue, and both were as brilliant in their thinking and presentation as any two speakers I have ever heard. The message, couched in different terms by each speaker, was essentially the same.

Donald Knuth of Stanford University, one of the keynote speakers, said, "Both theory and practice can and should be present simultaneously." He went on to say that blending the two has been "the main credo of my personal life."

Heinz Zemanek, retired head of the IBM Vienna Laboratory, speaking on "Formal Structures in an Informal World," said "We can only formalize what we understand at a basic level. We must start informally, then move to formalism."

In other words, informal practical thinking must precede—and proceed in tandem with—formal formulation of theory.

As Knuth gave examples of his credo from his experience, I thought back over an important one of my own. In the mid-1960s, after starting out as a scientific programmer, I was given my first data processing application—the job of writing three different report generators. There was a great deal of similarity between them, and as I struggled with the design problems of rolling totals and producing reports—problems that every data processing person has struggled with and by now mastered—I saw that the framework of those three products contained the nucleus of a generalized one. The result, when I finished delivering the reports, was that I produced one of the earliest report generator packages. But what is important in the context of this story is that my work in the specific construction of those report generators was an essential prelude to my ability to see the general problem that lay behind them. Without having done the informal or practical solution to those first three problems, in other words, it would not have been possible for me to form the formal, or theoretical generalized, solution.

That suggests to me two important corrections in my previous title and figure. It seems to me, with the benefit of the thinking of Knuth and Zemanek, that the title should be more like "Theory Plus Practice" rather than "Theory vs. Practice," and that Figure 7.1 should be more like Figure 7.2.

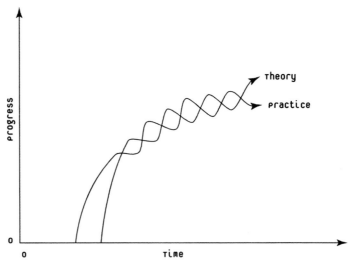

figure 7.2: Theory plus practice.

Now we can see that, although often the first glimmer of a new idea comes from the world of practice (don't we say "necessity is the mother of invention"?), the act of maturing both the practice and the theory can and should go on in tandem. Attempts to do otherwise, as we have been trying to do in the world of computer science and software engineering, lead inevitably to weak theory and stuck practice.

Knuth left his audience with a fascinating "challenge problem" to cause them to explore their own blending of theory and practice. Study what your computer does in one randomly chosen second, he challenged, and then think about what you have seen there. He posed these questions to help frame and direct those thoughts:

1. Are the programs that were executing correct? (Most of those he looks at, Knuth said, have one or more errors in them.)
2. Do the programs use existing theory?
3. Would existing theory help these programs?
4. Would new theory help these programs?

Zemanek, too, left his audience with a fascinating thought. "Fifty years ago," he said, "we had masters of the language," people who were articulate and even inspiring in their ability to speak. "Now," he went on to say, "we don't—and this is a very dangerous direction." The reason we don't, he said, is because our educational system has swung too far in the direction of formal methods and has neglected such informalisms as common sense and natural language communication.

Perhaps Knuth and Zemanek—and the others who care—can help us evolve theory and practice into a fundamentally sound working partnership.

7.3
Theory and practice: A Disturbing example

The relationship between theory and practice has been dealt with philosophically in the preceding essays in this book. Here, I would like to illustrate that relationship by a real live example.

Some years ago, at a prestigious computing conference, there was a paper presented on a very practical topic: how to decide when to terminate maintenance of older software and rewrite it. It is a topic at the heart of the maintenance effort, one confronted by every software organization in the world, dealt with in practice for over 30 years. Some companies, such as Ford Motor Company and Pacific Telephone, have created elaborate decision mechanisms just for this purpose.

However, this paper was written by academics. The research behind the paper was, in fact, done by an information technology department at a major university, and took no account whatsoever of the 40 years of practical history devoted to this "rewrite or maintain" decision. Instead, the researchers wrote the paper based on their analysis of projects described in the computing literature.

What was the result? Some academics who heard the paper congratulated the authors on a job well done. They had, after all, tackled an important topic with wisdom and insight.

But others in the audience, myself (and, I am happy to say, the academic discussant assigned to critique the paper) included, were dismayed. The paper not only was not based on the accumulated experience of our field, but it was patently erroneous in its conclusions.

The conclusions, in fact, are worth stating here. The researchers based their analysis of the decision to rewrite or maintain purely on a mathematical study of cumulative maintenance costs for the software product. Their assumption was that as software reached the point of rewrite, maintenance costs would be exploding upward. But that conclusion is naive. Often software reaches the point of rewrite because its original design envelope has been stretched to the point at which additional enhancements are simply impossible. At such a point, maintenance costs, far from going up rapidly, actually drop!

Additional conclusions, peculiar in themselves, were also presented by the researchers:

1. Software should be rewritten "less than halfway through its projected lifespan."
2. Software operational life:
   a. decreases with initial size (the bigger the software, the shorter its lifespan)
   b. decreases with structuredness (the more structured the software, the shorter its lifespan)
   c. increases progressively as the software is repeatedly rewritten (the more it is rewritten, the longer its lifespan)

Some of these conclusions are amazingly counterintuitive and counter-experiential. Could the researchers really have believed that, with findings like these, their analysis was correct?

What's the point here? There are topic areas where practice is far ahead of theory. In this millennium (and in the last), software maintenance is one of those topics. Researchers ought to be aware of what those topic areas are, and rely on practice to help build theory. Not only do most researchers not do that, they do not even seem to be aware that they could or should.

The result is weak theory that gets laughed out of the halls of practice. The flip side is stuck practice that does not upgrade to match the legitimate findings of theory. Neither theory nor practice is well served by what is happening.

What was my personal reaction? I quietly told the researcher, after his presentation, that he should go no further with his research until he considered the implications of practice. And I gave him a couple of names of software practitioners who could help him.

I wondered at the time if he would follow through. To get the contact points for the names I gave him, he would have needed to contact me, using the business card I left with him.

He never did.

7.4
The Flight of the Bumblebee

I first heard about it in the fourth grade, and I've heard it said many times since.

"There's no scientific reason," the saying goes, "why a bumblebee can fly."

What people who say that mean is that the theories of science do not hold an explanation for why this bulky, heavy bee with the stubby wings can do what it does.

Whatever you may think about this strange statement, one thing is clear. When we consider the puzzle of the flight of the bumblebee, it does not occur to us that the practice—the flight—is wrong. We all know intuitively that there is something wrong with the theory.

Perhaps there's a broader lesson here.

7.5
Theory vs. practice: A variety of laments

The issue of the relationship between theory and practice is a complicated one. But what is at least as interesting as its complexity is the number of viewpoints—and the emotional laments that arise from them—that we find if we explore the topic.

In a fascinating interview with the late Harlan Mills in *IEEE Software*, July 1988, Mills is quoted as saying "It's too bad that hardware grew so fast. You know, if we'd had these new processors ... for 50 years at least, mankind could really have learned how to do sequential programming. But the fact is, by the time that [Edsger] Dijkstra comes out with structured programming, we've got all kinds of people using multiprocessors with interrupt handling, and there's no theory behind that, but the IBMs, the DECs, the CDCs, and so on, they're all driving forward and doing this even though nobody knows how to do it."

What a wonderful acknowledgment that early on in a discipline, practice leads theory, and a lament that it does, all at the same time! However, just as there are those stuck in the world of practice who would prefer that theory go away, Mills illustrates that there are theory people saying "slow the world down, it's moving too fast for theory to keep up." Of course, both viewpoints are wrong. The world will move at its own pace, urged onward by practice and theory in turn, and none of us have the power to stop it. Would we really want that power?

Not all academics adhere to the Mills viewpoint, of course. Quite the opposite of Mills' lament is one expressed by Manfred Kochen [Kochen 1985] in a paper called "Are MIS Frameworks Premature?" Here, Kochen suggests that research has been guided erroneously by the belief that the construction of definitional frameworks should precede theory and experiment, with the application of theory coming last. He points to the mathematical notion of derivative, noting that it was first used, then discovered, then explored and developed, and finally defined, as the correct model for theory development in any new field. Kochen laments, in fact, something the opposite of Mills—that the search for definitional frameworks, given the state of the practice, is premature, and that "such a search diverts effort from problem-solving activities which, despite its imperfect definition and in absence of a framework, are likely to be more fruitful."

There are other lamentations in our field. David Parnas, in a surprising essay on computer science education [Parnas 1990], found major flaws in our pedagogy, many of them related to this same issue of theory vs. practice. "Academic departments and large conferences," he says, "are often battlegrounds for the 'theoretical' and 'applied' groups. Such battles," he concludes in a meaningful warning, "are a sure sign that something is wrong."

What does Parnas see as wrong? Plenty. "Computing science," he says, "focuses too heavily on the narrow research interests of its founding fathers ... The separation between academic computing science and the way computers are actually used has become too great. CS programs do not provide graduates with the fundamental knowledge needed for long-term professional growth."

Returning later to the value of practice in both pedagogy and theory, Parnas says, "Students do not get the feedback that comes from having a product used, abused, rejected, and modified. This lack of feedback is very bad education."

In another part of the computing forest, information systems specialist Peter G. W. Keen says something similar [Keen 1980]. "No one should be involved in MIS research," he says bluntly, "who is not a craftsman in some aspect of computer technology and techniques ... To want to be 'scientists' may be a praiseworthy goal, but if this involves an explicit disdain for 'application,' 'business,' or 'practice,' one wonders about the sense of ethics of the researcher being at a business school."

And, as the conclusion to this article, Keen says, in no uncertain terms, " ... the world of practice is central, not peripheral" to that of MIS theory and research.

In a more emotional and controversial article, Rustom Roy, quoted in an article in Newsweek [Roy 1991], questions the very value of research. Roy, the interview says, finds that "Many programs still have it backward. They start with basic principles and only eventually ... work up to application." Roy objects to that approach. "Only that which is connected to life will be remembered for life," he is quoted as saying.

Roy's objection seems more than a simple lament at times. He decries the quality of the theory development that does take place, noting that of the top-quality papers (by reviewing standards) published in various scientific fields, 45% were never referenced by other researchers in the five years following their publication. "The implication," says Newsweek, "is that nearly half the scientific work in this country is basically worthless." Roy calls researchers who believe they have a right to be supported by government funding "welfare queens in white coats."

Not all laments are that emotionally tipped. However, as we can see here clearly, when it comes to the issue of theory vs. practice, there is plenty of room for discussion—and strong opinion.

postscript

In a quotation that is peripherally related to this discussion, Steven Jones, one of the Brigham Young University physicists involved in the controversial nuclear fusion experiments, said this: "We have an experiment but not a theory. We have Cinderella, but we don't have her shoe." Dare we characterize practice as Cinderella without the shoe? Or is that characterization better applied to research?

References

Keen 1980—"MIS Research: Reference Disciplines and a Cumulative Tradition," *Proceedings of the International Conference on Information Systems,* 1980; Peter G.W. Keen.

Kochen 1985— "Are MIS Frameworks Premature?" *Journal of Management Information Systems* Vol. II, No. 3, 1985; Manfred Kochen.

Parnas 1990—"Education for Computing Professionals," *IEEE Computer,* January 1990; David Lorge Parnas.

Roy 1991—"Gridlock in the Labs," *Newsweek,* January 14, 1991; from an interview with Rustum Roy.

7.6

A Tabulation of Topics where software practice leads software Theory

I've been saying for several years now that, in a new discipline, sometimes practice leads theory. I've said it in print, and I've also said it in person before lots of audiences. Most of the audiences, be they practitioners or academics, listen with rapt attention and sometimes a furrowed brow, as if to say, "This is all very interesting, but do I really want to believe this nonsense?"

However, in front of one audience, a particularly rapt-and-furrowed listener finally challenged me on the subject. "OK," he said, "that's an interesting theory, but get specific. Where in computing and software does practice lead theory?"

That's a fair question, of course. Now it was my turn for a bit of rapt-and-furrowed. It's all well and good to express a theory about theory vs. practice, but could I make it become real in a practical sense?! (Do I detect a bit of something similar to recursion here?)

I'm not a terribly creative thinker standing on my feet in front of an audience. All that adrenalin that surges through my body parts to get me into a high-energy mode for speaking seems to sap the brain power needed to do new things with a few dozen or a hundred people watching. On the occasion when the listener challenged me, I mumbled some things about creative design and graphical user interfaces being areas in which practice led theory, but then I hastily looked at my watch, harrumphed about being behind schedule, and went on with my prepared speaking materials.

Back in the safety of my own office, after the adrenalin had calmed from a waterfall to a trickle, I began thinking about that question some more. Where, indeed, does practice still lead theory? Here are some of the thoughts I had.

software Design

People have been doing software design now for five or more decades. Many of those designs have been successful, some phenomenally so. Those designs that have succeeded have been the product of creative minds focusing on fairly complex problems; remember the Fred Brooks quotes about software being "the most complex task mankind has ever undertaken?" So there's plenty of evidence that the practice of design is a thriving enterprise.

What about the theory of design? Look at any textbook on software design, and tell me that you see there. I'll bet it's a bunch of stuff on methodology and a bunch of stuff on representation. Follow these methodological steps, the textbook implies, and you'll have some thoughts worth drawing with this representation. Well, not good enough. There's many a creative step twixt the methodology and the representation, and what's in the textbook leaves all of that out.

Plus, think about this: When did methodologies and representations arise in the software world? How about the 1970s? And when did practice start designing real production software? How about the 1950s? No matter what sword you use to slice it—a historic one or a contemporary one—practice has led and continues to lead theory here.

However, I think it is important to admit that theory is playing a good game of catch-up on this topic. The research into cognitive design by Bill Curtis and his folk, and Elliot Soloway and his, brought theory well into a position to catch up with practice on creative design. But that happened in the 1980s, and is sill not well acknowledged in the textbooks and theory work of our time. For a little while, at least, I would assert that the practice of software design still leads its theory. (We'll return to this topic in Part II of this book).

software maintenance

The first job I got in industry, over 50 years ago now, was one doing software maintenance. I wasn't very good at it then, but after getting lucky—I was given software by some pretty superb software developers to maintain—I was making significant strides in my maintenance maturity within a few years.

What did computer science and software engineering have to say that would help me do that software maintenance at the time? Absolutely nothing! In fact, there was no computer science or software engineering then, in an academic/theoretic sense. Those disciplines were to first grace the halls of ivy over 10 years later.

But is all of that ancient history still relevant today? I would assert that it is, and for a particularly sad reason. The theory world of software, until very recently, actually disdained the subject of maintenance. It wasn't just behind practice, it was refusing to try to catch up! The literature of software displayed an amazing paucity when it came to theoretic contributions to maintenance. I recall one academic making a presentation at a software conference the content of which was clearly behind, and could have benefited from an understanding of, the state of the practice! (That story was told earlier in this chapter.)

That is beginning to change now. Still it is sad to note that the places where the change has happened—the University of Durham in England, the University of West Florida, Arizona State, De Paul University, and a few others—can be counted on the fingers of one, or perhaps barely two, hands. There is still very little solid interest in software maintenance in the world of theory.

Now, there is a very well understood theoretic approach that theory can use—in any discipline—to catch up with leading practice. It is called "empirical studies," and it involves studying the best of practice in order to evolve theory. But software theorists have, to date, exhibited little interest in using that very effective bootstrapping approach, and as a result it is fair to say—as of the publication of this essay—there is little evidence that theory is making much progress at all in catching up with the world of software maintenance practice.

user Interfaces

Here is a nice example of an area in which theory and practice are proceeding neck and neck, and there is every reason to believe that theory is pulling out ahead. Still, it is an interesting example of what happens during the phase when theory catches up with practice.

The pioneering work in user interface development, as any computer-crazed schoolchild knows by now, was done at Xerox PARC several decades ago. Now, how do we count that work? Was it theory work? (It was done in an industrial setting.) Or was it practical? (It was done by theorists who, except for their industry identification, had all the trappings of academe.) It seems to me fair to take the position that this pioneering work was a mixture of theory and practice.

What happened next? Much of the work transitioned out into industry, where Apple made it into an industry standard, and based most of its long-term economic success on continuing to use and further develop the Xerox PARC concepts. Theory development continues, of course, but it is probably fair to say that the great theoretical/practical leap forward that happened all those years ago has not been equaled to date in either theory or practice.

programming in the Large

Pragmatic programming has always seemed like programming in the large. That is, every generation of practitioners has had the feeling that the software they were building was severely stretching their intellectual capabilities, and those of the hardware they were developing it on, to the absolute limit.

And, of course, every generation of practitioners has been trampled in the dust by the onrushing complexity of the problems tackled by the next generation. I still find it difficult to believe—but I can't refute the numbers—that software systems were 50 times larger, on average, in 1990 than they were in 1980 [Dekleva 1991]. That is a staggering commentary on the rate of change in the world of software practice.

What, in the meantime, has been happening in the world of theory? In most places, theory development is still based on small studies of small projects. Practitioners make fun of that approach by calling it "toy projects," but I would prefer to give it a little more dignity by calling it "research in the small." There are a few counterexamples of people and places doing research in the large—the work of individuals like Vic Basili at the University of Maryland and Chris Kemerer at the University of Pittsburgh, and a few key institutes like the Software Engineering Institute, Fraunhofer (in Germany and the U.S.), NICTA (in Australia), and Simula (in Norway) comes to mind—but for the most part, theorists are stuck trying to extrapolate findings from research in the small to programming in the large. And, as most people in software engineering have known since the term "software engineering" was invented over a quarter of a century ago, it just won't work.

Now here, of course, theory has a severe problem. It costs a lot of money to do research in the large, and most software researchers haven't developed access to the kind of money needed. So it is easy to understand why the world of theory has not grown to match the needs of practice.

However, at the same time, it is not unknown for some insensitive computing theorists to poke fun at practice for being stuck using old technologies and concepts. I sometimes wonder what would happen if computing practitioners poked the same kind of fun at theorists for doing the same thing?! I don't imagine that progress in the field would be helped by that kind of social interplay; but still, isn't there something about "sauce for the gander"?

It is time for the world of software theory to graduate to something that Vic Basili calls "full professor research." What does he mean by that? My interpretation is this: New professors tend to do research that involves making in-depth studies of disciplinary minutiae. That kind of work is consistent with what they did in their graduate studies, and is necessary to get them tenure. But the time comes when someone—preferably those who have leaped the tenure hurdle—ought to do more in-breadth examination of the key issues of the discipline. Full professors, and others senior in the field, are in an ideal position to do that.

Who is doing full professor research? In addition to those named above, it is interesting to examine the work of Mary Shaw of Carnegie Mellon, who has studied the origins and evolution of the various engineering disciplines for an understanding of the evolution of software engineering. There is a lot, she has observed, to be gained in understanding our own field through that approach.

With a stronger commitment toward research in the large, and/or full professor research, and with a large dose of funding thrown in to help make it happen, it is possible to get the world of research in the large moving faster. Perhaps, with enough help, it can even catch up with the practice of programming in the large.

Modeling and simulation

If you have ever worked on a large real-time software project, you know how much a part of the development of that kind of software modeling and simulation are. Models are developed and simulations run in order to:

7.6

A Tabulation
of Topics
where software
Practice Leads
software Theory

1. Analyze the concept of the system before starting to build it
2. Run design studies to check the viability of design approaches
3. Allow the execution of target computer software on a host computer with a different instruction set (because the target computer is not yet available, or not capable enough to support debugging)
4. Substitute for the real test environment during early environmental testing
5. Produce approximate test oracles for checking the test results produced by the as-built system during system test

That is a lot of modeling and simulation. The technology, you can see here, is an essential part of the real-time software practitioner's world.

How is the world of theory doing here? My own observation is, not much. When I judge by the number of courses that theorists introduce into their curricula, for example, I see virtually nothing on this subject. Yet in practice, instruction-level simulators and environment simulators and all the others we talked about have been absolutely essential in doing business for decades.

Modeling and simulation are, of course, heavily used in some fringe areas of computer science theory, especially those having to do with manufacturing applications; but that is far from the mainstream of computing theory. When they do appear in an academic discipline, in fact, modeling and simulation are usually taught in some other college, not the one housing computer science or even software engineering.

This is what I call a "gap" subject in contrasting theory and practice: a subject where practice has a presence and theory does not, thus identifying a gap in the underlying theory. And when there are gaps in the theory, it will take an awful lot of playing catch-up for theory to even begin to approach practice.

Metrics

This is a field where bifurcation has occurred. What theory is doing with respect to measurement of software work and what practice is doing are on two different planes, planes that are shifting in different directions.

Take a look, for example, at the encyclopedic theory work on metrics by Zuse, and compare it with the practical books by Grady. Or take a look at the complexity metrics work done by Halstead and McCabe, contrasted with the quality metrics work funded at the Rome Air Development Center (and documented in lots of studies filed with the National Technical Information Service). It is almost as if the two areas have given up communicating with each other.

I had the good fortune, as the editor of a software engineering journal, to read the comments that an anonymous theorist reviewer passed on to a theorist author of a paper on metrics. The message was basically this: Why are you bothering to propose unverified additional theoretic metrics when (a) the theory world is already full of other unverified metrics, and (b) the practice world has given up on all of this unevaluated theory and is rapidly moving on in its own directions? My personal bias is that this reviewer/theorist—who was unwilling to be identified because his theoretic colleagues might crucify him—is one of the few who has grasped what is happening in software metrics.

There is, of course, a bit of theory/practice overlap. Many enterprises doing software maintenance are using the commercially available CASE tools built to calculate the various theoretical metrics such as those of Halstead and McCabe, and say that the identification of complex code segments that they obtain in that way is very helpful, especially in planning reengineering activities.

However, there is another strange faction in the metrics world. There are many, both theorists and practitioners, who have explored the various complexity metrics and found them to be

7.6

A Tabulation
of Topics
where software
practice Leads
software Theory

dubious when theoretic justification is attempted, and of little value in a practical setting.

Perhaps the best summation for the topic of metrics is that here is a field where there is much turbulence in the relationship between theory and practice. However, I think it is fair to say that practice is very slowly beginning to evolve some practical, useful metrics, and that theory is still trying to decide whether its own work has merit at all. This is an area, I would assert, poised for explosive growth once these early difficulties can be sorted out.

There, then, is my response to my rapt-and-furrowed questioner. At least in these areas—software design, software maintenance, user interfaces, programming in the large, modeling and simulation, and metrics—software practice leads software theory.

Like all us human beings, it's the response I wish I had been able to make on the spot during my lecture. But perhaps, if that listener has happened to run across this essay, he'll recognize his question, and be glad for this belated answer!

Reference

Dekleva 1991—Article in *Software Maintenance News*, February 1991, reporting on a survey conducted by Sasa Dekleva.

chapter 8:
Industry vs. Academe

chapter contents

introduction to chapter 8

"Our [Japanese] children are drilled and our school system is imbued with ... uniformity ... Deviation from the standard is [barely allowed]. Creativity is punished ... The question 'why' is not interpreted as a healthy sign of curiosity—it is a personal offense toward the integrity of the teacher ... Brain power in Japan is limited; the nation works hard, but it does not think hard."

—Hisao Yamada
"Breaking the Mould" in *The Discipline of Curiosity*,
Janny Groen, Eefke Smit, and Juurd Eijsvoogel, eds.
Elsevier Science 1990

"A peculiar division of labor has established itself between East and West, a silent arrangement in which the United States and Europe do the basic science, and Japan turns their discoveries into marketable products."

—Horace Freeland Judson
The Search for Solutions,
Holt, Rinehart and Winston 1980
(Reprinted by permission of Henry
Holt and Company, Inc.)

How does this section on industry vs. academe differ from the previous one on theory vs. practice?

In the previous section, we explored intellectual differences between the world of ivy-covered walls and the world of profit motives. In this section, we will explore their behavioral differences.

It is true, of course, that much of theory is produced in academe, and nearly all practice is done in industry. However, even those somewhat absolute statements deserve the qualifications I gave them. I have done "research and development" work in industry (we called it "R&D," and tended to do a whole lot more R than we did D, so that it came out to be very close to the kind of theory work academic people did), and I have worked on practical projects in academe (mostly directing graduate-student projects, where a secondary goal was to produce something that might be useful in the marketplace).

There is, then, a logical reason for distinguishing theory/practice from industry/academe. It is possible to mix and match who does what where.

But a far more interesting theme here, I think, is how people in the academic world differ from those in industry. I've had an ideal career for exploring that question. After nearly 30 years in industry, doing most of the different kinds of things that industry people do (software development and maintenance and management and R&D), I've spent another decade or so in various facets of the world of academe. I've done teaching on a tenure track and contract basis. I've done research and had it published in some pretty good journals. I've done committee work and curriculum development and all the other lesser baggage that is part of academe. In short, my career has spanned these two very different worlds.

As an acid test of my bipolar background, I spent a year at the Software Engineering Institute. Whatever else you may think of the SEI, I think it is fair to say that it was then and still tends to be now a strange and somewhat unsuccessful mix of the worlds of industry and academe.

People from academe directed and worked on projects that have a major impact on industry. People from industry gave input to projects with a largely academic focus. Different organizational entities in the SEI were populated largely by people from one particular camp or the other. Many of the industry people were those who spent much of their industry career doing the R of R&D, making them really only semi-industry people.

Why do I say the mix is somewhat unsuccessful? Because industry people struggle to be heard at the SEI. Because real industry practitioners tend to lose out to industry research people. Because academic people display so much disdain of industry people that it is difficult for an industry person to gain sufficient respect to help steer what the SEI does. If a cultural study of computing ever looks at the behavioral and intellectual worlds of industry vs. academe, and how successfully or unsuccessfully they work together, the SEI is the perfect cultural melting pot in which to conduct the study—except that the melting pot contains undigested chunks whose cultural identities have never really been melted into the whole.

In the absence of such a study, the collection of essays that follow is my attempt to make a small initial contribution to the field of computing cultural anthropology.

Before we start reading on, let's do the definition thing:

Industry, my dictionary says, is "the production or manufacture of goods; the quality of being industrious." (Notice, once again, how the smokestack America philosophy is solidly imbedded in the dictionary!)

Academe, by contrast, is related to academic: "of a school, college, or university; scholarly as opposed to technical or practical; of theoretical interest only, with no practical application."

Surely, more than the other word pairs we have dealt with in this chapter, the dramatic contrast between the two is self-evident in the definitions.

On to the essays ...

8.1

The Interesting/ useful Dichotomy

Everyone should have an ethic.
    It gives the person a touchstone, a cause, and even an enthusiasm.

There is, however, a problem with ethics. By their very nature, they are rarely subject to personal compromise. Name your favorite ethic. Are you willing to discuss the possibility that it may be faulty?

Even that rock-steadiness of ethics is both good and bad. It's good because it makes people relationships dependable and predictable. But it's bad because it makes people relationships over the subject of ethics inflammatory and divisive.

Enough philosophy. What does ethics have to do with software?

Let's take a look at the academic world of software, and the industrial world of software, for a while, and the relevance will soon become clear.

In the academic world, the researcher pursues those subjects he considers to be interesting. He is rewarded for doing so by the esteem of his peers.

In the industrial world, the researcher pursues those subjects he considers to be useful. He is rewarded for doing so by the esteem of his management.

The dichotomy between studying things which are interesting or useful is not a small dichotomy. The academician looks with some disdain on things which are merely useful. The industrial worker looks with some disdain on things which are merely interesting. Thus each side is making judgments about the basic goals of the other.

In fact, the pursuit of interesting work is an ethic to the academician, and the pursuit of useful work is an ethic to the industrial worker. It is an ethic so strong that it brooks little compromise. Believers in each of the ethics question the wisdom and even the morality of the other.

Are there some less philosophic examples of this dichotomy? Yes, all around us in software.

Is proof of correctness interesting? Yes. Is it useful? No.

Is testing interesting? No. Is it useful? Yes.

Are requirements languages interesting? Yes. Are they useful? Not as often as we would like.

Are requirements reviews interesting? Largely, no. Are they useful? Yes.

Is symbolic execution interesting? Yes. Is it useful? Not very.

Is peer code review interesting? No. Is it useful? Big time!

The dichotomy is all around us, and it is very real.

It is also very bad. Because the researcher who pursues primarily interesting problems communicates badly, if at all, with the researcher who pursues primarily useful ones. Mutual disdain is a poor basis for sharing knowledge.

The dichotomy is made worse, not better, by the researcher who works interesting problems believing erroneously that they are useful, or who works useful problems believing erroneously that they are interesting. The bridging of the dichotomy must be genuine, and not contrived. It must be based on knowledge, and not ignorance.

It is time for academic and industrial people to review their ethics. It is legitimate to work interesting problems. It is legitimate to work useful problems. What is not legitimate is to represent one as the other. What is not legitimate is to disdain those who make the other choice.

There is a fascinating concept we all grew up with that I call "local loyalty." We all knew our grade school was the best in the city. And so was our high school the best in the county. And so was our college the best in the state. And so was our city, and county, and state the best in the country.

Our religion is the best in the world. And so is our ethic.

Local loyalties are useful. They are also absurd. The likelihood that my personal grade school, or high school, or college, or city, or county, or state is really best ... is nil!

Understanding is the answer to overcoming absurd local loyalties. It is also the answer to overcoming conflicting ethics.

Everyone, as we said at the beginning, should have an ethic. Everyone, perhaps we would now agree, should mesh that ethic with a large dose of understanding.

8.2
The Individual/
Team Dichotomy

The boundary layer between the academic world and the industrial world is subject to turbulence.

Some of the turbulence is well known—the student moves from learning to earning as the prime motivator, for example.

Some of that turbulence is not so well known. This is a note about one of those less well known areas.

In the academic world, the student functions as a competing individual among competing individuals, and group activity is often thought of as cheating.

In the industrial world, the employee functions as a team member, and group activity is the primary way things happen.

In the academic world, the individual is given credit for what he or she does.

In the industrial world, the individual's role often dissolves into anonymity.

In the academic world, students building on the work of others is questionable at best.

In the industrial world, building on the work of others is common sense. (The other alternative is called, with considerable disdain, "re-inventing the wheel.")

In the academic world, copying is wrong.

In the industrial world, cutting and pasting from previous documents to make new ones is expeditious and wise.

The transition from wrong to right comes suddenly. The transition from competition to cooperation is unexpected. The transition from individual importance to individual anonymity may be painful.

Whatever else the transition is ... it will be turbulent. Boundary layers are like that!

8.3
Two pop culture sayings

One of the things computing academics say about software practitioners is that they do too little thinking about what they are about to undertake. The pop culture saying for that is:

Ready, Fire, Aim

Practitioners, stung by that criticism, might be pardoned if they found a similar accusation for academics. Given their propensity to find fault with practice, the pop saying for that might be:

Ready, Blame, Fire

8.4

of understanding, acceptance....and formal methods

I made a fool of myself at a computing conference last winter. I argued with a speaker. I disrupted the session. I did all the things I hate when someone else does them.

What happened? Why did I get so involved?

The speaker was explaining a concept. It was a spirited presentation of the concept, and, in the spirit of the moment, he was expressing exasperation that not everyone agreed with his concept, and in fact began to put down those who did not. Since I didn't agree with the concept, I became increasingly uncomfortable. Finally, I couldn't take it anymore. I spoke out, trying to point out that it was possible to understand what the speaker was saying but still not accept it.

The more I spoke, the more the speaker sought to explain his concept; and the more he explained, the more disagreement I expressed. We were mired in a difficult loop that finally flamed up in anger. The remainder of the attendees and speakers in the session grew quiet. Discomfort settled heavily around the room. When the session ended, I slunk from the room, wishing I hadn't been there.

As I ruminated afterward over what had happened, I began to realize that the speaker and I were operating under two different communication models. In his model, it was sufficient to make me understand the concept he was presenting. If I did not accept the concept, it was because I didn't understand. If I didn't understand, then more explanation was in order. And if I still didn't understand, it must have been either because I was pretty stupid, or because I wasn't listening carefully.

However, in my communication model, two notions were decoupled. The first notion was understanding, the one the speaker was working on. But the second notion, one entirely separate from understanding, was acceptance. I understood the concept he was presenting; I simply did not accept that understanding.

As I mulled over the problem, I related it to some deeper social implications, and I began to realize that there was a problem of more general interest here. (This is my rationale for including a conference squabble in these pages!) Through the early part of our lives, as our maturation process is led by authority figures, the notions of understanding and acceptance are, in fact, identical. The parent or teacher explains a concept, and the child or student accepts it. But as the student or child matures, a gap slowly begins to emerge between understanding and acceptance. It is not enough for the parent of a teenager, or the teacher of a graduate student, to present an understanding of an idea. They must also seek its acceptance, a far more taxing and complex task. This is because understanding is accomplished simply by absorption of conceptual material, whereas acceptance is about fitting the concept into the framework of other understandings. The richer the listener's framework of past understanding, the more difficult the task of reaching acceptance becomes.

(The typical authority-figure reaction to the growing decoupling of understanding and acceptance in the maturing person is perhaps best typified by the plaintive cry that all parents will relate to—"... because I'm your mother, that's why!")

I remember when this distinction first became important to me. I had finished reading, several decade before, Shirer's Rise and Fall of the Third Reich. And I realized, as I ruminated over what I had read, that I understood what Shirer had to say about Hitler's reasons for killing the Jews, for the Holocaust.

And I was horrified. Because, in my personal history to that date, I had equated—as a child or student must—understanding and acceptance. Did I accept Hitler's rationale for the Holocaust? Of course not—I rejected it with all my being. And yet I understood it. At that moment, the decoupling of the terms became totally necessary.

Now let me return to my more recent ruminations, and try a little harder to make this discussion relevant to systems and software. Frequently, in the computing literature, I find a discussion of some new concept (e.g., formal methods) followed by the exasperated statement that those involved in the practice of software have not adopted this new concept because they are ignorant of it.

However, I think I understand the practice of software fairly well, and it is my belief that practitioners may or may not be ignorant of such concepts, but it matters a lot less than whether they accept them or not. And it is frequently the case—formal methods are a particularly good example here—that the real basis for lack of adoption by the world of practice is not lack of understanding, but lack of acceptance.

What happens when an academic begins to realize that their new concept is not being used? They work harder at explaining the concept. They seek understanding. And when they provide that understanding, and find that the concept is still not accepted, in exasperation they blame the practitioner for being stupid or not listening. (Sound familiar?) After all, in the world of authority figures, isn't understanding equal to acceptance?

The message imbedded in these thoughts is this: It is necessary for authority figures, as well as students and children, to decouple understanding and acceptance. The degree to which the authority figure permits the student or child to decouple the two notions is symptomatic of how well the authority figure respects the maturation of the student or child and has achieved some personal maturation of his or her own.

Once that decoupling occurs, the authority figure can then go about the two important tasks for which he or she is responsible:

1. Explaining a concept in such a way that it can be understood
2. Supporting that understanding with a rationale for why it should be accepted

I believe that there is an absence of an evaluative component to most contemporary software research. My view of the current state of the art in our research is that it involves a lot of definition, a lot of explanation, a lot of advocacy, and very little evidence to support that advocacy. Evaluative research, whose purpose would include providing such evidence and which is a rich part of the tradition of our more scientific brethren, is largely absent from our research.

(The one piece of evaluative research on formal methods with which I am familiar shows a 9% benefit in "total development cost" to the use of the formal specification language Z [Ralston 1991]. In the larger world of cost-benefit tradeoffs, where formal methods must compete with 4GLS and CASE tools and methodologies and downsizing for management attention and funding, a technology that promises a 9% benefit and large learning costs simply isn't going to rank high in the technology transfer queue.)

Perhaps the near absence of evaluative research is partly due to our authority figures not yet decoupling understanding and acceptance. Perhaps there is a general feeling, not well understood and certainly not articulated, that the job of the researcher is simply to provide understanding. Perhaps this is partly because the authority-figure researcher has not really accepted yet the increasing maturity of the software practitioner. Therefore, they do not yet see the need to supplement explanation with rationale.

Over the years, I have mused about the differences between the world of academe and the world of practice. I believe, for example, that academics are often poorer listeners (the typical lecture hall setting is not conducive to building listening skills in the lecturer) and less goal-oriented (academics do in order to learn, rather than learning in order to do). And perhaps, now, I should add to those differences my belief that practitioners have done a better job of decoupling understanding and acceptance than academics. (Try selling a new concept to upper management on the basis of understanding alone, and you won't make that mistake more than once!)

Ah, well, enough of these ramblings. The truly important question is, what's the bottom line regarding that conference squabble? Well, I really do believe that I made a fool of myself, but I can't quite bring myself to be sorry that I did it!

Reference

Ralston 1991—"Formal Methods: History, Practice, Trends and Prognosis," *American Programmer*, May 1991; T.J. Ralston and S.L. Gerhart.

8.5
structured Research?
(A partly tongue-
in-cheek Look)

There is a problem hardly anyone wants to talk about, but I think it's time to bring it out into the open. It's what I'd like to call the "software research crisis."

The software research crisis? What is this crisis? I hear you saying.

It's the tendency of research to be over budget, behind schedule, and unreliable. And it's a real crisis. When did you last hear of a research project that worked to a tightly controlled budget, came through on a predictable schedule, and was reliable enough to be put to immediate productive use?

I am not here just to bemoan this crisis. I have positive suggestions as to what we should do about it.

First of all, I think it is time we structure our research. In fact, I would like to propose a structured revolution for research.

What do I mean by structured research? First, we need a disciplined, rigorous, orderly, straightforward process for doing research. None of those random opportunistic "goto's." None of that slovenly, uncontrolled, freedom-loving serendipitous stuff out of the past. We will have a research life cycle, carefully controlled milestones for monitoring research accomplishments, and a set of research documents to be produced along the way so that management can get visibility into research progress.

And research metrics. We need ways of measuring both the productivity and the success of research projects. (Perhaps we could measure person-hours per Source Line Of Published research Paper (SLOP). In order to compare future research under this new paradigm with the undisciplined research of the past, we'd better begin collecting these metric data now. Contemporary research metrics data collection is perhaps the most urgent need of the research crisis.

Ah, and then we need to define research process. Perhaps we could even define a research process model, and invent a process language in which we could define the activities of research and monitor a specific project against that model.

What would be in the process model? First of all we would have all the elements of the research life cycle. We would define the requirements for the research in a formal, rigorous, mathematical language so that we could clearly convey them to our funding sources. In fact, with a rigorous enough language, perhaps we could look forward in the future to the automatic generation of research findings from these rigorous requirements languages.

And then we would have research design. Perhaps we could have a research design methodology, the Rational Research Methodology (RRM), a set of orderly steps and processes for doing design. And when we finished the design, we could represent that design in a collection of structured languages: idea flow diagrams (IFDs), in which the flow of ideas and the processes that manipulate them could be shown; research structure charts (RSCs), in which a hierarchic view of the research functions could be represented; and research modeling languages (RMLs), in which we could represent in a rigorous way the many minuscule details of the design. In fact, even without automatic generation of research from requirements specifications, we could probably, with the help of rigorous and thorough design representations, use technicians to finish the research once thorough designs were written.

And then research implementation. With all the formalization of the preceding processes, research implementation should be straightforward. We will have research design folders (RDFs), a sort of repository in which we put everything pertaining to the research implementation for the future use of whomever looks at RDFs, and we will hold research structured walkthroughs (RSWs), in which research peers will examine and critique research implementation findings. And we will get ready for the research testing process.

There are two possible approaches to structured research testing. The traditional approach, of course, is via the use of sample inputs, either structured or random (statistical), where test cases are run against the implemented research in order to seek flaws in its implementation. Or there is formal verification of the research, in which mathematical proof processes are used on the research findings to both seek errors and to prove the correctness of the results. Either way, these testing processes will be performed to structured test plans and be reported in structured test reports.

And maintenance? Well, of course, there is no maintenance problem in research (or if there is, it is the same as the research development process) and so we will not define a separate research maintenance process. (Note that here alone we have saved 40 to 80 percent of the research budget.)

Now, with this rigorous approach to research, we can finally get control of these researchers. We can estimate the time it will take to do research from estimates of the lines of published papers that will result. And with appropriate estimates based on these structured and rigorous approaches, we can then more tightly control and monitor research, eventually solving the research crisis.

There is one more facet of contemporary research approaches to be dealt with. Current research is heavily ego based, with both institutional and self-belief intimately tied to the work and its publication. Research must be freed from its ego dependence. To do this, regular reviews will be held, matching the phases of the

8.5

structured research? (a partly tongue-in-cheek look)

research life cycle, to monitor progress in front of both managers/customers and research peers. Then there will be aperiodic audits performed, to check troubled research projects for inherent flaws, and of course to enforce the structuring process on those projects that are trying to avoid its use. The result will be a team-based, egoless approach to research.

And there it is. With a well-defined research process program, appropriate discipline applied to researchers, a research life cycle with milestones by which we can measure research progress, reviews and audits for getting visibility into the process, and metrics to evaluate how well we did when the research ends, we can begin to control this elusive area.

Researchers of the world, rejoice! The structured revolution is at hand, the enforced discipline of rigorous and formal methods is coming, and the research crisis will soon be solved!

(This research was funded by the International Theological Society for Research and Other uncontrolled Things (ITSROT), and the author wishes to thank them for making this work possible. In particular, it is important that the sponsors did not insist that this research be subject to the proposals contained herein. These ideas, of course, are for other researchers and for software engineers, not for elite people such as myself.)

8.6
The Drifting Talk/ Listen Ratio

One of the nicest guys I had ever met had just walked into my office. I was pleased to see him, and told him so. However, the message from my gut, the one that told me how I really felt, was somewhat different. There was a queasiness there, and I wondered what it was all about.

This nicest of guys was a faculty member, the one who had the office next to mine. He taught in one of the engineering disciplines; over the ensuing years, I have forgotten which one. He was a caring, thoughtful kind of guy. What possible reason could there be for my stomach to launch a rebellion?

I was relatively new to academe at the time. After nearly 30 years in industry, it was fun to try a new field. I had loved my software-building and software-maintaining experiences over those industry years, but in the back of my mind there had always been this career alternative—teaching. Now, I was trying out that alternative. I was a software engineering faculty member at a university that had chosen to make a splash in software engineering. I was in the right place at the right time, and I was loving it.

The conversation began between this nicest of guys and me. We chatted pleasantries, sampling a few of the relevant conversational topics du jour, and we moved toward the more interesting subjects slowly, as conversationalists usually do. Finally, we launched into a deeper topic, one we could truly wrap our minds around. Ah, these were the kind of conversations it was worth joining the academic world to have!

But then it began to happen, so slowly that I didn't see it coming at first. The tilt of the conversation, well-balanced at the outset, was beginning to slide in the direction of the nicest of guys. As time went by, his talk-listen ratio climbed higher and higher, and mine (commensurately) fell lower and lower. It was happening all over again, as it had happened before. My visitor loved to talk, but not to listen. My stomach growled an "I told you so."

My pleasant smile began to freeze on my face, as I tried to be nice to this nicest of guys; but I was rapidly losing interest in the conversation, in the guy, in all of it. What had begun as a two-way conversation had turned into a lecture. And I was no longer enjoying it.

As the conversation moved on without me, I began to muse over what was happening. Certainly, I had run into people who talked but didn't listen before, but what I was experiencing with this nicest of guys was an experience I'd had before, with other academics, not as nice as this guy, of course, but still reasonably nice people. There seemed to be, my new insight was trying to tell me, an epidemic of talk-not-listen in the academic world. What had been an occasional problem in industry was a thriving disease in academe.

How strange, I thought to myself, the smile still frozen on my face. There seems to be something in the environment of a university that causes people to lose their listening skills. What could it be?

The answer was fairly obvious, of course. What do academics tend to do for a living? They lecture. Who do they largely do it with? Undergraduate students. And there, as I teased those two facts around a bit, lay my obvious answer. Academics talked instead of listened because that's what they were paid to do, trained to do, best practiced at doing. Their motivation to listen was low because the people they normally talked to (I was beginning to think it was really talking at, not to) had much less to contribute to an equal conversation than the lecturer. Everything in the workaday world of the academic moved him or her in the direction of talking and away from listening.

There is, of course, a problem with this mindset. The mind that fails to listen rarely obtains new insight; and without insight, a mind can atrophy. And that, of course, is the worse possible thing that can happen to an academic. If the mind does not personify what the academic offers to the world, what does? An academic with an atrophied mind is a wasted academic.

My mind had drifted far enough down this path, as the conversation wore on, that I almost failed to notice that the conversation was coming to a halt.

"Gotta go now," the nicest guy was saying. And, with a genuine and warm smile, he left the office. I came back to reality with a start.

Two starts, in fact. One, that I had returned to the world of participation, and it was up to me to begin to do something, to take some action. My time of passive listening had ended for awhile.

And the other start? This one came as a shock. As I realized how much I had tuned this nicest guy out during our talk, as I realized that I missed the last two-thirds of what he was telling me, the horror of what that meant began to wash over me. I had been an academic just long enough, I could see now, that my own listening skills were atrophying. I hadn't learned to compete at the talk level, but I was certainly losing my ability to listen actively. My reverie about talk-not-listen was a symptom that I had begun the voyage to that undesirable land already.

I resolved, that day, to fight that tendency. But who knows how well I have succeeded at it? I can't seem to get anyone to talk with me long enough to find out. Could that mean ...?!

postscript

There is a particular aspect of this problem that really troubles me. I believe, and I have believed for decades now, that there is a communication chasm—not just a gap—between the academic and industry worlds of computing and software. Academics don't listen to practitioners, and practitioners don't listen to academics. How does this chasm manifest itself?

1. Practitioner jargon and academic jargon don't mix very well. The academic, who can point to the origins of his or her jargon in the textbooks and papers of the literature of the field, doesn't understand why the practitioner can't use the proper terms, the proper language. Academics sometimes say, "They got it wrong." That can mean a lot of different things, but one of them is, "They don't speak the correct language." Although the academic who says that may in a sense be correct, the lack of understanding that under-lies such statements can be a real deterrent to meaningful dialogue.

2. Academics seem to genuinely believe that practitioners don't know very much. They talk about "dumbing down" presentations to practitioners, they speak of a "software crisis" as if some large percentage of practitioners don't know what they are doing, and they pay little attention to the system-building and system-maintaining skills that the practitioners do excel in. How do these academics think we succeeded in reaching out into space, for example, if there weren't some capable, even brilliant, practitioners doing their thing successfully?

3. Academics don't seem to know what they don't know. Somehow they have come to believe that if they are aware of the state of the art, as it is defined in the literature of the field, then they are totally knowledgeable about the field. They do not seem to be aware that there is a state of the practice, which is sometimes—perhaps even frequently—ahead of the state of the art, and is certainly, in real and important ways, different from the state of the art.

4. In short, some academics—a small but disturbing number of them—are arrogant and ignorant.

That is, of course, a fairly one-sided picture of the communication chasm at work here. Practitioners who don't read the literature and who ignore powerful new ideas must carry their share of the blame, too.

But still, it is interesting for me to muse, sometimes, about how much of the chasm lies in this very simple difference between academics and practitioners: academics, I believe after sampling both worlds, have decidedly atrophied listening skills. And that, of course, doesn't bode well for overcoming the chasm.

8.7
The Non-goal-oriented committee meeting

The faculty committee meeting droned on. It was our third meeting on the same subject, and I was beginning to think we were never going to get anywhere. Little did I realize at the time how right that thought was going to be.

The meeting was about defining a core curriculum. It was an important meeting. Whatever we decided would be in our core, all of the university's undergraduates from then on would be required to take. No matter what their major. It was hard to imagine a more important committee assignment than this one.

Why, then, was our progress so slow? There was the usual internecine warfare, of course, as the different disciplines tried to force their way into—or out of—the core. (I hadn't yet realized what a drag so-called "service courses"—courses given to non-majors in the subject—were to the professor. Teaching those students who had to take a course was the worst teaching assignment possible, I was to learn. No wonder some disciplines wanted none of their material in the core.)

However, it wasn't politics that was the real problem. The real problem seemed to be—and here, I still have to fumble for words, looking back on the experience a decade later—that no one really cared whether we got anywhere in the meeting or not. There was a joy in collegiality among the meeting attendees, to be sure, but there was little if any sense of mission.

Collegiality, not mission. That's a cumbersome way of saying what I really want to say here. What I really decided, after experiencing it so many times in my academic life that there was no doubt in my mind that it was true, was that academic people simply weren't goal-oriented. Whereas a meeting in industry would have come to order, come to the point, and been dismissed, these academic meetings seem to exist of and for themselves.

At one level, I still see that as an accurate conclusion. At another level, I suppose, it is unfair. After all, what industry has for goals and what academe has for goals are very different. Academics do in order to learn, we have probably all heard by now, whereas industry people learn in order to do. Academics pursue things they find interesting, whereas industry people pursue things that are useful. Those are not just words, they are profound social differences; and they affect a lot of what people in each area do.

However, there is nothing like working toward a common product to motivate people to get on with what they are doing. And my colleagues at this core curriculum committee meeting simply didn't see the final product as being important enough to spend a lot of energy working toward.

(Later, I came to see the problem as even deeper than that. When industry people disagree over methods or approaches, the eventual need to produce a final product forces them to overcome their differences and row in the same general direction. When academics disagree over methods or approaches, there may be nothing to pull them together. Without the need to strive for a communal product, there is little to force diverse interest groups to work together. Disputes can smolder unresolved in the academic world for ludicrous amounts of time. The fact that teaching students and performing research are the real underlying institutional goals doesn't help overcome these differences, since teaching is generally regarded as something of a necessary evil, and research is often individual and thus not dependent on group agreement.)

The fourth and fifth meetings of the core curriculum committee brought us only slightly closer to our stated goal, defining an agreed-upon core. And then, wonder of wonders, the summer holidays intervened. We could not meet during the summer, of course; presumably, we would return to our task in the fall.

And then an interesting thing happened. During the summer, by a process that none of us could ever see or feel, the core curriculum in fact got defined. When we came back in the fall, there were no longer any committee meetings. It seemed a blessing too good to be true.

Or was it? What in fact seemed to have happened, I concluded with the advantage of hindsight, was that the administration went ahead, over the summer, to define their notion of a core; a notion that they probably had had all along. However, and this is important, it was a notion that no one on the committee now had the least inclination to oppose, because in fact we didn't want to hold any more committee meetings!

So what had really happened here? The core curriculum committee had been, in the jargon of technology transfer and change management, an instrument of grass-roots involvement. The faculty members of that committee had had the opportunity to affect the process, to steer toward a goal. The fact that they had not reached a goal, and had left a rudderless ship at the end of the spring semester, had in fact been very predictable. However, the net effect was a decision made by the goal-oriented administration that had the look and feel of involvement at the faculty level, a decision that the faculty could feel some sense of participation in. Not only had the faculty members not been terribly goal-oriented, but their administrators had known it would be that way—and had taken advantage of it!

However, I am afraid we digress here. The preceding analysis is

about the effects of this fundamental industry-academe difference;

but this essay is about the difference, not the effects. And that difference is goal orientation. Industry people are generally well-focused on their goals; academics either are not focused on goals, or have a kind of goal so different that it is not at first apparent that goals are even involved.

And any attempt to build bridges across the industry-academe communication chasm had better take this difference into account

postscript

There is another interesting way in which this difference in goal orientation manifests itself in industry and academe. We have already seen that industry people are product-focused, since the product, for most disciplines, is clearly the goal that matters.

It has become common in recent times for academe to take the position that process is the best way to achieve good product. With that thought, a great deal of effort is focused on defining better process. The whole of the Software Engineering Institute Capability Maturity Model work for example, is focused, on that premise.

However, it is important to be careful here. The natural tendency of the academic world is to focus on process over product. That's part of "doing in order to learn," it's part of "interesting rather than useful." The fact that academics tell us that good process is the best way to good product should be seen as what it is: the natural tendency of a non-goal-oriented group to focus on things of interest to themselves, not necessarily of usefulness to their more goal-focused colleagues.

In other words, it is OK for industry people to focus on process, but never to the exclusion of product. And goal-oriented industry practitioners should never lose track of that fact.

8.8
Rigor vs. Relevance

Aclassic dilemma in any academic field with practical implications is the issue of rigor vs. relevance—that is, is it more important to do impeccably sound research (rigor), or research that has the potential of being useful to practice (relevance)? That becomes particularly important to software practitioners who expect that academic research is going to in some way be useful to them.

To the naive, this may seem like needless controversy. Isn't it possible, after all, to be both rigorous and relevant? The answer to that question, perhaps surprisingly to those not in the research field (and even to some who are!), is a resounding "no." Rigorous experimental research, for example, demands a highly controlled, limited-scope environment. But for research to be useful to the world of practice, it should be conducted in an environment as close to that real world as possible. And the real world is hardly highly controlled and of limited scope. (The wonderful saying, "reality is the murder of a beautiful theory by a gang of ugly facts" comes to mind!)

Perhaps nowhere is the rigor vs. relevance dilemma more difficult than in the field of Information Systems (IS). IS is, after all, the computing academic field devoted to the application of computing solutions to business problems, a field with about as much potential relevance as one could imagine. (The other academic computing fields, such as Computer Science and (to a lesser extent) Software Engineering, are all too often disinterested in application topic areas).

The issue has troubled the academic IS field almost since its inception, several decades ago. Periodically, discussions arise in IS academic circles focused on facets of the dilemma. The issue assumes several guises: What, precisely, is the scope of the Information Systems field? What are its primary foci? What is its relationship with Computer Science, and what should it be? What is its relationship with other reference disciplines? Does IS research lead practice, or trail it? If it is trailing, is that a proper role for research? These are healthy questions, and yet the failure to resolve them over the years signals some confusion in the field, a confusion that is shared by both academics and practitioners.

There are also plenty of attempts to identify a resolution to this dilemma. One recent academic paper [Vessey and Rosemann 2005], for example, proposed that research studies undergo "reality checks" to make sure that they meet such practice-relevant criteria as understandability, relevance, timeliness, applicability, and publication in a place that practitioners might see.

Recall our earlier discussions in this book about the temporal relationship between theory and practice. Obviously, academic IS has never gotten quite comfortable with the idea that in some cases it is inevitable that theory trail practice. At the same time, practitioner IS has grown weary of waiting for academics to produce results that will be useful to them. The issue has gone well beyond that tempest in a teapot.

What brings this issue to the fore now is a recent explosion of internet discussion over the relative roles of rigor and relevance in IS research, a discussion that took place on an academic IS email server. The discussion was lively, and in some cases barbed. This section of our book is a summary, from a practitioner point of view, of that discussion:

To bring some order to what was essentially a collection of very personal beliefs and opinions, I have abstracted below several pithy quotations from the discussion, categorizing those quotations in a way that I hope will make them meaningful to both practitioner and academic readers. (Note that I do not attribute the comments below to the individuals who expressed them. In this article, I am more interested in the viewpoints, than in who presented those viewpoints. Note also that, although what follows is not presented within quotation marks, it is in fact direct quotes from some of those emails).

why is is Academic Research the way it is?

We do research primarily to survive in academia. The attainment of tenure at most schools requires some level of research productivity ... It is a game played by academicians who wish to prosper...

A few (fortunately not many) of my instructors had no relevant work experience, and little understanding of how things work in the real world.

The real yardstick for IS research should be "Have we learned anything about information technology since our field was created? I think the answer is yes."

I think we should classify the strengths of academic as opposed to industry research as follows:

1. Dealing with issues contrary to commercial interests
2. Addressing unsolved problems
3. Addressing issues economically unattractive to industry
4. Addressing issues where management aspects are more important than technical ones
5. Conduct research on teaching IS

In 1967, Doug Engelbart produced some research at Stanford Research Institute that practitioners thought was not relevant. He had a hard time getting anyone to listen until eventually, five years later, Xerox became interested. The research was the windows and mouse interface. It was not relevant in 1967; it is very relevant today.

The issue of relevance to business practice is ... culture dependent. Such an issue would not have been given this weight if the cultural environment were not the western "free enterprise" (capitalistic) system.

Why should the relevance of our research to current business practice be used as the metric for judging IS research?

The views of anyone speaking for the interests of the business community should not be a basis for determining the relevance of the work. What's good for General Motors is not necessary good for the country.

why is practice the way it is?

I never read a journal when I worked in industry, and I honestly don't think I know anyone who did.

There are even two sets of journals, that attend to the needs of each group—Information Systems Research, MIS Quarterly, etc., for basic research, and Datamation, CIO, etc. for applied research (author's note—it is interesting that this academic emailer was not aware that some of those "applied research" journals (a) didn't really report on research, and (b) were no longer in existence!).

I don't know why my staff avoids academic conferences. There are a number of PhDs on the team, and I do pass along to them all the interesting conference calls.

Much of what I know about practice gets obsolete very rapidly.

The biggest thing the work experience can provide is an appreciation of the need for accuracy, testing, and quality.

The Gap Between Academe/Research/ Theory, and Practice

There is a chasm between academia and industry. Part of the problem is caused by a lack of understanding of the nature and purpose of IS research.

There are probably no academic findings of any importance in IT and few, if any, from business schools in general. The evidence is few, if any, business people bother to waste their time with academic journals.

We do not have any evidence of any potential impact of IS research on practice.

Research is often not timely or relevant to the applied world. Conferences are behind by a couple of years, and journals have review times of 1-3 years.

We are definitely behind practice!!! The MIS academic discipline is broken. We are not leading industry in any way that I can see. Practice doesn't respect us because we don't respect them.

In other fields, theories are proposed, then they are tested over and over again, as everyone tries to tear them down. What emerges is a theory that works in the real world. We don't do that, to my knowledge.

Using the expectations of business people to evaluate academic research will likely be as frustrating as using a hammer to plant a tree, or a shovel to drive a nail.

Academics and practitioners have a different worldview. Academics favor the creation of general concepts and ideas, and the refinement of theories and concepts.

There is no reason to make an "either-or" distinction in rigor/ relevance, theory/practice; we have the option of "both-and."

Much of IS research is based on empirical evidence from practice. In many instances of IT applications, practice leads theory. But there are other examples.

Many in academia are unable to relate to practitioners who are concerned with the specific application of theory to a specific problem.

There's an old saying—theory without practice is sterile, practice without theory is blind.

Consultants get paid very well to make academic research relevant to today's practitioners.

computer science vs. Information systems

Basic research is absolutely essential, but such developments come out of Computer Science, not IS. When I want to learn more about emerging technologies, I consult Communications of the ACM or other computer science publications, but rarely our own.

The incumbent territoriality of Computer Science and Engineering has tended to insure that IS never got technical enough to threaten their turf.

I never hear from my Computer Science colleagues about issues like relevance or impact. Maybe it has something to do with creation. When you create (as computer scientists tend to do), you get an identity. The alternative is a kind of "parasitic" discipline, which merely surveys, analyzes, and proposes some bizarre hypothesis about how practitioners work.

My (practitioner) teammates seem less interested in IEEE and ACM meetings than ever before.

what should be Done?

Maybe junior faculty should have to jump through tenure hoops, but it would be nice if senior faculty were tasked with making a reputation for themselves and their institutions out beyond the ivory towers.

Why don't we embrace the Medical discipline model, where academia and practice must be integrated. Medical schools are located nearside and inside hospitals, and most of the researchers are also practitioners, or at least active consultants. We should try to persuade the giant companies, such as IBM, HP, Oracle, Microsoft, etc., to act as "hospitals" for us.

I went to a conference recently where the keynoters were all academics, and the paper presenters were mostly practitioners. The thing that intrigued me was the questions practitioners had for the academics: Are we doing the right thing? How do we measure success? Are we having an impact?

Isn't it time to start thinking about a strategic alliance with Computer Science?

Does it not behoove us to have required coursework for Ph.D. candidates and graduate students that includes 3-6 credit hours of "applied work"? We ask our undergraduate students to do this kind of work, but many graduate students escape it completely.

Doctoral candidates need some practical work experience. All of us need periodic updating (to the state of the practice, not just the state of the art).

Is there a place for a new kind of doctoral program—call it a "practitioner scholar" program—that brings highly skilled, mid-career folk from industry and educates them at a doctoral level? If our IT research and teaching efforts are to be "relevant," wouldn't IT programs benefit from having a complement of such "converts"? Wouldn't industry benefit from educating their brightest and best at a doctoral level so that they can bring the latest "relevant" academic research to the work world?

Exchange programs with industry would benefit all of us, including tenured, experienced professors, and practitioners getting classroom experience.

Reference

Vessey and Rosemann 2005—"Linking Theory and Practice: Performing a Reality Check on a Model of IS Success," working paper, Queensland University of Technology Center for Information Technology, 2005; Iris Vessey and Michael Rosemann.

chapter 9
Fun versus Getting Serious

chapter contents:

introduction to chapter 9

"Creativity and the chance to be creative is really fun ... People are creative, they have more fun, they come up with better solutions."

—*Claire Arnold*, CEO, Leapfrog Services, Inc. in "The Creative Edge," *Atlanta Business Chronicle*, September 16, 2005

"There clearly follows the impossibility ... of increasing machines to immense size ... enormous ships, palaces, or temples."

—*Galileo, Dialogues Concerning Two New Sciences* as quoted in The Search for Solutions, Horace Freeland Judson, Holt, Rinehart and Winston 1980 (Reprinted by permission of Henry Holt and Company, Inc.)

Now it's time to really get down to it. All the rest of that talk in this chapter, about discipline and satisficing and qualitative reasoning and process, is just mental gymnastics. This is where the truth really comes out!

Software development is and always has been fun. That's what makes the field of software go round. You do it, and if it goes well you feel good. It just don't, as the beer commercial says, get any better than this.

Take it from an old-timer. I got in on the ground floor of computing, way back in the 1950s. In those days, those of us in computing had to be in it for the fun of it, because there was a price to be paid in society for being a computist.

What price? We were, to put it simply, considered weird. We were doing something with our minds that most everyone else did with their hands—crafting a product and making it do phenomenal tricks (in our case with the aid of a box of mysterious electronics that few people understood).

It wasn't the same as today's hackers. Hackers do a fairly normal thing in fairly weird ways. We pioneers did what were considered to be weird things, and no one cared much how we did them. We pioneers were weird to the core of our professional selves; hackers engage in weird behavior, but their profession itself goes unquestioned.

I can still remember the first time, flying on a business trip, that I discovered a seat mate who spoke computerese (it was in the '70s, on a flight from Albuquerque to Austin). I had been in the field for a couple of decades by then, and had never before met anyone who had anything meaningful to say on the subject. Contrast that with today's social world, where the chance that you will meet someone who knows nothing about computers and has no opinions on them is virtually nil.

That weirdness was part of the fun of the field. We really were pioneers, doing something that most people couldn't even imagine. Our frontier was invisible and had no shape or weight. Even explaining it to non-computer-people was a task doomed largely to failure! What fun all of that was.

But that fun paled in contrast to the fun of doing software things: figuring out how to use some new instruction in the instruction set of the latest computer; figuring out how to rewrite last year's software and make it better using this year's computer (we did it all the time, because the pace of computing hardware change then was far faster—believe it or not—than the pace of change now); debugging a program, playing detective and trying to ferret out mysterious clues to determine what they were telling us; and seeing the results of our handiwork in the form of real answers, correct answers even, spilling out onto our printers or terminals.

Most of that fun persists today. We may be figuring out some feature of a new programming language instead of a new instruction on the computer. We may not have to rewrite our software on a regular basis (and we're probably thankful for that!). However, we still feel the joy of the chase in debugging, and the pleasure of creation in results. I sometimes marvel at how lucky I was to find myself getting paid to work in a field that was so much fun. Do we really need money to do this sort of thing?!

But something has gone wrong over the years, and I can't quite figure it out. Computing, as you will see in the final essay in this section/chapter, isn't as much fun anymore. Is it me who's changed, unable to mix frivolity and productivity? Or is it the field that's changed, driving software people to distraction with impossible cost and schedule targets? I don't know the answer, although I suspect it's some of both. If this is a theme that interests you, I'd love to hear from you.

Be that as it may, let me stand aside here and let you get on to the material at hand. Do we need to define fun? Why not: "light-hearted amusement." (Imagine yourself not knowing our language, and trying to make something out of that definition! Light-hearted indeed.)

What about serious? "Solemn and thoughtful, not smiling; sincere, in earnest, not casual or light-hearted."

That does it ... we're going to have to look up light-hearted as well: "cheerful, without cares; too casual, not treating a thing seriously."

Talk about overloaded words. Which would you rather be, a fun person or a serious one? Somehow, that part about "not smiling" says a lot to me.

But enough wordplay. On to the subject at hand.

9.1

TOΓΠ BETWEEN FUN and TEDIUM

It's interesting how seldom you hear about the fun aspect of building software. Oh, there's a bit about it under the surface of the open source literature—after all, having fun must be one of the biggest reasons why someone would choose to build software and not get paid for it!

But fun *per se* is almost never the subject of anything else you read in our field. There's little "fun" in the popular-press computing literature. And there's certainly no "fun" in the academic literature (sometimes I think academics make a fetish out of not appearing to have fun. How else can you explain the boring way in which so many academic papers are written!)

Because of all of that, it was with delight that I learned that a friend of mine, Bruce Blum, had not only thought a lot about fun in the software field, he had actually written a paper on the subject [Blum 1991]. I quickly talked him into letting me publish it in my newsletter (that's the citation I used above).

Let me share with you some of what Bruce had to say about fun.

He began writing about fun by lamenting on how seldom his "input file labeled 'FUN' seems to build up." No matter how much you want fun in your software life, he was saying, it's a hard commodity to come across.

How do we come across fun? Here Bruce took two different perspectives—a life cycle one, and a software history one.

In the life cycle perspective, he talked about which phases of the life cycle tend to be fun, and which aren't. You might want to play a little game with me as you read what follows. How much do you agree with Bruce's life-cycle fun-source assessments?

Phase one of Bruce's life cycle is what he calls "selling the concept." You can't build software until someone thinks it's a good idea that you do so. And selling the concept, Bruce says, is almost purely a fun activity. "It's problem solving in its freest, most stimulating form. With a wave of the hand almost any objection can be overcome … The only tedium here is trying to find nonstop flights, making last-minute changes to the visuals, and working with narrow-minded people." Here we have a 100-0% division between fun and tedium, he is saying.

Phase two, Bruce says, is developing the statement of requirements. This, he says, "is equally divided" [50-50] between fun and tedium. The fun part is coming to understand a stimulating problem, and the sense of working toward creating a new system. The tedium is writing it all down, making sure that what has been written is correct and conforms to the promises already made. "Still, at this early stage, a lot can be done with a wave of the hand," he concludes.

Phase three is top-level design. Here, Bruce says, "we can see the tedium creeping in. There are promises to keep, and now we have to find out how to keep them. As the amount of documentation increases, we lose the freedom to make up solutions on the spot. The source of the growing tedium" [and Bruce puts the fun/tedium ratio at about 40-60] "is obvious. All those documents have to be read, more documents have to be written, and—most distressing of all—we have to be sure that what we are saying is consistent."

In phase four, detailed design, Bruce says "It only gets worse." [Bruce suggests a 33-67 ratio]. That's because all the arm-waving joy of top-level design now has to be fleshed out into something that actually makes all that free-form stuff happen. Getting down to brass tacks is absolutely necessary, but have you ever met anyone who thought brass tacks were fun?!

On the other hand, Bruce loves programming, phase five. "Programming," he says, "is mostly fun. That's why it is a hobby; that's why [programming magazines] are so thick and filled with advertisements. You know, whenever things get to be too bad, I just go to the computer and write some programs. It's therapeutic, it makes me feel better." [Bruce puts the fun/tedium ratio here at 75-25].

Above, I suggested you might want to think about your own allocation of fun vs. tedium. It's at the programming phase, I think, where—if I could put my ear to this page of this book—I might hear the strongest rumblings of disagreement. I'm with Bruce on the fun in programming, as you've no doubt already guessed. But I meet a lot of freshly-minted students of the computing field in various academic institutions who can't seem to wait to get finished with programming and become managers of others who program. Makes me wonder, as you might imagine, why they chose to major in computing in the first place!

Ah, but I digress. Bruce has a couple more life cycle phases to deal with.

Testing, he says, is phase six. Here, Bruce quickly sees the fun part slipping away again [to 33-67]. Obviously, he and I have different viewpoints on the potential for fun in this phase. Recall from above that I see it as a detective story phase, putting together clues to eventually flush out and repair those bugs that I found it hard to believe I'd accidentally placed in my code. But Bruce sees it another way. "Frankly, I get defensive in an adversarial situation." (Bruce is seeing his programmer relationship with formal testers as adversarial. But, in a sense, the computer, in executing the actual (and faulty) code I wrote, is also my adversary!) "I am sure I would have found [those darned bugs] myself if I hadn't had to spend so much time [dealing with] testing," he says in exasperation. And, to be honest, I can share his joylessness about the adversarial aspects of testing. There I am, expecting—as usual—my code to run correctly the first time (it rarely does, of course!), and there is the tester or the machine showing me up as a failed human being all over again. Who needs that?!

Testing isn't the end, however. It may be the end of the development cycle, but then after all that development is complete comes the (drum roll!) maintenance phase. My ear on the page is hearing a lot of rustling out there! And, if I can interpret what I'm hearing from you correctly, dear reader, you are agreeing with Bruce. "This is almost pure tedium" [0–100], he says. Hardly anyone in the software world likes doing maintenance. Why else would we find that the vast majority of newly-minted programmers get assigned to maintenance tasks? Why else do we find such a high percentage of "last-hired, first fired" people doing maintenance? (Because senior people, as you know, avoid maintenance like the plague). (By the way, I don't agree with making any group—except perhaps sluggards—the last hired and the first fired, but for whatever reason there are people (women, for example) for whom that's true. Go to a meeting of any software maintenance organization, and you'll find an astonishingly high percentage of women there).

I do need to interject here that I actually find maintenance to be kind of fun. I have been lucky enough, however, to maintain code written by some of the best and brightest, and I learned a lot and matured professionally during the time I did maintenance. (There's an interesting story to the effect that a young Bill Gates filched listings of the vendor operating system from his university's computer center dumpster in order to learn how to become a better programmer!)

I began all of this discussion by saying that Bruce presented two different perspectives on fun vs. tedium. We've finished the lifecycle perspective. Now for the software history one.

"In the beginning," says Bruce, "...programming was a small-scale, problem-solving activity ... There were few firm requirements. Programmers worked with prototypes and used them to extend their knowledge as they created new products. In doing this, they maximized fun ..."

But it couldn't continue that way, Bruce says. "As the programming technology matured and larger systems were being designed, the inherent problems of this ad hoc approach became obvious. Teams of 100 programmers could only work if there were fixed requirements and designs. Thus, software engineering turned to the optimization of process conformance rather than fun."

"Clearly," Bruce went on, "the discipline introduced by this [next] phase of software engineering did improve the process. It instituted a form of mathematical rigor. The requirements were taken as axioms, and the designs were produced as theorems ... This shift to a disciplined process proved to be very effective for large and constrained projects."

But all of that discipline wasn't enough, Bruce says. There are problems that don't lend themselves to an all too rigid axiom/theorem/disciplined approach. No matter how much we wish it were so, some problems aren't constrained the way those approaches require.

"Here, then, is the underlying problem," Bruce says. "A software process optimized for fun is only good when the tasks are small and the motivation for quality is based on an individual's insight. A software process optimized for phased compliance," he goes on, "is only valid for firm and stable requirements. It fails when there is uncertainly regarding the requirements ... It also fails when the requirements are not stable. Thus both the natural intuitive approach and the managed response to it have proven to be poor models for controlling the software process."

It's been a lot of years since Bruce wrote that last, and yet I'm still oh-so impressed by it. Read that last paragraph over again, if you don't mind. Here is Bruce, way back in 1991, talking abut why almost none of our software construction approaches are working as well as we'd like. In a sense he's predicting the whole agile thing, the whole open source thing, and all the other flailings we have tried over the years as we try to deal with those new problems that don't seem to match either our fun approach, or our phased compliance approach.

Time to lighten up here. "Perhaps," Bruce concludes, "you would like to know how software should be developed. Actually, the answer is simple. What we need is a structured, object-oriented, knowledge-based prototyping paradigm based on formal specifications and proofs of correctness that combines the main features of composition and decomposition in a CASE environment using methodology-independent methods and visual programming in Ada. As soon as my [research] grant is approved, I'll show you how it works; it really makes computing fun."

Yea, right! Well, at least Bruce has shown us once again that, even though software work isn't as much fun as it used to be, writing about it still can be!

P.S. You may have been wondering about the use of the word "tedium" in Bruce's discussion. It's a nicely chosen word, and I applaud him for choosing it. But there was another meaning here. Bruce really had done a lot of research on a system that would "automate the tedium of the software process." He called that system TEDIUM. Like so many other bright ideas in the software field, nothing much ever came of TEDIUM except some books that Bruce wrote about it, and some in-house use at Johns Hopkins where Bruce worked before he retired a few years back

Reference
Blum 1991—"Torn Between Fun and Tedium," *The Software Practitioner*, May 1991; Bruce I. Blum.

9.2

open source: the fun returns

In the beginning, software was free. Back in those pioneering days 50-something years ago, there was no marketplace for software—it was "bundled" free with computer hardware. And all software was open—if you wrote something particularly useful or good, it was contributed to a communal software parts repository like that of the IBM user organization SHARE, whereupon any software developer could read and use the code as they wished.

And producing software was fun. Most of the people in the software profession deeply enjoyed the creative act of building software, so much so that they might have built software for nothing if it hadn't happened to be true that there were companies willing to pay them handsomely to do it.

That was then, this is now. In between, software became a product worth money, so much money in fact that one software entrepreneur became the world's richest person. But something negative happened along the way—for some software practitioners, at least, building software became a lot less fun. Huge and complex projects, rigid and required methodologies, schedule-driven project estimation, and stern management oversight resulted in diminishing that fun, the fun that had been such a powerful motivator in software's early days.

Consider the now. There has been a movement afoot for a decade or so to return those notions of "free" and "fun" to the world of building software. And that Open Source movement seems to be hitting its stride as the second edition of this book is being written. Open Source programmers seem to build software largely for the fun of it.

Oh, there are other motivations. They build software that they want to use. They build software because they are good at it. They build software to be accepted (or even lauded!) in a community of other software builders. They build software because they don't like the existing proprietary software industry, particularly Microsoft and its role therein.

But, nearly at the top of that list of motivators, they build software for fun. In fact, there was a recent study [Hann 2004] that showed that, when all the motivators of Open Source software builders are considered, fun (the study called it "recreational value," but you know how academics can't resist using a long word when a short one would do!) came in at number two. The findings about these motivators were:

- 27% of open source programmers participated in projects for the "use value" of the result
- 19% participated for that recreational value
- 12% participated because they thought it would have a positive effect on their career

There. Open Source software project participation is, demonstrably, about fun. (Incidentally, this paper was chosen as the "Best Theme Paper" at the conference where it was presented).

There's a lot more that could be said of course, about the Open Source software movement. Some say that Open Source programmers are the cream of the programming crop, produce the most reliable and secure software, and that Open Source is the inevitable future of the field. Others resist or decry or refute such claims. Advocates are accused of being zealots, and opponents are said to not understand what they are talking about. Politics has even reared its ugly head in the Open Source battlefield, with Open Source advocates trying to get governments worldwide to use their wares to the exclusion of proprietary products, and proprietary companies trying to prevent Open Source code from being used on certain kinds of projects. It has all gotten pretty ugly at times.

If you want to get a broader exposure to the Open Source movement, with both pros and cons presented therein, try the recent book [Feller, et al. 2005], which is a collection of solicited writings about Open Source from some well-known software writers and Open Source "experts." If you want to remain current on the fast-paced topic of open source, read such publications as *Cutter IT Journal* and *The Software Practitioner,* which regularly carry articles or special issues on this topic. If you want to know more about whether it's possible to combine participation in the Open Source movement and still make money doing it (you capitalist, you!), see such articles as [Bollinger 2004].

You may have felt like that previous paragraph was kind of a brushoff, one that precedes an abrupt ending of this section on Open Source. You would be right! There are a lot of things that can be said about the Open Source movement, but this is not the place to say them. In this book about creativity in software construction, topics are included when they are at least somewhat clearly related to that topic. There may be some who would claim that Open Source is a more creative way of building software, but I think that's kind of a stretch. There's no evidence one way or the other, I would assert, on where the truth lies on that issue. But—and this is the point of this section—Open Source has restored the fun part of the building of software (er, that is the "recreational value"!), and we celebrate it here for that reason, and that reason alone.

references

Bollinger 2004—"How to Make Money Writing Open Source Software," *The Software Practitioner*, July 2004; Terry Bollinger.

Feller et al 2005—*Making Sense of the Bazaar: Perspectives on Open Source and Free Software*, MIT Press, 2005; edited by Joseph Feller, et al.

Hann 2004—"Why Developers Participate in Open Source Software Projects," Proceedings of the 25th International Conference on Information Systems, Washington DC, December 2004; Il-Horn Hann, Jeff Roberts, and Sandra A. Slaughter.

9.3
A peculiar project

By Dwayne Phillips
Originally published in Cutter IT E-Mail Advisor, December 2005
Used with permission (dwayne.phillips.home.att.net)

"Peculiar: adj: beyond or deviating from the usual or expected, a curious hybrid accident"
—*Wordnet 2.0,* Copyright Princeton University

I am working on a peculiar project. I have worked on a few peculiar projects in my life, but they have been greatly outnumbered by normal projects. This time, however, I have been fortunate enough to notice the peculiarity of this project and to enjoy it. I have identified a few characteristics of peculiar projects and have learned how to make these the norm, or at least occur a little more often.

My current project is, as the definition above states, "deviating from the usual or expected." I think of it as peculiar because all the problems are technical in nature while all the joys involve the people on the project.

Technical problems and people pleasures are not the norm in my career. Most projects have a few technical problems but the frustrations involve the people. People bicker over approaches and processes; people come in late for work and leave early; some people work 16-hour days and become tired and grouchy; other people become bored and leave the project without leaving a guide for what they had and had not accomplished. My list of people-related headaches is almost limitless.

In contrast, the people working on my current project are for the most part motivated, happy, and pleasant to be near. People are not entering and leaving the project at a pace that leaves the rest of us restarting every month. When people do leave, they do so happy and at a good break point. This allows new people to come onto the project and pick up their work without requiring the rest of us to stop and train them.

It is a pleasure to work on this peculiar project. Dare I even say that it is fun?

I cannot take credit for this peculiar project. To my credit, I have grown in my ability to manage work and communicate with people, but I still work on many projects that are normal. This project has gotten me wondering why such a pleasurable project is peculiar. Why can't most of our projects be fun? I think the main reason is that we don't expect them to be. Since we don't expect the pleasure of working with motivated people with good attitudes, we don't work to create such projects.

I've examined myself and my practices on past projects. Only once in 25 years have I scribbled a list of attributes about the people with whom I wish to work. (That one project was also peculiar; maybe there's a pattern here.) Instead, I have thoughtfully written a work breakdown structure, sketched a schedule having a critical path, denoted the risks and mitigations, and other such good practices. Most of those projects succeeded; that is, they delivered the desired product on time and within budget. Few of them, however, were fun.

Here is a suggestion for creating peculiar projects and maybe making them normal instead of peculiar. This technique is called "incremental consensus" and was described to me in a private conversation with consultant and author Jerry Weinberg [Weinberg] (I describe this technique in [Phillips 2004]).

Incremental consensus begins with two people who want to work in a mutually pleasing manner and succeed on a project. This team grows one person at a time. When one team member finds another person who wants to join the team (emphasis on the desire to be on the team), the current team members must agree that they would like that person on the team. No one enters the team without the consensus of the existing team. This team is likely to be peculiar because everyone on the team is accepted by everyone else.

My peculiar project team wasn't formed using incremental consensus, as it comprises some 100 people. The ten team leaders, however, were added to the team one at a time, with each person wanting to be on the existing team (there is that desire again).

My peculiar project may not succeed. We are facing several technical problems that threaten to blow our budget and delay deliveries. There are no guarantees on projects, especially when you are inventing hardware, creating algorithms, and trying to write new software to fit the custom hardware. What is peculiar is that we talk openly about our technical problems and seek ways to solve them as a team devoted to project success and to one another's well being. When the latter is present, the former seems to follow.

References

Weinberg—Jerry Weinberg, see http://www.geraldmweinberg.com.
Phillips 2004—*The Software Project Manager's Handbook:
Principles that Work at Work*, IEEE Computer Society and Wiley-Interscience 2004; Dwayne Phillips.

9.4
can you Help me find it?

Fun. That's what software is all about, right? Those of us who eat, sleep and breathe computing and software do it because it's fun.

Oh, sure. We also do it for the money, the status, the professional advancement, and all those other mundane things that people write books about. But basically, we're in it for fun. That's why no one has ever written a book called The One-Minute Programmer ... not because programming takes longer than that, but because who could ever quit after one minute?

Now that I've said that, though, I have a confession to make. Software used to be fun for me. After 30 years, it's not nearly as much fun any more. And as I work my way into my third mid-life crisis, I'm trying to figure out why. I'm writing this story to see if any of you readers out there can help me.

Here's where I've gotten so far. I've established some candidate explanations to try on for size.

1. Employers think 30-year people are too valuable to let them program. The last time anyone really asked me to write a program for money was so long ago I can't remember when. Oh, sure, I get to study requirements, or write proposals, or do research, or write papers. But it's not the same. The

fun in programming is programming. Nothing else really hacks it (cough). And employers believe that a fresh young programmer is just as good as an experienced older one.

2. Programmers suffer burnout. What's fun about programming is also what's awful about it. It's weaving a thousand tiny, intricate details into a functioning tapestry, an executable work of art. And after awhile, tangling with those details becomes less like fun and more like work. Why else would so many programmers aspire to become managers ... what's the fun in that?

3. The older you get, the more uptight you get. Now there's a truly revolting thought! Have we learned so little about life, we experienced folk, that it becomes more of a burden as we live it, rather than less? Growing older should, in part, be a refinement of the ability to have fun. Looking about me at my age-peers, I don't believe I see that happening.

The list could be longer. That's one thing I'm counting on from you, dear reader. But let me wrap up this story by telling you what brought this issue to a focus.

I don't know how better to put this: I now have a second-generation programmer. Thirty something years ago I had a son, and darned if he didn't decide to follow in his father's footsteps, cow pucky, program bugs, and all. So now there's a new generation programmer out there with my name on him. And as I watch his career progress, I see him having fun. Nostalgia and déjà vu ... just like I used to.

It was his write-protect-ring story that got me. There he was, sitting around on a laid-back Friday afternoon at his particular employer's software factory, mellow after a week of hard work. And darned if one of the crew didn't throw a write-protect-ring at someone else (you know the write-protect-ring? The badly-named plastic gizmo that allows you to write on a tape when it's present, and protect it from writing when it's absent?). And, as will happen among spirited folk, the volley was returned. Write-protect-rings were flying through the air like bugs in an un-debugged program. Even the corporate vice president got into the act (you know how small some of these contemporary software houses are, and how young their executives!). There was my son, a big smile on his face, happily telling me this story. And there was me-the-listener, analyzing my reaction and finally identifying it as envy. What was flashing through my mind was those halcyon days at the beginning of my career, when I swapped stories, shot rubber bands, and played ten-second chess on the job just like God intended us to do. So what happened?

What happened, indeed? I got more experienced. I got paid more, got to feeling more responsible, somehow. I wrote some books, authored a column or two. I did research, wrote a paper or two. I got successful, just like All-American boys and girls are supposed to dream about.

But somewhere along the line, I think, I lost something. Can you help me find it?

9.4
can you help
me find it?

part 2
making creativity happen

294

introduction to part II

"There are two main phases in the ... creative process ... and in the ... development of new ideas; an imaginative phase and a practical one. In the imaginative phase, you generate and play with ideas. In the practical phase, you evaluate and execute them.

"In the imaginative phase, you ask such questions as 'What if?' 'Why not?' 'What rules can we break?' 'What assumptions can we drop?' 'How about if we looked at this backward?' 'Can we borrow a metaphor from another discipline?' The motto of the imaginative phase is 'Thinking something different.'

"In the practical phase, you ask such questions as 'Is this idea any good?' 'Do we have the resources to implement it?' 'Is the timing right?' 'Who can help us?' 'What's the deadline?' 'What are the consequences of not reaching the objective?' The motto of the practical phase is 'Getting something done'."

—*Roger von Oech*
A Whack on the Side of the Head, Warner Books 1990

I t is one thing to believe that creativity is an essential part of the work of software; it is another to make creativity happen. **295**

If the previous Part of this book has been about philosophy and motivation, then this is the "how-to" part

Much has been written in both the popular press and the more serious journals about how to make creativity happen; but very little has been written, as we are about to see, in the computing literature. It is as if the focus on disciplined, formal, quantitative approaches to software development that we discussed in Part I of this book has blinded us to the need for more creative approaches as well.

Fortunately, one academic saw this problem and set out to overcome it. In this Part, scattered through its several chapters, we present some material derived from the work of the late Professor J. Daniel Couger of the University of Colorado at Colorado Springs. Couger's interest in creativity in the field of computing resulted in both significant research in the topic area, and in the founding of a Center for Research in Creativity (CRC) at his institution. I strongly recommend that you buy and read Professor Couger's various books on this subject.

But enough admiration and plugging! Let's return to how-to. Let's suppose, for the moment, that you've become convinced by all the prior material in this book that creativity is, at least to some extent, an essential part of the process of building software. Let's further suppose that you're in charge of a group of software people, and you're eager to increase the creative capabilities they possess. What do you do next?

That's where Professor Couger's material comes in. In the chapters to follow, particularly in Chapter 11, we note that he presents a solid academic framework for thinking about creativity in information system implementation, and then he moves quickly to a discussion of where, when and how in the software process creativity can and should be important. His case study, included as the last section of Chapter 11, is a stunning contribution to the field of making creativity happen! He presents a set of techniques for enhancing creativity, discusses a program that taught those techniques, and elaborates on what happened at the enterprise in question when they were taught and applied. Although we tend to think of innovation entering an organization top-down, in this material Professor Couger talks about making it happen bottom-up, and even suggests that it may work better that way!

There are other major contributors to this material. Perhaps surprisingly, Watts Humphrey, he of software process fame, says some pretty significant things about "managing for innovation" in chapter 10. Humphrey's insights here make an interesting complement to the work of Couger. From Humphrey we learn that managing for innovation requires some new thinking from software managers, and he talks about what form that new thinking should take. If this short summary of Humphrey's earlier book whets your appetite, I strongly recommend that you buy Managing for Innovation—or its sequel, Managing Technical People—as well.

But now … on to the how-to part.

References

Some interesting reading beyond what we present in what follows on making creativity happen in the software world:

- "Creative License," *Better Software*, March 2005; Patrick M. Bailey.
- "Imaginate," IEEE *Software*, September 2004; Andy Hunt and Dave Thomas.
- "Provoking Creativity: Imagine What Your Requirements Could Be Like," IEEE *Software*, September 2004; Neil Maiden, Alexis Gizikin, and Suzanne Robertson.
- "The Creative Edge" (a roundtable discussion), *Atlanta Business Chronicle*, September 16, 2005; Powell Goldstein.
- "The Creativity Issue," *Fast Company* magazine, December 2004.
- "Innovation and Language Action," *Communications of the ACM*, May 2006; Peter J. Dennin and Robert Dunham.

chapter 10
creativity in the software organization

introduction to chapter 10

"The day your vision, what you think needs to be done, is bigger than what you can do single-handedly, then you have to make a move toward management. The bigger the issue, the further in management you have to go."

—*Richard Hamming*
"You and Your Research," transcribed from his presentation at the Bell Communicatioon Research Colloquium Seminar, March 7, 1986

There is an interesting diversity of viewpoints in this chapter, all strung on the common theme of how to make the software organization more creative.

There are two different pairs of authors, Peter DeGrace/Leslie Stahl, and Stan Rifkin/Charles Cox, who point out the huge differences that exist between a freewheeling software organization and a tightly disciplined one (I'll bet you just pre-judged what those authors are going to say in their respective sections based on those adjectives "freewheeling" and "tightly disciplined"! You may need to re-think that judgment when you read their material!) We pursue where Watts Humphrey's Managing for Innovation material takes us, as we mentioned in the intro to Part II. And there's an analysis of the value of strategic information systems, based on the controversial Nicholas Carr article "IT Doesn't Matter," that may surprise you regarding what it was Carr was really trying to say when he riled so many IS people!

10.1

Greece vs. Rome: two very different software cultures

Discovering the writings of Peter DeGrace (and his co-author Leslie Hulet Stahl) was, for me, a particularly wonderful experience. It's not just that he said the kinds of things I was trying to say myself. It's not just that he said them so well. It's also that he added a neat cultural breadth to his discussions. Take, for example, the distinction he offers in his "Greece vs. Rome" dichotomy in [DeGrace 1993].

DeGrace describes the workplace and working culture of Greeks and Romans, noting huge and, I think, relevant, differences there. Greeks, he said, worked as individuals or as self-motivated members of teams. They owned their own tools, taking them to work with them and back home afterwards. They worked as individual, independent contractors, providing a service for a fee. They were their own people.

This contrasts mightily with the Roman approach. In Rome, a worker's first duty was to the status group to which he belonged. This meant sacrificing himself for the good of the organization, giving up his individuality, and closely identifying with his group. In a Roman environment, a worker would go to work, take up his company tools, and do what the group said should be done. He would not be an individual; he would be owned by the organization body and mind for as long as he worked there. He

301

was, however, substantially rewarded for following this approach. Rewards came in the form of security, money, and power.

Later in this material, DeGrace protests that in his description of the Greek and Roman approaches "we are not making any moral judgments here." He goes on to say that, rather than taking sides on whether the Greek or Roman approach is the preferable one, he is simply pointing out what he sees as a present-day imbalance in our field, one where most gurus favor the Roman view at the expense of the Greek one.

But I smile a little wryly at that. Note the stuff in the Greece and Rome quotes above about who owns the body and mind of the individual worker. None of us, I suspect, wants our body and mind held hostage by our company. I worked at the same aerospace company where DeGrace worked when he wrote his books, for a number of years. It was definitely a Roman company, at that time, and we employees may not have felt that our bodies and minds were being held hostage, but we definitely did feel that the company placed little value on our contributions as individuals as opposed to those of our group. (In fact, I began my career as a writer of computing tales as a kind of pseudonymed "sanity outlet" from this stifling culture! And I know from personal conversations with DeGrace that he suffered from these same kinds of effects.)

There are worse things, of course, than being part of either a Greek or Roman organization. Some less civilized shops, those that inhabit the lowest rungs of the organizational sophistication ladder, could be considered to be "Barbarian."

Let's translate this Greek vs. Rome dichotomy into categories specific to the working world of software. And, just for fun, let's add a Barbarian factor as well (thanks to Steve McConnell for suggesting it). As you read the list that follows, think abut the software organizations where you have worked.

- Greeks organize things, Romans organize people, Barbarians barely organize anything.

- Greek methodologies are informal, Roman ones formal, Barbarian ones nonexistent.
- Greeks write programs, Romans manage projects, Barbarians leap to coding.
- Greeks are motivated by the problem at hand, Romans by group goals, Barbarians by heroics.
- Greeks minimize the amount of documentation produced, Romans maximize it, Barbarians take pride in doing no documentation.
- Greeks work in small groups, Romans in large organizations, Barbarians work solo.
- Greeks use things as tools, Romans use people as tools, Barbarians avoid tools.
- Greeks are democratic, Romans are imperial, Barbarians are anarchist.
- Greeks are empirical/inductive, Romans analytical/deductive, Barbarians unthinkingly emotional.
- Greeks are intuitive, Romans logical, Barbarians impulsive.
- Greeks are a meritocracy, Romans a "function-ocracy," Barbarians a "fear-ocracy."
- Greeks emphasize substance, Romans form, Barbarians lines of code.
- Greeks do things, Romans plan things, Barbarians break things.

In some ways, this whole distinction seems strangely like a precursor of the Agile vs. process debates to follow nearly a decade later! (We have already visited that topic earlier in this book). Greeks would fit pretty well into the Agile camp, Romans would be working mightily to improve their CMM level, and Barbarians would say "huh?" if you mentioned either one!

At the end of his discussion, [DeGrace 1993] tells a wonderful yet terrible story, one that is not unique to DeGrace but has been told by others in other times and places. Once upon a time, there are two programmers, the story goes, who are given the same identical problem to solve.

The first programmer sees the problem as one to which he can apply orthodox methods. He creates a team to produce the solution. He engages in a great deal of visible activity: meetings, plans, documents, reports, etc.

The other programmer sees the problem as an opportunity to apply his problem-solving skills, and spends his time thinking about a solution with little apparent (visible) outside activity.

The first programmer produces an elaborate solution, with equally elaborate schedules for repair and testing. The other programmer produces a simple solution with no known problems.

How did this all end? The first programmer was rewarded, because (for example) his productivity rate in lines of code produced was higher. But the second was chastised. His solution may have been impeccable, but it was not accompanied by reams of planning or documentation, and it was produced with little visible effort.

In this particular Greek vs. Roman parable, justice was clearly not served. It ended as a case of "punish the virtuous, and reward the sinners," I would assert. I suppose this should not surprise us (although it most certainly does disappoint us) in today's software world where the Roman view is indeed favored by gurus over the Greek one.

It is interesting to speculate on adding a Barbarian programmer to this story. He might, for example, code like crazy but introduce a ton of bugs. Still, he might finish his task sooner than the others who were burdened with doing it correctly, thereby earning initial accolades. And then, as the error reports start rolling in, the Barbarian programmer puts in a lot of overtime to fix them, finds himself on the critical path more and more often, and emerges as the hero who pulls the project's fat from the fire. (Never mind that he built the fire!) In this case, the ultimate sinner reaps the largest rewards!

That is not, of course, a happy ending to this analysis of Greece vs. Rome with a dash of Barbarian thrown in. But it does say some things nicely that are relevant to the remainder of this book!

Reference

DeGrace 1993—*The Olduvai Imperative,* Prentice-Hall 1993; Peter DeGrace and Leslie Hulet Stahl.

10.1

Greece vs. Rome: Two very Different software cultures

10.2

control and corporate culture

Companies seem to have a corporate culture that emphasizes either of the following:

- Management, with the goal being to control in order to improve
- Technologists, with the goal being to experiment in order to improve

Certainly, that is the message of the Greek vs. Roman material we have just seen. The deeply felt view of Peter DeGrace and Leslie Hulet Stahl is clear: there are Greek organizations focusing on the skills and talents of the technologist as the best way to good product, and there are Roman organizations focusing on the orchestration and control offered by management as the best way to good product.

Is The Olduvai Imperative the only place that dichotomous view is identified? As it turns out, the answer is no. Independently, and in a completely different part of the software forest, Stan Rifkin (then of the Software Engineering Institute—SEI) and Charles Cox came to the same conclusion at about the same time [Rifkin 1991].

Whereas DeGrace and Stahl spent their formative years at an aerospace company, Boeing, participating in software projects of various kinds, Rifkin and Cox came to their similar cultural conclusions during an SEI-supported study.

The purpose of the study was to explore what made certain institutions better at generating and using software metrics than others. They visited one or more divisions of the following companies in pursuit of that question: Contel, Digital Equipment, Hewlett-Packard, Hughes Aircraft, IBM, McDonnell Douglas, NASA, NCR, and TRW. What did they learn there?

Interestingly, what they learned is what the lead sentences of this article say. That is, Rifkin and Cox came to the conclusion that some companies are management/control-driven and others technologist/experimentation-driven, and were saying that publicly and independently at about the same time that DeGrace and Stahl were putting the finishing touches on their book!

But Rifkin-Cox added one dimension beyond the experienced and educated opinions of DeGrace and Stahl. In their study, Rifkin and Cox clearly found that the companies which emphasized technology and experimentation were the leaders in the successful use of metrics. And the other companies, the ones that focused on management and control? Their metrics programs were not as successful.

Rifkin cited Digital Equipment and Hewlett-Packard as examples of engineering-focused companies. Most companies, he said, are of the other kind. They are characterized by a hierarchical organizational system with an emphasis on control.

What do the successful metrics companies do?

- They tend to have achieved an SEI process level of 4 or 5 (very good) without ever having passed through level 3. That is, they measure and use feedback to improve their software process without ever having invoked a defined process! (That is, of course, the epitome of technologist/experimentation vs. management/control.)

- They have "decriminalized" errors. People talk openly about what they have done wrong as a means of self-improvement. There is no need to hide failure; management is not allowed to, or simply does not, use it against you.
- Measurement is part of "how we do business." That is, there is no management mandate or policy that causes measurement to happen, but rather a common understanding that it is the only reasonable way to build product.

What we learn from Rifkin and Cox, then, is that not only is there support for the DeGrace/Stahl view of Greek and Roman software cultures, but there is some evidence—fairly narrowly focused, to be sure—that the Greek way (the technologist/experimentation way, in Rifkins/Cox's terms) can be shown to be the better way.

Neither Rifkin/Cox nor DeGrace/Stahl focus heavily on the word "creativity" in their discussions. However, it is not too much of a stretch of the imagination to say that the technologist/experimentation method would provide more opportunities for creativity than the management/control one. Perhaps Michael A. Cusmano best makes the linkage in his book Japan's Software Factories when, while discussing the benefits and problems of a software factory approach, he says [Cusmano 1991]:

"On the one hand, too much emphasis on individual creativity and independence might create problems in controlling development costs, quality, and long-term maintenance. On the other hand, too much structure and control might stifle creativity, innovation, and the ability to change—as well as prompt rebellion from managers, developers, and perhaps customers."

Certainly, our intuition would agree with Cusumano's words, that creativity and control are, to some extent, enemies. And that, in turn, supports the notion that the technologist/experimentation way is linked more closely than the management/control way to software creativity.

References

Rifkin 1991—"Measurement in Practice," CMU/SEI-91-TR-16, also published in *Proceedings of the Sixteenth Annual Software Engineering Workshop*, NASA Goddard Space Flight Center, December 1991; Stan Rifkin and Charles Cox.

Cusmano 1991—*Japan's Software Factories*, Oxford University Press, 1991; Michael A. Cusmano.

10.3
Managing for Innovation

Watts Humphrey is best known for his work on software process at the Software Engineering Institute. His *Managing the Software Process* [Humphreys 1989], and his subsequent writings on that subject, are likely among the most significant works in the field of software engineering, and that work on process has been at the heart of most important discussions of software engineering topics for at least two decades.

Two years before his first process book, Watts wrote another book, *Managing for Innovation* [Humphreys 1987]. This earlier book attracted almost no attention over the years, and yet in many ways it may be just as important as the better-known one. It was republished 8 years later as Managing Technical People [Humphreys 1997], and, to the best of my knowledge, that version 2.0 book remains as little-noticed as the earlier one.

The subtitle of the innovation book is "Leading Technical People" (it is interesting that this subtitle graduated to the title of the version 2.0 *Managing Technical People),* and the idea behind both books is that people matter a lot in building software product. The books are about innovative technical software people and the role of managerial leadership in enabling that innovation. That makes the books a fascinating juxtaposition with Humphrey's later process work, since in that later work he has taken the position that process (not people) is the key to software success.

But back to the earlier Humphrey book and its successor version 2.0: What is the relationship between innovation and creativity? Humphrey—quoting Theodore Levitt—puts it very succinctly:

"Creativity is thinking up new things. Innovation is doing new things."

Humphrey goes on to add, "While innovation requires creativity, it also involves a great deal of hard work."

The book is about both creativity and innovation, although Humphrey is clearly more interested in the latter, because it is in the "doing," the "hard work," that management's role comes to the fore.

What does Humphrey have to say about the intricate relationship between management and the creative technical person?

Regarding control, he reports findings from the literature that "managers who tightly control the way their people work generally get significantly less creativity than those with a looser and more informal style."

Regarding management technical knowledge, he reports other findings that "when the manager's ability was limited, innovation was highest when the group was given the greatest freedom.

"When the manager was highly skilled in administration, personnel, and technology," Humphrey went on, "the results were mixed; sometimes freedom helped, but sometimes it did not." Humphrey concludes with an old saying: "If you don't know what you're doing, then stay out of the way!"

Looking at the matter from a different point of view, Humphrey examines studies of successful and unsuccessful groups. "In the most innovative the managers personally involved themselves in the work and maintained close technical contact with their people. For the least innovative the managers were less active and more remote."

Is there a lesson to be drawn from this material? Perhaps it is "the most innovation comes when (a) the manager has technical skills and involves himself or herself in the group's work, while (b) maximizing the amount of freedom given his technical people."

Is technical creativity the most important factor in successful innovation? According to Humphrey and the studies he cites, the answer is "no." In fact, the "persistent tendency of technical people to confine themselves to the laboratory and not to seek a detailed understanding of the user's needs" is one of the foremost reasons for research and development failure, he says.

What is the alternative to the laboratory-confined technologist? "Successful product development depends more on market astuteness than on technical competence," he says, quoting a University of Pennsylvania study. The most innovation, in fact (according to another study), comes "when the users were technically competent." That is, users, understanding the application problem to be solved, are more likely to produce innovation than computer technologists, who understand only the computing problem to be solved. Humphrey goes on to cite another study that found "75% of all innovations ... came from market sources, but the highest percentage of technically driven innovations given by any single study was only 34%." That is, customer need, rather than technological progress, determines whether an innovation is likely to be successful or not. (Sounds familiar, doesn't it? It's a new variation on the old theme, "necessity is the mother of invention.")

An interesting aside in the book deals with the issue of "how age affects creativity." Although there is a common belief that creativity and innovation peak at a fairly early age (it has been cited as being anywhere from 21 to 29), Humphrey says there is "an increasing body of evidence that points the other way." In one study, the researchers found that "performance peaked at an early age but declined very slightly thereafter." "The precise point at which this peak occurred depended on the technical field; it was earlier in the more abstract fields of mathematics and theoretical physics and later in such pragmatic specialties as biology and geology. The initial peak fell in the mid-30s, but they also found a late peak in the mid- to late-50s. This double peak phenomenon occurred in all the groups of engineers and scientists ... studied, and the dip between these two peaks was not very significant."

Humphrey summarizes with an encouraging (at least, for older readers!) thought: "For creative people, the late 30s and early 40s is a highly stressful period. Once they pass this hurdle, however, many engineers and scientists will continue their creative work for many years ... many of Thomas Edison's 1100 inventions were produced late in his 84-year life."

From the point of view of "managing for innovation," then, the good leader must know that any of his people, of any age, may contribute creativity and innovation.

There is one strange and somewhat jarring part of Humphrey's Innovation book. Before he joined the SEI, Humphrey spent a number of years with IBM. Many of Humphrey's anecdotes, and much of the focus of his acknowledgement section of (especially the first) the book, is about his IBM heritage. In today's era when IBM's past troubles are well known, an era in which every computing columnist feels free to pontificate on "what went wrong with IBM," it is a little strange to read a book with statements like "IBM is a leading example of corporate technological success. It has demonstrated a remarkable ability both to make the right decisions and to make its decisions right." It is important to get past this early impression of the first of these books (Humphrey wisely downplayed his laudatory view of IBM in version 2.0), however, because what Watts Humphrey has to say here about innovation—and creativity—and managing technical people—is well worth reading.

References

Humphrey 1997—*Managing Technical People*, Addison-Wesley 1997; Watts S. Humphrey.

Humphrey 1989—*Managing the Software Process*, Addison-Wesley 1989; Watts S. Humphrey.

Humphrey 1987—*Managing for Innovation*, Prentice-Hall 1987; Watts S. Humphrey.

10.4
creativity and strategic information systems

There is a great deal of controversy surrounding the topic of Strategic Information Systems (SIS). Those who believe in the importance of those systems, and there are many of them, refer to them by a sort of pseudonym, "Competitive Advantage Systems," the implication being that a successful strategic system will bring about competitive advantage for the enterprise that implements it. And what more powerful benefit could information technology bring to an enterprise than to provide it with an advantage over its competitors?

But there are detractors to the notion of SIS, as well. Perhaps the most visible of those detractors was Nicholas Carr, who created a monumental stir in the information technology field, not to mention the business field in general, with his infamous "IT Doesn't Matter" essay [Carr 2003]. The essence of what Carr really had to say, buried in the essay and not visible in the provocative title, was that strategic information systems were becoming less and less likely. It wasn't that IT in general didn't matter, as the unwashed masses of those who rushed to refute the article presumed based on that title, but SIS in particular.

Why did Carr pick on SIS? Because, if you look at the litany of successful SIS's that occur in almost every IT 101 textbook these days, most of them are several decades old. There were successful

SIS's, Carr (and anyone who looks at the field objectively) would have to admit, but there have been awfully few of them lately. That litany includes such golden oldies as airline reservation systems (American Airlines did the pioneering one over four decades ago), and warehouse/distribution systems (Wal-Mart has been using its now for several decades). Every single enterprise would dearly love to have an SIS, these naysayers are saying, but the likelihood of obtaining one today is fairly small. That's why "IT Doesn't Matter" – it's not that IT doesn't help the enterprise, it's just that it rarely helps the enterprise in strategic/competitive ways.

(It's interesting to draw an analogy between Carr's "IT Doesn't Matter" and Fred Brooks' famous "No Silver Bullet." Brooks took the position in his essay that the truly significant silver bullets (breakthrough advances) in software engineering had already happened in the distant past, and that managers should not expect a fresh one to come along and revolutionize their ability to build software systems. And Carr is saying quite the same thing about SIS/competitive advantage systems).

But, given the importance of SIS to the enterprise, that absence of recent successes doesn't mean that the enterprise can or should give up on finding them. There's a reality to be considered here: efforts to obtain competitive advantage through information technology are more than likely to fail. But that should never prevent an enterprise from trying to succeed at it.

Given that fact, how should an enterprise go about trying to identify and build an SIS? Here we lean for help on authors who have had a lot to say on that topic over the years. In two academic papers [Galletta, Sampler, and Teng 1992] and [Galletta and Sampler 1993], for example, we find a fascinating collection of ideas about how to generate the ideas that lie behind a successful SIS. And the essence of that collection of ideas, these authors point out, is creativity. To come up with a truly advantageous competitive system, they say, requires the ultimate in creative thinking.

However—and there is irony here—Galletta and his colleagues note that few early authors who studied SIS seemed to realize that. There is almost nothing in the SIS literature, they say after considerable literature review, that links SIS to creativity. Perhaps the absence of a consideration of creativity's role is why the early expectations for the ubiquitous generations of SISs have been so far afield. After all, if it doesn't take creativity to identify and implement an SIS, then any enterprise should be able to do them all the time! But if it does, then no wonder we have had so few of them.

These papers then tend to focus on how to stimulate the kind of creative thinking that can possibly result in successful SISs.

Their review of the SIS literature led them to identify several frameworks used by both practitioners and academics to search for SIS ideas. They include:

1. Analyzing a firm's competitive forces. Such forces can include (a) creating barriers to entry of competitors, (b) increasing the cost of customers switching away, (c) building power in relationships with suppliers, (d) achieving dramatic cost reductions, and (e) generating new products or services.
2. Focusing on a firm's value chain, from receipt of raw materials to delivery of the product or service.
3. Focusing on the customer resource life cycle, identifying the processes through which customers interact with the enterprise.
4. Employing strategic option generation, asking such questions as (a) what is our strategic target, (b) what strategic thrust can we use against that target, (c) what strategic mode can be used (offense, defense), (d) what direction should that thrust take, and (e) what information system skills can we use.

But Galletta and his colleagues also note, wryly, that there is some disagreement about whether any of these approaches can work. They point out that one author has taken the position that "strategic systems come through a long-term adaptive process, rather than through a major breakthrough that brings quick rewards ... we cannot set out to develop an SIS."

In spite of that, however, these authors proceed on the assumption that it is indeed possible to position one's enterprise for the creation of SIS, and that further efforts to induce creativity are bound to help toward that end. They then identify three sociological levels within which that creativity stimulation can occur, and discuss ways of doing so:

1. Creative people. Galletta and his colleagues point out that researchers have spent considerable effort in finding ways to identify creative individuals. Creative people may simply have (a) innate creativity (although it is nontrivial to identify who those people really are!); creative people probably will have considerable (b) factual expertise (although of course this is a necessary but by no means sufficient trait), and creative people must be (c) motivated (if they are to make something out of whatever it is they bring to the table) (once again, this is a necessary but by no means sufficient trait).

2. Creative groups. There has been a great deal of work in the research community on how to stimulate creative thinking in groups. Some of that thinking will be reflected later in this book. For the purposes of this discussion, we will simply mention in passing that such approaches include "boundary examination" (by means of which assumptions are questioned, "wishful thinking" (where "impossible" solutions are allowed to play out), "goal orientation" (where the logical mind is turned loose on the problem and its needs/obstacles/constraints), "brainstorming" and "reverse

brainstorming" (where various solutions are proposed and evaluated), "nonlogical stimuli" (where various "way out" approaches are encouraged), and "nominal group technique" (where individuals propose and the group decides).

3. Creative organizations. Perhaps the most thorough treatment in the work of Galletta and his colleagues in the role of creativity in SIS is devoted to this topic. They suggest quite a large number of approaches:

   a. Encourage the use of the SIS frameworks mentioned above.
   b. Use creative people (this begs the question discussed earlier about how to identify them)
   c. Use people with some depth (those who know the problem area well)
   d. Use people with some breadth (those good at connecting seemingly unrelated facts)
   e. Use cognitive aids (use tools, notes, pictures, diagrams, analogies)
   f. Promote intrinsic motivation (and avoid extrinsic rewards like bonuses and overly ambitious deadlines which are generally thought to negatively impact creativity)
   g. Provide group diversity (utilize a variety of expertise and experience levels)
   h. Use creativity techniques (these will be discussed later in this book)
   i. Support the group (provide realistic deadlines, freedom of discussion, commitment to the goal, etc.)
   j. Remove organizational barriers (explicitly support cross-functional perspectives)
   k. Encourage risk-taking (allow failure to be an option)

By attacking the SIS problem on all three of these sociological levels, these authors are saying, the enterprise maximizes its chances of coming up with a truly significant SIS.

One of the problems with SISs is that they must provide sustainable advantage, of course. Once a successful SIS has become public knowledge, it is simply a historic fact that every other enterprise rushes to put an analogous one on the air in their enterprise via their IT shop. American Airline's early advantage of its reservation system vanished in the next decade as every other airline built its own. Wal-Mart may still have a highly sophisticated distribution/inventory system, but there is not a retail enterprise in the big business category that doesn't have its own version as well.

So there are two categories/phases to SIS development – the early winners, those who conceive of the truly original idea and put it on the air successfully, and the copycats, those who recognize a good thing when they see it and rush to play catch up. It is interesting to speculate on what distinguishes the early winners from the copycats. It is easy to assume that creativity plays a huge role in the former, and is considerably less important to the latter. If that is true, then the creativity approaches outlined above can be significantly important to early winners, and are perhaps less so to copycats. (Note that, given the importance of the SIS to the enterprise, one should not cast aspersions on those who play the copycat role. Today's early winner may very well play tomorrow's copycat to a competitor's own unique idea).

references

Brooks 1995—"No Silver Bullet," originally published in 1986 in the *Proceedings of the IFIP Tenth World Computing Conference;* later became the cover article for an issue of *Communications of the ACM;* subsequently published in *The Mythical Man-Month* (anniversary edition), Addison-Wesley 1995; Frederick P. Brooks, Jr.

Carr 2003—"IT Doesn't Matter," *Harvard Business Review,* May 2003; Nicholas G. Carr.

Galletta, Sampler, and Teng 1992—"Strategies for Integrating Creativity Principles into the System Development Process," *Proceedings of the 25th Annual Hawaii International Conference on Systems Sciences,* January 1992; D.F. Galletta, J.L. Sampler, and J.T.C. Teng.

Galletta and Sampler 1993—"Creativity: The Missing Ingredient in Identifying Strategic Informaton Systems," working paper WP-703RR, University of Pittsburgh, Katz Graduate School of Business, September 1993; D.F. Galletta and J.L. Sampler.

10.5
creativity vs. the law

Looming over the topic of "Making Software Creativity Happen" is a Sword of Damocles. That Sword, oddly enough, is the law. Like it or not, the law has a great deal to do with how creativity manifests itself.

What law are we talking about here? The law that is designed to protect intellectual property: patent law, copyright law, trade secret law, even "work for hire" law.

That law is subject to some of the most fascinating controversies in the world of software today. Do these intellectual property laws stimulate creativity? Or do they inhibit it?

It is the purpose of this section to explore that issue, but certainly not to resolve it (in fact, it is beyond the power of the author of this book, and in fact the legal system in general, to resolve this particular dispute! The dispute will rage on in the legal and software worlds long after this book has gone out of print and vanished from your shelves and ours).

Here's the gist of the dispute:

In one corner, wearing the Blue trunks of Emphasizing Social Freedom for the Individual, is the Belief that intellectual property law inhibits creativity because it builds walls around new ideas and restricts the ability of innovators to share information about them.

In the other corner, wearing the Red trunks of Emphasizing Profit and Business Freedom for the Individual and/or Corporation, is the Belief that intellectual property law enhances creativity because it protects the innovator from copycats and others bent on stealing ideas and profits.

The key issue distinguishing these two viewpoints is Motivation. Are innovators motivated to do what they do because they love being part of a process of intellectual freedom, standing on the sturdy shoulders of innovators who have gone before them? Or are innovators motivated because they are striving for the achievement of profits, a motivation so strong that they would not choose to do what they do without it? Although some people try to make it so, there's really no right and wrong about this issue. There are just different viewpoints.

We software folk tend to think that this dispute is a product of our time, one spawned by the quick rise and spread of software as a discipline, as a product, and as a profit-maker. But that's not at all the case.

The dispute is as old as innovation. In [Wagner 2004], for example, we see that the same dispute was alive and well 120 years ago. Thomas Edison, still today one of the largest patent holders in the U.S., had filed 1093 patents on his various discoveries. Opponents ranged from questioning the validity of the things he patented, to deriding the U.S. Patent Office as "under-quali-fied" to judge Edison's work. That new-fangled thing called the "light bulb," for example, raised what the article calls a "swirl of controversy." Was is really an original discovery, or was Edison relying on the work of others to the extent that his contribution was minimal? Was it significant enough that issuing a patent for it really mattered? Did the Patent Office know enough to pass judgment on these issues?

Patent law, of course, is not the only source of controversy. The arguments for the relevance of copyright and trade secret laws are at least conceptually similar. The Open Source movement (and related currents), which would tend to come down on the side of wearing the Blue trunks of Social Freedom, has invented legal frameworks it calls "Creative Commons" and "CopyLeft" that in many ways are the opposite of Copyright because they focus on the freedom to distribute software products, rather than the restrictions to be placed on such distribution. And, of course, when source code is "Open," all possibilities of trade secret protection fly out the window.

There are, in fact, a history and some identifiable trends to these issues of intellectual property protection. Roland Coles, an attorney, sees the era for trade secret use to be pre-1975; for copyright, 1975–1990; and for patents, 1990–the present [Cole 2005]. That explains why so much of our attention more recently has been focused on patents, pro and con.

There is an interesting middle ground to this whole discussion. Steve McConnell, in discussions about the revision to this book, saw the dispute as something of a tempest in a teapot. Software and its products change so quickly, he believes, that it is nearly impossible to be sure that some particular approach is new/innovative/protect-able and not a revision to something that has been around a long time. ("There are so many different ways to do the same thing," he says, "that the current protection approaches aren't really useful"). An interesting case in point, according to [Wagner 2004], was a suit filed by a company named Eolas Technologies against Microsoft. The suit claimed that Eolas had patented some ways of doing Web page plug-ins that Microsoft had appropriated for its own products, specifically Internet Explorer. But the Patent Office disagreed, noting that the work that Eolas had patented was based on pre-existing work, having been originated by Tim Berners-Lee a decade or so before. (Note also that the patent office may have made a mistake in accepting that original patent, but its litigation processes allowed it to correct that mistake when it really mattered).

How serious is this dispute? Critics of the current legal system envision "the death of software innovation." Others see just the opposite, plenty of innovation happening, pointing to huge new industries built around new software products (linked to the Internet, for example) that didn't exist until fairly recently.

It's a case of "you pays your money and you makes your choice." Is it really "creativity vs. the law," as our section title above states (mostly to provoke your curiosity and get you to read this section!)? Or is it "creativity plus the law," where the law really stimulates innovation while protecting it? It's your call. And however you call it, no one is going to be able to prove you wrong!

Reference

Cole 2005—Cited in "Open Source Myths and Realities Presented," *The Software Practitioner*, May 2005.

Wagner 2004—"For Innovation's Sake," InternetNews.com, November 9, 2004; Jim Wagner .

chapter 11
creativity in software technology

chapter contents

introduction to chapter 11

"Software applications are limited mainly by human imagination. Since human creativity is so vast in potential and computer hardware is still evolving by leaps and bounds, it would be foolish to think of software technology as being mature."

—*Michael A. Cusmano*
The Business of Software, Free Press 2004

This is where the material by Dan Couger that we mentioned in the Introduction to Part II really comes into its own. Here, in the work of a man who successfully devoted his professional career to the intersection of creativity and the development of information systems, we find some exceedingly valuable material. His case study, for example, is enough to breathe excitement into anyone contemplating advocating creativity-building approaches in a software development organization. The benefits of creativity approaches that he cites are hard to ignore!

creative Approaches to Information systems Implementation

Most computing/software professionals would agree that creativity is an important part of being able to build software systems. There might be some discussion about precisely where in the software process this creativity is needed—we have already seen several discussions of that earlier in this book—but there would be little or no disagreement about whether it is needed.

It may seem odd, then, that the subject of creativity is almost totally absent from the literature of the computing field. The late Prof. Daniel Couger was one of the few to explore creativity's role in his specific interest area, information systems. He studied the creativity literature and learned this:

- More than 4000 articles on creativity have been published in the literature (as of his literature search a decade or so ago)
- Only 5 of those articles on creativity had appeared in the 35-year history of the information systems literature

Prof. Couger called this "enigmatic." It is almost as if the computing/software profession has been so inwardly-focused on the technical challenge of building successful software systems, that it has spent little energy in looking outside its own narrow boundaries.

It became something of a life challenge to Prof. Couger to try to overcome this lack. He wrote frequently and well on the role of creativity in information systems, and his contributions to that otherwise sparse literature are quite profound. Perhaps his strongest such contribution is his book Creativity and Innovation in Information Systems Organizations [Couger 1996] which, although more than a decade old at this point, is astonishingly comprehensive and up to date. In this section of this book, I will rely on his work relating creativity to the software life cycle to focus in particular on ways of making software people more creative [Couger 1990].

Academics normally begin any discussion of a relatively new topic to their field with appropriate definitions, and Prof. Couger was no exception. He struggled a bit, however, to define the key word creativity, discovering more than 100 (varying) definitions in the literature! In the end, he relied heavily on what he called "the most comprehensive definition," found in [Newell and Shaw 1962], who said that creativity in a solution must satisfy one or more of the following conditions:

- The product of the thinking has novelty or value (either for the thinker or for his/her culture)
- The thinking is unconventional, in the sense that it requires modification or even rejection of previously accepted ideas
- The thinking requires high motivation and persistence, taking place over a considerable time span (continuously or intermittently) or at high intensity
- The problem as initially posed was vague and ill-defined, so that part of the task was to formulate the problem itself

Couger summarized all of that by saying that his work in the creativity area chose to characterize his subject matter by its uniqueness and utility.

Now, about the software life cycle as Couger saw it. He saw a need, at the outset, to set aside time for "creativity evaluation" in the overall life cycle—points at which the system builders would pause to consider the possibility of more creative approaches than those they had initially chosen. He saw those points following each of what he saw as the up-front life cycle phases: requirements definition, logical design, physical design, program design, and programming. He saw those strategic pauses consuming a minimum amount of overall project resources—less than half of one percent, he said, based on his educated estimates for typical projects and the activities necessary to consider creativity.

However, he noted "unfortunately, we cannot acquire actual data on the use of creativity techniques in IS development" ... because "the author has not found any organization using them." (Later in this book, we will explore Prof. Couger's case study in which he sought to overcome this lack, injecting creativity approaches into an actual practitioner organization in real time, and evaluating the results!)

Although he broke the use of creativity approaches down into the various life cycle phases in his work, there was one creativity technique that kept recurring in all the life cycle phases: Prof. Couger called it the "5Ws and the H." By that, he meant asking the questions Who, What, Where, When, Why, and How in order to ensure that the full range of options to a problem and its solution are being explored. (Journalism students will recognize this as the set of questions to be asked to determine if their story-in-the-making is complete).

He applied 5Ws in the requirements phase of an IS project by suggesting this set of questions:

• Who are the customers for this solution, and who else might be interested?

- What is the overall significance of the problem to be solved; what competitive advantage might we derive from this solution?
- When would be the optimum time to install this system, and what impact would any delays have?
- Where in the organization could this solution be employed?
- Why would we want to provide this service to our users/customers?
- How might this application be used for other purposes?

But 5Ws is not the only creativity approach that Couger suggests. In the logical design phase, for example, he suggests one borrowed from the famous mathematical problem-solver Polya, in [Polya 1971], called "Checklist," in which the problem solver works through a checklist of stimulating questions, such as "Have I encountered this problem before? In the same or different forms? Is there a related problem that could prove helpful? Is there some piece of theory that might be useful?"

For physical design, Couger suggests an approach in which a set of verbs is established to help manipulate the problem in order to see it from multiple points of view. This "manipulative verb" approach of [Koberg and Bagnall 1981] proposes 32 such verbs, including these:

- Multiply—can we generalize some parts of the system to make it apply more broadly?
- Divide—can we divide users into sets of similar interests, such that a small collection of user interfaces can satisfy a very diverse set of users?
- Eliminate—can we avoid some of the special tailoring that at first appears to be necessary?

(The other verbs are: subdue, invert, separate, transpose, unify, distort, rotate, flatten, squeeze, complement, submerge, freeze, soften, fluff-up, bypass, add, subtract, lighten, repeat, thicken, stretch, extrude, repel, protect, segregate, integrate, symbolize, abstract, and dissect.)

Program design brings rise to yet another creativity approach, which Couger calls "attribute listing," citing the work of [Crawford 1954]. Here, the system developer lists the attributes of the problem to be solved, withholding any evaluation of them but rather tinkering with the attributes to see if their modification can lead to a better solution to the problem.

It is interesting that Couger concluded this particular aspect of his work by noting the possibility that creativity can be universal. He quotes Carl Rogers as saying "It is my belief, based on my experience, that creativity exists in every individual and awaits only the proper conditions to be released and expressed." It is not entirely clear why Couger included this quote at the end of this work rather than at its beginning, up next to that definition of creativity, but perhaps his reason was simply to say that no matter where we are in the software lifecycle, the people responsible for that phase can quite likely employ creative techniques when the need arises. That is, systems analysts can be creative; designers can be creative; programmers can be creative. It is not a matter of IF, but rather HOW, that creativity can be freed and employed.

References

Couger 1990—"Ensuring Creative Approaches to Information Systems Design," *Managerial and Decision Economics II*, pp. 281–295, 1990; J. Daniel Couger.

Couger 1996—*Creativity and Innovation in Information Systems Organizations*, Boyd & Fraser Publishing Co. 1996; J. Daniel Couger.

Crawford 1954—*The Techniques of Creative Thinking*, Prentice-Hall 1954; R.P. Crawford.

Koberg and Bagnall 1981—*The Universal Traveler: A Soft-Systems Guide to Creativity, Problem-Solving, and the Process of Design* (Revised edition), Crisp Publications 1991; Don Koberg and Jim Bagnall.

Newell and Shaw 1992—"The Process of Creative Thinking," in *Contemporary Approaches to Creative Thinking*, edited by H.E. Gruber, et al., Atherton Press 1992; A. Newell, J.C. Shaw, and H.A. Simon.

Polya 1971—*How to Solve It*, Princeton University Press 1971; G. Polya.

creativity and software Design: The Missing Link

There is tension and conflict growing between two polar software points of view. The first point of view is that the construction of software is best done using formal, disciplined processes. The second point of view is that software should be constructed using creative, freeform processes.

This conflict is seen in presentations at software conferences and papers in the software literature, as well as in the approaches used in software-producing organizations. At this writing, the dominant voice in the software literature is one that advocates formalism. Formal methods are seen as necessary for the construction of large-scale software, and appropriate to software of any scale. We see papers on formal approaches saying such things as "... Software engineering leaders are beginning to call for more systematic approaches: more mathematics, science, and engineering are needed" [CSTB 1990]. Creative approaches, from this formal point of view, are seen as counterproductive—sometimes effective, but more often unpredictable.

However, the counter view is also beginning to appear in this same literature. We find a growing questioning of formal approaches. For example, in [Denning 1991] we find, "There is nothing wrong with formality. It has demonstrated remarkable technological power. I am saying it limits what we can accomplish. We need to go beyond formality ...."

Nowhere is this conflict more focused than in the topic of software design. The formal, disciplined approach to design is generally seen as:

1. Follow a life-cycle methodology, a series of steps calling for activities performed in a particular order, with specified deliverables produced at the end of each step. The steps involving design are called such things as preliminary, or logical, design, and detailed, or physical design.

2. During design itself, attack large problems by decomposing them in hierarchic fashion into smaller, more manageable problems. Within those smaller problems, employ high cohesion (focus each solution on a cohesive set of problems) and loose coupling (make each solution stand as much on its own as possible).

3. When the design is complete, represent the design in some formal, often graphical, language. Candidate languages over the years have included UML, dataflow diagrams, structure charts, and program design language (pseudo-code).

Those who favor more creative approaches say that there, in design, is where the problems of the formal approach are most easily seen. Although the steps of a methodology, and the use of a representation, are an important part of the design process, these people say, there is clearly something missing. Nothing in the methodological steps and the representational techniques is actually a design activity. Instead, they represent preparation for design and completion of design. Where, this point of view says, does design really take place?

With that question in mind, a couple of decades ago several software researchers began exploring ways of discovering the actual design process. This search was characterized by some as the pursuit of a "missing link"—the link between methodology and representation—that represents the true act of design.

The findings of that research, which at first thought might be seen as badly dated by now, are still kept fresh and useful by two factors:

1. No other researchers have revisited this approach to studying design in the interim.
2. The nature of design itself has not changed in the intervening years.

In Pursuit of the Missing Link

In pursuit of this missing link, these researchers looked to the best of practice. After all, successful software designs have been produced for over 50 years. Even though the theory of design, these people say, has a missing link, the practice of design does not. Peter J. Denning [Denning 1991] says, "The time has come to pay more attention to the murky, imprecise, unformalizable domains of everyday practice, which is, after all, where design is judged."

That is precisely what these researchers did.

Two approaches were taken to examining design through its practice. In one, top design practitioners were interviewed. In the other, actual design sessions were videotaped, and the process used by these designers was abstracted into a theoretical description of the process. The two approaches, though rather different, have produced some interesting resonance in their resulting findings, as we will see in what follows.

In the interviewing approach, again, two rather different approaches were used. Veteran software specialist John Nestor, at the time working at the Software Engineering Institute, identified what he believed to be the top ten software designers (based on his experiences in working with them) and set out to interview them, presenting the results in an internal SEI briefing. Journalist Susan

Lammers, on the other hand, interviewed a collection of successful microcomputer software entrepreneurs, and published the result in a book [Lammers 1986]. We will present a quick summary of Nestor's findings here; the Lammers' findings, on the other hand, will be presented scattered through the remainder of this section.

What did Nestor learn from his top designers? He asked several questions, including "What is design?" and "What makes great designers?" He got answers like the following:

- Great designers have a large set of standard patterns.
- Great designers have lived through failing projects and have learned from those failures.
- Great designers have absolute mastery of their tools.
- Great designers have a strong predilection for simplicity.
- Great designers are able to anticipate more kinds of possible change.
- Great designers are able to put themselves in the user's shoes.
- Great designers have no fear of complexity.

There are flaws, of course, in research conducted as subjectively as this. The choice of designers and the choice of conclusions was entirely dependent on one person's view of design. Still, there are some fascinating themes to Nestor's findings. Top designers apparently must have had some experience, including experience at failure, and must have been able to abstract from those experiences a collection of models for use in future design efforts. (I like to think of these top designers as carrying a pack on their back full of analogies into which they can reach to find a starting point for a new design. The more full their analogy pack, the better they are at design.) Top designers are also able to tackle extremely complex problems and try to find simple solutions. There is no doubt that; in spite of the subjectivity of the approach, Nestor's findings are important.

The videotaping Approach

The videotaping approach, the second approach to researching the nature of design through an examination of practice, escapes the dilemma of subjectivity. The process for this research was as follows:

Individuals or groups of designers are videotaped while designing a solution to an assigned problem.

During individual design sessions, designers are quietly urged to "think aloud" so that the thought processes employed can be captured.

Videotape sessions, although inevitably intrusive, are designed to interfere with the design process as little as possible.

Results of several video sessions with several design groups are reviewed to identify common themes and activities.

A theoretical description resulting from the above reviews is constructed.

The theoretical description is tested by applying it to further videotaped sessions to see if it matches what is happening.

The theoretical description is exposed to the design session participants to see if they agree that it describes the process they used.

This series of steps is called "protocol analysis," and is used in many kinds of observational research. The researchers who used it in pursuing the question of software design include Elliot Soloway, then at Yale University (and more recently of the University of Michigan), and Bill Curtis, then at the Microelectronics and Computing Consortium (MCC) (and more recently of the Software Engineering Institute, and then Borland). The findings of this research were published in the late 1980s [Curtis 1987, Guinon 1987, Adelson 1984, Adelson 1985, Soloway 1987].

What, in fact, did these investigations into the nature of design discover? There were two levels of findings:

In the first, the researchers found that design involves

1. Understanding a problem
2. Decomposing the problem into goals and objects
3. Selecting and composing plans to solve the problem
4. Implementing the plans
5. Reflecting on the design product and process

At this level, the findings were interesting but not terribly illuminating. Some, in fact, have criticized these findings on the grounds that they describe the general process of problem-solving, rather than the specific process of design. That criticism seems warranted—looked at objectively, these steps are really another wording for the concept of the software life cycle, a notion well defined and understood long before this research was begun. If this level of findings had been all that these researchers produced, their findings would have died a quiet death.

striking paydirt

But it was at the next level down that the researchers struck pay dirt. They explored more deeply the issue of "selecting and composing plans," to see what activities that task implied. And there they found what many now believe to be the essence of creative design.

People composing design plans, they found, performed these steps:

1. Build a mental model of a proposed solution to the problem.
2. Mentally execute the model to see if it does indeed solve the problem. Often this mental execution (also called a "simulation") takes the form of providing sample input to the model to see if it produces correct sample output.
3. If the sample output is incorrect (as will often be the case in the early stages of design), the model is expanded to correct its deficiencies, then executed again.

339

4. When the sample output finally becomes correct, another sample input is selected, and steps two and three are repeated.

5. When sufficient sample inputs have passed the test in step four, the model is assumed to be a suitable design model and representation of the design begins.

It is important to note two things about this process. The first is that the process is entirely cognitive—that is, all of the steps are conducted inside the mind, at mind speeds. This is important because the design activity must occur extremely quickly in order to succeed. Use of pencil and paper, or even computerized support, at this stage would significantly slow down and thus degrade the design process.

The second thing to note is that the process is iterative. That is, a designer repeats certain steps in the process in a trial-and-error fashion until a potentially successful design is achieved. Researchers call such a trial-and-error process a "heuristic" method.

What is especially significant about both of these things is that they are, to some extent, at odds with the more formal, methodological approaches. Since the steps of the design process occur inside the mind, it would be difficult—and counterproductive—to subject them to any formal, disciplined process. Since they are heuristic, they are almost exactly the opposite of formal approaches (formalists often mention heuristic approaches as the "erroneous" opposite of their preferred formal methods). Thus here, in this cognitive essence of design, we have found one point at which formal approaches simply are not useful.

This finding did not surprise those who have been concerned about formal approaches all along. For example, H. Dieter Rombach has said [Rombach 1990], "While formalization ... is a solution for more mechanical processes ... it is not feasible for design processes." Here, we can see why.

Let us return for a moment to the other research approach to studying design, that of conducting interviews. Recall that the results of one set of interviews was recorded in a book [Lammers 1986]. It is interesting to note some quotations from that book:

> "The first step in programming is imagining. Just making it crystal clear in my mind what is going to happen. In this initial stage, I use pencil and paper. I just doodle ... because the real picture is in my mind." (This from Charles Simonyi, designer of the Multiplan spreadsheet product.)

> "At some point, the [design] gets explosive and I have everything inside my brain at one time ... All sorts of things go on in my brain that I can't put on paper because I'm always changing them." (Gary Kildall, designer of the CP/M operating system.)

> "You have to simulate in your mind how the program's going to work ... When you're creating something ... and you have that model in your mind, it's a lonely thing." (Bill Gates, founder and CEO of Microsoft.)

> "You constantly try to hold the state of the entire system you're working on in your head. If you lose the mental image, it takes a long time to get it back into that state." (John Page, designer of PFS:File.)

The resonance between these interview findings and the findings of the videotaped protocol analysis process are almost amazing! The interview subjects put into lifelike words the more analytic findings of the researchers. It is particularly interesting to note that the interview subjects used words like "model" and "simulation," and talked about the "loneliness" of the creative designer

341

who, during the act of design, must not "lose that mental image." Clearly, these words describe a creative, not formal or disciplined, process.

empirical research

Research of this kind based on an examination of practice is generally known as "empirical." Many of the findings of these empirical studies were originally presented at a series of conferences devoted to empirical research, known as the "Empirical Studies of Programmers" conferences. (The unfortunately chosen acronym, some in the formal methods community have noted, is "ESP"!) More recently, such empirical findings are published in a journal devoted to the subject, Springer's Empirical Software Engineering. It is important to note that the findings of this empirical research have moved well beyond this discovery of heuristic approaches.

For example, ESP researchers have stepped back from the details of the cognitive design process to examine its broader elements. They have found that design involves several components:

- Those oriented toward the problem to be solved
- Those oriented toward the nature and notion of design itself
- Those oriented toward the involvement of the human designer
- Those oriented toward the use of computer tools to support the designer

In this list of the components of design, some ESP researchers are becoming more and more convinced that the difficult problems of design are not those involved in the design process itself, but those involved in designing a solution within the context of a particular application problem. For example, the designer must know not only some basic facts about the application domain (problem-oriented) but also some specialized facts about design approaches unique to that domain (design-oriented). (For example, designers of report programs must understand how to produce columns of figures totals lines, with multiple levels of totals of totals; and designers of scientific programs must understand how to perform iterative mathematical solutions on a finite-precision computer.)

The Designer as Human Being

However, perhaps the most fascinating components in the design process are the contributions and limitations of the designer as human being.

Recall that the inner nucleus of the design process is a cognitive, heuristic activity. What advantages and disadvantages does the human mind bring to this activity?

To begin with, psychologists have discovered that the human mind consists of two different portions, "short-term memory" and "long-term memory." (The analogy between these components and a computer's main memory and external memory is interesting.) Short-term memory is exceedingly fast but has limited capacity; long-term memory is comparatively slow but appears to have unlimited capacity. The capacity limitation of short-term memory is, in fact, extremely severe; researchers from the 1950s (and since) have found that this portion of the mind can hold only about five to nine distinctions at any one time. (Psychological researchers have referred to this as the "magic number 7 plus or minus 2.")

Because cognitive design must happen at lightning speed, it must happen in short-term memory; but this magic number 7 constraint is a severe limitation on the designer. Fortunately, according to psychologists, the mind has developed a workaround solution for that limitation. It performs an act called "chunking," in which several distinctions are "chunked" together into one, and the mind can then hold seven of these things. (For example, when humans identify another person, they do not remember the looks of that person through a set of lower-level facts like "lip shape" and "eye color" and "facial hair," but rather they form and remember a gestalt or chunk, perhaps one called "face.") Thus, designers are able to overcome part of the natural human limitations on short-term memory by chunking. However, in spite of that, the constraints of memory are a serious problem to the designer. For example, recall the "loneliness" of the designer who cannot be interrupted for fear of losing the state of a design. Here we see the volatility and low capacity of short-term memory at work: A short-term memory interrupted is a short-term memory unable to reconstruct its contents, and the problem is made all the worse because that short-term memory was necessarily full of complicated chunks of information rather than a large number of simple facts.

There are two other important findings of these empirical researchers regarding design. The first has to do with the beginning of design, and the second with its ending.

Beginning of Design

One of the key findings of the ESP researchers is that designers begin a design, whenever possible, with the reuse of an existing design. (Recall the "analogy pack" on the designer's back, where he or she reaches for a past design used in a similar problem.)

That first model used in the heuristic process of cognitive design may very well be a reused model rather than one created by the designer in response to this particular problem. Visser discovered that, for problems encountered before, designers employ an "example program" as their starting point, and then observed, "Designers rarely start from scratch" [Visser 1987]. This was echoed in one of the interview findings from [Lammers 1986], where veteran mainframe and microcomputer software designer Butler Lampson is quoted as saying, "Most of the time, a new program is a refinement, extension, generalization, or improvement of an existing program. It's really unusual to do something that's completely new...."

There is another interesting empirical finding about design. Although textbooks and the literature frequently refer to design as a top-down process, design is in fact rarely top-down. Bill Curtis has said, "The unperturbed design process is opportunistic"—that is, rather than proceed in an orderly process, good designers follow an erratic pattern dictated by their minds, pursuing opportunities rather than an orderly progression. Some say that design is really "hard-part first" design—that is, the designer seeks out sub-problems that appear to be difficult to solve, and solves them before any easier problems, in order to be sure that the complexity of an unknown solution does not come along to destroy the predictability of earlier, known solutions. It is interesting to note that David Parnas, a noted computer scientist, has recommended "faking" a top-down process—that is, even though design does not take place top-down, the recording and representation of that design should be top-down, because only in that way can observers or reviewers understand the design product.

Again, this notion of "opportunistic" or "hard-part-first" design is echoed by the interviews in [Lammers 1986]. We find these quotations:

"You start at the point where you think it's too hard to solve, and then you break it down into smaller pieces," says Gary Kildall, designer of CP/M.

"Once I've dealt with the hard parts in isolation—maybe by writing a little program to prove out some theory—I can go about structuring the program," says John Page, designer of PFS:File.

ending of Design

If the beginnings of design, involving reuse of existing designs and an opportunistic, hard-part first approach, were a surprise when compared to textbook views of design, what have ESP researchers learned about the ending of design? There are some surprises here as well.

The textbooks tell us that design proceeds down to the level at which a competent programmer can begin writing code. But what does that really mean? Top designers seem to have a well-defined criteria for ending design—they quit when what remains to be designed is analogous to something they've already done before, and done it so many times that they can code it with no further creative thought. They call these pre-solved problems "primitives." But the question naturally arises, "Do all designers have the same set of primitives?"

Clearly, the answer is "no." A designer's primitives emerge not just from their knowledge of design, but (as we saw earlier in this paper) from their knowledge of one or more application domains and domain-specific design approaches. Thus, designer "A," when designing a data processing report generator, might stop at a fairly high level of design if he has designed and coded many of them before, whereas designer "B," who might have just as much experience as designer A but be inexperienced in report generation, might produce a much more elaborate, detailed design. This produces no problem, of course, as long as the person who writes the code is the same as the person who produced the design. However, more and more often, particularly in very large systems, there is a handoff from the designer to the coder. If the primitive set of the designer matches that of the coder, this handoff can go smoothly.

But consider two situations where the primitive sets do not match:

- The designer has a stronger primitive set than the coder: Here, the designer stops at a fairly high level, but the coder cannot write code from that level of design and must do further design work before writing code.
- The coder has a stronger primitive set than the designer: Here, the coder may be offended by what he or she may perceive to be an unnecessary level of design (and, in fact, the design may be erroneous or more complicated than the coder knows to be necessary), and the coder discards portions of the design before writing the code.

The point here is that the end of the design process is far from the simple "competent programmer" textbook solution. It is often true in practice that when a design handoff occurs, further design or discarding of design takes place.

There is one other consideration at or near the end of the design process. It is a characteristic of software design that, on occasion, some difficult design problem lurks at the lowest level of design, such that the entire design solution to that point is found to be infeasible, and the designer must discard it and begin again. What happens in this case is that the designer has overlooked a "hard-part" portion of the design, waiting to do it last, only to find that the design-to-date does not allow a solution to the hard-part problem. Most designers confess to having encountered this problem on occasion, but no research has been done to try to characterize the types of problems that cause this effect, or to define warning signs to allow anticipating such problems.

Once again, these thoughts are echoed by quotes from [Lammers 1986]: "Carry the design down to a level ... where two things are true. First, I already know about the primitives I write the programming in—they have been implemented many times before ... Second, I understand the primitives well enough to estimate within a factor of two or three how much memory they are going to cost ... I can be fairly confident that it's possible to implement a function, and I can roughly estimate its performance. Of course, it's possible to do that and overlook something very important. There's no way around that," says Butler Lampson.

summary

What is it possible to say about the nature of software design as a formal process and as a creative process? Certainly, we can say that the formal processes of methodologies and representations form an important under-pinning for design; but just as certainly, it is clear that they do not get at the essence of design.

The essence of design, it has been discovered by researchers looking at the best of design practice, involves:

1. A heuristic, cognitive process not susceptible to formal approaches
2. The need for experience in constructing suitable reusable design starting places
3. An opportunistic rather than top-down approach to the steps involved in design
4. A person-dependent, primitive-dependent process for determining when and how design shall end
5. The possibility of lurking, unspotted "hard-part" problems that can destroy an apparently complete design at the last minute

This set of findings may be upsetting to those who believe that formal approaches are the only way to build software, but the realization that formal processes must be supplemented with creative ones may be the beginning of a more complete understanding of what is necessary to build superior software products.

References

Adelson 1984—"A Model of Software Design," report from the Dept. of Computer Science, Yale University, October 1984; B. Adelson and E. Soloway.

Adelson 1985—"The Role of Domain Experience in Software Design," *IEEE Transactions on Software Engineering*, October 1985; B. Adelson and E. Soloway.

CSTB 1990—"Scaling Up: A Research Agenda for Software Engineering," a report of the Computer Science Technology Board of the National Research Council," *Communications of the ACM*, March 1990.

Curtis 1987—MCC Technical Report Number STP-260–87, "Empirical Studies of the Design Process: Papers for the Second Workshop on Empirical Studies of Programmers," September 1987; B. Curtis, R. Guindon, H. Krasner, D. Walz, J. Elam, and N. Iscoe.

Denning 1991—"Technology or Management? An Editorial," *Communications of the ACM*, March 1991; Peter J. Denning.

Guinon 1987—MCC Technical Report Number STP-283–87, "A Model of Cognitive Processes in Software Design: An Analysis of Breakdowns in Early Design Activities by Individuals," August 1987; R. Guindon, B. Curtis, H. Krasner.

Lammers 1986—*Programmers at Work*, Microsoft Press 1986; Susan Lammers.

Rombach 1990—"Design Measurement: Some Lessons Learned," *IEEE Software*, March 1990; H. Dieter Rombach.

Soloway 1987—"E Unum Pluribus: Generating Alternative Designs," Dept. of Computer Science, Yale University 1987; E. Soloway, J. Spohrer, D. Littman.

Visser 1987—"Strategies in Programming Programmable Controllers: A Field Study on a Professional Programmer," *Proceedings of the Empirical Studies of Programmers, Second Workshop*, Ablex 1987; Willemien Visser.

11.3
creativity meets
reality: a case study

You already met Prof. J. Daniel Couger in previous sections of this book. It will probably not come as a surprise to you at this point that Prof. Couger decided to apply the things he had learned about creativity and the software process to a real-live organization, and to use that application as the basis of a case study.

What follows are case-study excerpts from his book Creativity and Innovation in Information Systems Organizations [Couger 1996]. The organization where he conducted the case study was an Information Systems organization of the United Technologies Microelectronics Center (UTMC), which was located in the hometown of Prof. Couger's University of Colorado at Colorado Springs (UCCS). UTMC tends to specialize in high-reliability military and aerospace products, and the organization at which the case study was conducted was responsible for development and maintenance of the computer applications used to support UTMC corporate management (it did not perform, for example, such scientific/engineering applications as Computer Aided Design, which were done in another organization).

At the outset of the study [Couger, McIntyre, Higgins and Snow 1991], the organization was considered by UTMC management to be "quite effective." It was rated above average, and often excellent, on such factors as meeting commitments, training users, timely output, minimal errors, solving problems, ease of use, and providing status information. Prof. Couger reasoned that, if a creativity improvement program could be shown to be useful for an already-excellent IS organization, then the application of such a program to others could have widespread appeal.

A two-pronged approach was chosen:

1. Improvement of the organizational environment for creativity and innovation
2. Training in specific techniques for creativity generation and evaluation

A training program was the first step in this approach. We will see later below what topics were chosen to be taught. They will form, as you might imagine, an excellent beginning for any other organization that wants to employ these same approaches.

The second step in the approach was to reinforce what had just been taught through the application of those ideas taught, and discussions of those applications.

First, let's discuss the topics that were taught. The list that follows is an enhancement of the topics presented in the previous section, where one or more techniques were presented as components of each stage of the software life cycle. Based on Prof. Couger's analysis of the creativity literature and his own interpretation of its application to the field of information systems, here are the creativity techniques he taught the UTMC case study software people:

A Description of the Creativity Techniques

Analogy/Metaphor—An analogy is a statement about how objects, people, situations or actions are similar in process or relationship. Metaphors are figures of speech. Metaphors and analogies can be used to create fantasy situations for gaining new perspectives on problem definition and resolution.

brainstorming—This technique is designed to produce a large quantity of ideas in a short period of time by a process that stimulates ideas. Idea generation is separated from evaluation as a means to encourage ideation.

blue slip—Ideas are individually generated and recorded on a 3×5 sheet of blue paper. By anonymous recording and sharing of ideas, people feel more comfortable about expressing ideas. Using a single slip to record ideas facilitates sorting and grouping of ideas.

extrapolation—A proven technique or approach is applied to a new problem.

progressive abstraction technique—Alternative problem definitions are generated by moving through progressively higher levels of problem abstraction until a satisfactory definition is achieved. When a problem is systematically enlarged in this way, new definitions emerge that can be evaluated for their usefulness and feasibility. Once an appropriate level of abstraction is reached, possible solutions then can be more easily identified. The major advantage of the technique is the degree of structure provided to the problem solver for systematically examining problem substructures and connections.

5Ws and the H technique—The Who-What-Where-When-Why-How questions aid in expanding an individual's view of a problem or opportunity to try to make sure that all related aspects have been considered.

force field analysis technique—The name of this technique is derived from the technique's ability to identify forces contributing to or hindering a solution to a problem. The technique can stimulate creative thinking in three ways: 1) define direction (vision),

2) identify strengths that can be maximized, and 3) identify weaknesses that can be minimized.

peaceful setting—The objective of this approach is to enable people to mentally remove themselves from present surroundings to enable a less cluttered, more open mental process. They visualize themselves in a favorite, relaxed setting such as beachside or mountainside.

problem reversal—Sometimes it is useful to reverse a problem statement to provide a different framework for analysis. For example, in trying to improve the climate for creativity, it is useful to consider the opposite—how to "ruin creativity."

associations/images technique—This approach builds on the natural inclination of humans to associate things. The linking or combining process is another way of expanding solution space.

wishful thinking—This technique is particularly useful for people who typically take a very analytical approach to problem solving. It enables them to loosen their analytical parameters to consider a larger set of alternatives than they might ordinarily consider. It is designed to permit a degree of fantasy in the solution process, and this loosening-up may result in some unique approaches. Bu taking unusual positions to start the problem solving process, a perspective might arise that would not ordinarily be brought forth.

Following the training and application of this collections of techniques, the UTMC organization engaged in an analysis of the effects of these approaches. That analysis was, of course, quite subjective (in the battle between research rigor and research relevance, it is often difficult to succeed at both ends of the spectrum. Case studies tend to be low on rigor and high on relevance. This one is no exception).

353

Prof. Couger employed a survey instrument to capture perceptions of the participants. They hypothesized that:

- Individual (self-perceived) improvement was about 23% per
person
- Departmental improvement was about 27%

But there was more than this perception component to Prof.
Couger's findings. The employees each kept "creativity logs," in
which they recorded the use they had made of what they had
learned. Those logs showed 12 specific improvements in project
work effectiveness, and 6 additional improvements in efficiency.
These improvements included:

- Reduction in time for a database expansion from 60 hours to 4
- Processing time on year to date computations reduced from 24
hours to 45 minutes
- Bookings forecast report processing reduced from 6 hours to 5
minutes
- Programming maintenance time reduction of 10-15 hours/
month

Based on these fairly spectacular improvements, the president
of UTMC asked that additional staff be trained in these same
approaches.

Because the numbers quoted above are so impressive but at the
same time rather emotionally cold, we present here a discussion of
the specific improvements made in the words of the UTMC IS staff:

creativity Improvements in UTMC IS Department
The following descriptions were developed by the analysts and
programmers; the first person "we" was retained to show the
pride of authorship of personnel in reporting their team's creative
accomplishments.

1. enterprise modeling: The MIS department was examining approaches for an enterprise model for the company. While we were conducting discussions with vendors and consultants about different approaches, UTMC's CEO attended a seminar on seven planning techniques for solving business problems. He wanted to create a UTMC culture to use this methodology. Picking up on his interest, the MIS department utilized "what if " questions to modify and integrate these planning techniques into a unified methodology for an enterprise model. We also deviated from the normal procedure of modeling the current business to modeling the "ideal" business. This approach should identify opportunities to reengineer the UTMC business process flow. The MIS department is teaching these techniques to a large number of UTMC managers who will participate in enterprise modeling.

2. CAM Restructure: Earlier in the year, we had a project to work with Production Control to bring up a manufacturing planning module that was part of our vendor-supplied CAM (computer-aided manufacturing) system. This CAM system had first been brought into UTMC seven years ago when our business was completely different. For instance, we did not have our own wafer fab facility and only built products for UTC. We now supply products to commercial customers, as well as UTC customers, resulting in a very different focus. Thus, we were having difficulty in getting the manufacturing planning module to work properly with our existing route and facility structure. Instead of trying to force-fit a system that would never work properly, we decided to step back and completely redo our CAM system structure to prepare us for the 1990s. We used the "5 Ws and H" and brainstorming creativity techniques to conduct structured interviews of all functional groups utilizing the CAM system. We developed a three-year plan for a major upgrade to our system in support of company business objectives for the 1990s. We presented the plan to senior management, got approval and have begun work on the project.

3. **Evaluation of CASE tools**: The MIS department needed to evaluate different CASE (computer-aided software engineering) tools to improve our productivity and software quality. We used the "problem reversal" creative technique to list the factors that were causing poor productivity and quality in MIS. This allowed us to quickly select the major factors that needed to be addressed by the CASE tool and generate a CASE tool comparison matrix that narrowed our selection evaluation to three tools.

4. **CAM Database expansion**: Our CAM database contains all of our manufacturing data and is constantly expanding. In order to maintain good response time for database accesses, the database must be periodically reorganized. Previously, we would unload the database, make the changes, and then reload the database. This process took around 60 hours to complete. One of the MIS section managers was looking at ways to improve system performance; he discovered a new way to modify the CAM database size without having to unload/reload the database. We were able to apply these techniques to our specific site and reduce the database expansion task to four hours (resulting in 46-hour time savings). This is a good example of extrapolation, using a proven solution approach in a new application area.

5. **Automated GL report structure cleanup**: Our GL (general ledger) report structure needed to be cleaned up because it contained reporting structures that were obsolete, had missing reporting structure entries, and had centers that would sum to the wrong summary center. The financial department planned to manually conduct this clean up project. The process would have taken several personnel-months to complete. Instead, we suggested that use of the "wishful thinking" technique to help the finance people identify how they desired the GL report structure to be. We then wrote a computer program to automatically clean up the reporting structure. As a result, more than 40,000 obsolete reporting struc-

ture entries were deleted, more than 10,000 missing reporting structures were added and 2,505 errors were corrected to properly summarize the reporting structures. Automation of this process not only saved Finance many months of manual activity, but it also ensures consistent reporting across UTC, UTMC, and for government reports.

6. **use of RDB to Replace Ingres**: Currently, most of our financial systems use the INGRES (vendor name) relational database software package; we are also developing a major marketing system on INGRES. We like the flexibility that the relational database gives us, but it is expensive to license on multiple VAX systems. We currently have a VAX cluster but only have INGRES running on one VAX 8650. As more and more applications run on INGRES, it will become necessary to add the software to more machines. Additional INGRES licenses will cost us significant dollars. By asking "what if" types of questions (5 Ws and H technique) and brainstorming, a suggestion resulted that may provide a cost effective way of using existing INGRES implementations on multiple machines. DEC has an RDB (relational database software package) whose engine is supplied free on all VAXes. INGRES frontend tools can use the DEC RDB engine. We will test the feasibility of using this INGRES-RDB combination to allow our INGRES-developed systems to run on all computers on our VAX cluster.

7. **CAM Report Distribution**: CAM reports are automatically produced monthly, weekly or daily depending upon frequency requirements. The system determines the frequency by using hard-coded command procedures to indicate when the report was to run, as well as for whom the report was being generated. While this procedure worked, it required programmer time to keep it current. Using the "what if" question (5 Ws and H technique), a file-based system was developed. We created a file that contains all the

required information to run the reports. The result is a reduction in programmer maintenance time by 10–15 hours a month. The output also provides visibility to the user community on who gets what reports—which is especially useful when someone goes on vacation.

8. STAR screen Driven/Report Driver: We are developing a new sales order system named STAR. We needed to introduce some "user-friendly" features, such as the capability to move directly from one function to another function without going through the menu structure. We also needed a friendly front-end to reports to more easily select criteria and specify desired sorting for reports. We used brainstorming techniques with senior MIS analysts from different groups to derive a solution that was easy to maintain. We repeatedly asked the question "what could we do ..." to arrive at the ultimate solution. We developed several powerful tools that can be used on any INGRES application.

9. Program Management Reports: A user came to MIS requesting help on his personal computer inventory program that he was using to manually track information about key UTMC programs. We used the "wishful thinking" creative technique to determine that he desired a report pulling data from our general ledger, labor collection and the Viewpoint program management system. We were able to accomplish his "wish" by using the UDMS (User Data Management System) report writer tool. So for the first time our company can base key decisions on integrated UTMC program data.

10. 12-Month Window: UTMC needed to implement a business practice that allows the booking of an order only if its customer-request-date was within a 12-month window. A previous attempt to implement this capability had been unsuccessful because the programming logic was difficult in the existing Order Entry System. We used the brainstorming technique with senior MIS

analysts to evaluate what went wrong last time and how we could successfully implement the window this time. The result was a sound design with a completely different file structure concept.

11. Forecast Projection System: UTMC needed salesmen to be able to update their forecast projections from the field in order to improve the accuracy and timeliness of sales forecasts. Resources were committed to other projects and were therefore not available to undertake this major upgrade to the forecasting system using normal procedures. Instead we used the prototyping technique with the INGRES RDB and UDMS report writer, then hired a contract programmer for two weeks to provide an interim capability until the major upgrade can be performed. This approach provided UTMC with a timely solution; it also provided valuable input into the requirements for the ultimate system. The "what if" approach, along with an emphasis on a creative environment, fostered teamwork among personnel from MIS, marketing, sales and our vendor-contractor.

12. User Interface For INGRES Scrolling Region: INGRES has a built-in capability that does not work the way a user would normally scroll areas. Instead of using the TAB key to move from field to field, the user has to use the Enter key. This feature is not "friendly" for the user and made the system difficult to use. By asking "what if" questions, we were able to develop a clever modification to our INGRES code to allow the interface to work "normally" within a scrolling area. This modification made the STAR system more friendly and reduced potential operator errors.

13. Year-to-Date (YTD) Overhead: UTMC needed to be able to calculate YTD overhead during its normal closing cycle, but since it took 24 hours to run the program it was not possible to do so without delaying the output of other important jobs. MIS needed to step back from the way that we were using YTD overhead to come up with a new solution approach. We used the "5 Ws and H" technique and determined that, since this was a set-oriented problem, we could convert two major COBOL programs to DCL (digital command language) and SQL (structured query language) and reduce the run time to 45 minutes.

14. BOOKINGS FORECAST REPORT: Because the booking forecast report extract normally requires six hours of elapsed time to run, the information is not available in a timely manner for the forecast projection business cycle. To find a better solution, we used the "5 Ws and H" creative technique. It produced the suggested use of INGRES instead of RMS (records management services) files. The elapsed run time was reduced from six hours to six minutes, and the CPU time was reduced from 15 minutes to seven seconds, enabling a timely forecast projection.

15. POSTSCRIPT PRINTING: To produce more readable enterprise model charts, we used the "wishful thinking" creative technique to ask the question, "could we print the Freelance PC graphics on a new VAX Postscript laser printer?" This approach led to development of the capability to print reports generated from a PC on the laser printer connected to a VAX. It also led to encoding print characteristics into a file name so the users would not have to know the details of generating a report or graph. This capability is used in the forecast projection reports.

16. CAM RECOVERY: A disk failure destroyed a major CAM disk, making our CAM system non-operative. Our manufacturing process is heavily dependent upon this system, so we had to recover as quickly as possible to minimize the impact on our business. An MIS analyst and a key user used the brainstorming technique to come up with procedures to automatically update the missing data instead of entering the data into the system by hand. These proce-

dures saved many hours of manual data entry, provided an explicit
audit trail and avoided many hours of CAM system downtime.

17. cam reporting: In attempting to use a vendor reporting package
to develop reports needed by Production Control, we ran into a
major program restriction. We used the "5 Ws and H" creative
technique to get around the restriction on accessing DBMS group
keys that contain numeric values by "borrowing" an unused DBMS
record field to parse the correct search field.

Post-mortem interviews after all of these successes had been
achieved help reinforce the glow of these findings. Subjects made
such comments as:

comment 1: "I used to have to be more secretive about the time I spent
on coming up with 'far-out' ideas—I felt that I should be working
on very practical solutions. Now I don't worry about people getting
the impression that I am day-dreaming—we have the confidence of
management that we are good at generating good ideas."

comment 2: "In our meetings many of us hesitated to bring up a 'wild
idea,' not certain if it would be ridiculed. Now we feel comfortable with generating 'wild ideas.' The ideas are sometimes met
with laughter but we know it is more a spirit of playfulness than
criticism. We feel comfortable in responding to laughter with a
comment like, "Hey! I'm just trying to be creative!"

comment 3: "When I've scheduled a meeting with our users, I try to
think if one of the creativity techniques might be appropriate for
some portion of the agenda."

comment 4: "I'm not comfortable yet in suggesting the use of a
creativity technique with a group of people who have not been
through the creativity workshop. But when a group gets stuck,

unable to come up with a solution, I find myself suggesting one of these techniques to get us unstuck, to get back on track."

comment 5: "One of the surprising outcomes for me was a new tolerance for some of my users who I always considered to be uncreative. Now I tend to tell myself 'Be patient, let them come about it using their own approach.' I find they are more creative than I thought—they just use a less logical approach to reaching a solution."

comment 6: "In response to the question, "Would I have come up with those creative solutions on our list without the introduction of the creativity program?' I'd respond that some of them—undoubtedly. However, now I tend to be on the lookout for more creative solutions."

comment 7: "Within the new creative environment, we find ourselves less constrained in our thinking. For example, yesterday Theresa came up with a solution that was a quantum jump ahead in thinking. That is not untypical for any one of us in the new environment."

comment 8: "One measure of our creativity is the improvements we've made in the accounting package. We've been able to identify and implement some improvements that the experts—the developers of the package—were surprised about. Their technical staff is many times the size of ours and yet we introduced some significant changes."

One of the things important to Prof. Couger in all of his work on IS creativity improvement was the notion that it should be conducted in a bottom-up fashion. That is, whereas most of the information systems and software engineering literature focuses on top-down improvement, techniques authorized and blessed by managed and trained under their auspices, Prof. Couger saw bottom up as a superior approach for enhancing creativity. He conducted his training program on a democratic basis, with managers and technologists receiving the training together. Such an approach, Prof. Couger noted, leads to a management that is more open to new ideas and the facilitation of their implementation than the more traditional top-down approach. Further, in the UTMC study specifically, he found that 90% of the improvements could be implemented without having to obtain any management approval at all. This led to staff empowerment; one technical subject noted, "this has been the most exciting period of my career."

There was a bottom line to Prof. Couger's case study. One of the managers of the organization in question said, "In the near term, the benefits have included creativity improvements in systems development, business systems processes, employee hiring, cost effectiveness, and system efficiency. The long-term benefits are even more exciting. Creativity is now a part of our culture. We have become significantly more effective as a change agent within UTMC. And have already begun to enhance the way the company works."

This description of the application of creativity techniques to information systems applications occurred fairly early in Prof. Couger's explorations of this topic. Later, in [Couger 1996], he found a more quantitative way to describe the benefits to UTMC. The Return on Investment (ROI) for the cost of the creativity training used at UTMC, he said, "was a factor of six."

We have already noted that creativity case study research is rare to nonexistent in our field. For another interesting case, an exception to that rule, see [Maiden, et al. 2004], which describes a situation in which requirements activities were subjected (successfully) to applied creativity models.

Not bad results from this case study application of creativity to the real world. Certainly, at least in that corner of Colorado, those results appear to have been spectacular. Isn't it too bad that both the literature on creativity, and the capture of case studies like this one, are so sparse and infrequent in our field?

References

Couger, McIntrye, Higgins and Snow 1991—"Using a Bottom-Up Approach to Creativity Improvement in Information Systems Development," *Journal of Systems Management,* September 1991; J. Daniel Couger, Scott C. McIntrye, Lexis F. Higgins, and Terry A. Snow. Excerpts used with permission.

Couger 1996—*Creativity & Innovation in Information Systems Organizations,* Boyd & Fraser Publishing Co. 1996; J. Daniel Couger.

Maiden, et al. 2004—"Provoking Creativity: Imagine What Your Requirements Could be Like," *IEEE Software,* September 2004; Neal Maiden, Alexis Gizikis, and Suzanne Robertson.

chapter 12
creative milestones in software history

chapter contents

Introduction to chapter 12

"I think one of the characteristics of creative people is that they're never happy with what is."
—*Ken Higa*, Marketing, Lord, Aeck, and Sargent, Inc.,
"The Creative Edge," *Atlanta Business Chronicle*,
September 16, 2005

"There is an increasingly important category of work – knowledge work – that you can best manage by not enforcing a detailed, in-advance set of objectives – even if you could."
—*Bill Walton*,
in his opening statement to the *Cutter IT Journal* special issue on "The Role of Strategy, Planning, and Budgeting in an Agile Organization," February 2006.

Our society is always celebrating milestones. Things like the 200th anniversary of the buggy whip, or the 100th of the running board. We love to look back at what people were looking forward to all those many years ago.

There are plenty of celebrations, for example, of computing hardware history. In the last decade, we've celebrated such seemingly ancient computers as the ENIAC and the EDSAC, and several others. Name an early-days computer, and we've undoubt-edly celebrated its history and significance. Given the current moment in history, these were quite likely 50th anniversary celebrations.

But do you know what? There's almost no event in the history of the computing software field that we celebrate. It's not so much that we want to celebrate the birth of the punched card or the flowchart template or the coding pad. But there are some big milestones in software's history that ARE worth celebrating, I would assert. That's what this chapter of the book is about. I list my notions of those milestones here; I would be interested in knowing what your notion is.

12.1

The first creative milestone

First of all, we could celebrate the advent of the first software program. But that's clouded in some kinds of historic doubt. For example, some say that Ada Lovelace, after whom the Ada programming language was named, was the world's first programmer because she made Baggage's Inference Engine do the things that it was designed to do. But programming was a far different breed of cat all those many (150 or so) years ago, and that's not an event that most of us could dig a good, healthy, celebration into, I'm afraid.

The same thing is also true of all the early mathematical/scientific applications. World War II was a fertile time for beginning to make useful objects out of computers and software, and a number of programs were written to help the war effort along. But they tended to be things like calculators of tables of data, a worthwhile task, to be sure, but not so much of a milestone one.

So as I poked around in the dusty historic artifacts I have collected in my approaching 60-something years in the field, an idea began to form. What we should celebrate as perhaps the most significant software milestone of all time was the development of the first business applications software. Programs that massaged business data, and produced management-focused reports. Pretty mundane stuff, to be sure, but at the same time so essential to the development of business as we know it today. And, to this day, the application domain for which the largest percentage of today's software is still written.

Now, I suspect what I say next is going to be something of a surprise. The earliest business applications software was developed in 1951. That may not surprise you as much as it does me, but I remember the 1950s very well and when I got my first industry job in 1954 I thought I was a real pioneer in that field! And it turns out I was about three years late in coming to the party.

Who were these astoundingly early pioneers? It won't surprise computing historians that it was a company in England, I suspect, since England was a big-time pioneer in the early days of the computing field. But it may very well surprise everyone that it was an English company called J. Lyons (a company whose business was tea, tea shops, ice cream, and cakes! There'll always be an England, I suppose).

The most astounding thing about the J. Lyons pioneering computing work was that the company not only wrote the first business software application, they actually also built their own computer hardware in order to be able to run that software! That computer later came to be called the LEO, and it was a business production version of the EDSAC computer developed at England's Cambridge University.

Now you might imagine that the J. Lyons business applications software vintage 1951 was fairly primitive. Get ready for yet another surprise! The programs they wrote in that small English company weren't what you'd think of as your Grandma's business applications. There was transaction data processing, of course, as you might imagine if you've ever written any business software. Sales, inventory, stuff like that ... the rudimentary parts from which significant business applications are made.

But there was more. Results of those transactions were compared to pre-set standards, forecasts, and budgets. Variances were identified and dealt with by specifically assigned lower-level managers. "What if" explorations requested by senior management could also be undertaken via the software. The result was a real-time approach to management information processing coupled with a decision support system that would be the envy of some companies even today! What Lyons put on the air all those years ago would be considered akin to the Business Process Analysis and Reengineering work that forms so much of what we now think of as "avant garde." Writers who described the Lyons system say things like "It is ironic that the current rhetoric suggests that the way ahead lies in following the precepts [exhibited] over [50] years ago at J. Lyons."

My source for all of this early software history is the writings of Frank Land of the London School of Economics, who was an early member of the Lyons computing team. Frank has written in many places about his experiences at Lyons, but my favorite of those places is the article he contributed to my book [Glass 1998], which is a collection of anecdotal reminiscences by early software pioneers, including Land (and myself). (If you prefer a more encyclopedic look at computing's early history from a pioneer's viewpoint, see [Lee 1995]).

Now that I've identified what I consider to be perhaps the most important early milestone in the history of applications software, especially business applications, I have one regret.

My regret is this: we in the software field should have made a big thing out of the 50th anniversary of this milestone event. But that 50th anniversary should have happened in 2001, five or so years ago.

I suppose we have missed our chance to put one more ritualistic event into our calendar of other such events. And that's a shame. Because what, in this Age of Computing, can be much more important than celebrating the role of software in making that Age possible?!

Ah, well, I suppose we can celebrate the 100th anniversary, in the year 2051. Will you take responsibility for reminding the world of that when the time comes, please?

References

Glass 1998—*In the Beginning: Recollections of Software Pioneers*, IEEE Computer Society Press, 1998; Robert L. Glass.

Lee 1995—*Computer Pioneers*, IEEE Computer Society Press, 1995; J.A.N. Lee.

12.2

Later "silver bullet" milestones

In the previous section, I discussed the earliest creative milestone in software history, the development of business applications software and an application-specific computer called LEO, by the J. Lyons (Tea) Company in England, in1951. It was an astonishing event in the history of the software field, and it deserves to be celebrated as one of the leading events in computing history, I said there.

But the J. Lyons work was only the beginning of a long chain of creative milestones in computing and software history. It's the other events in that chain that I want to discuss here.

Why pour back over the dusty history of how software got to where it is today? After all, what's exciting about the computing field is what big tricks we can make it do today, not what (by comparison) small tricks we could make it do back then.

Just this. There's a lot of forgetting, and a lot of "never knew that," in our field today. People discuss the history of computing and get it badly wrong. And then others come along and reference those erroneous discussions, and compound the error by producing nicely citation-supported discussions that are also wrong!

There's another factor besides getting it wrong. I was recently writing an article on some concepts that remain very real to me, like the structured methodologies and CASE tools, and a young colleague pointed out that a lot of today's readers may not know what those are, and that worse yet any reference to them would date the article I was writing. I had to agree that this young colleague was right, of course. Events that happened back in the 1970s and 1980s, like the structured approaches and CASE tools, are pretty well off the radar screen of today's programmers who may very well have been born at about that time!

But at the same time, I had a second reaction. That reaction was that these are pieces of history that we shouldn't forget. Not just because they represent important lessons learned, although it's hard to overstate the importance of that factor. But also because a lot of what we think we know today is directly (or indirectly!) traceable to those historic milestones. They represent a rich history, I would assert, of material on which we will continue to build the future of the software field.

So let me take you on a quick trip through software's historic creative milestones:

First, back in the time of J. Lyons, came bare computers that were coded in machine language. And machine language was a creation of computing hardware people, useful as all get out (all of a computer's tricks could be performed using it) but definitely human-unfriendly. (Think of writing programs in all-numeric operations and data addresses, and think further of those numerics being not in decimal but in bi-quinary or octal or hexadecimal or one of the other number systems that computers used back then).

Fortunately, that era passed fairly quickly. First came assembly languages, and instead of coding in numerics we now coded operations and addresses in symbolics. From a milestone point of view, this was a fairly mild one, since it wasn't that much of a leap forward in our ability to build software. But from a creative point of view, assembly language marked the beginning of thinking about the use of computers in symbols instead of numbers. And most of the remainder of software's milestones are based on that notion.

One of the most fundamental ideas in the software field emerged about the same time as assembly language. We began to create software in modules, separable pieces of software that performed a task that could be invoked by a program proper. This mid-fifties idea remains, to this day, the arguably most important advancement in software history. Oh, it was expanded by generations of software practitioners to come, and by academics a decade or so later, but the idea of building software from (reusable) separate parts is one that many people find exciting (and think they're discovering afresh!) today.

Surprisingly quickly after assembly language and modular programming came two of the most important milestones in software history: the advent of the high-order programming language and the operating system. Both came along in the mid-late 1950s, and to be honest I can't remember which came first in the computing practitioner shops where I worked. But these were perhaps the most profound tool-based breakthroughs in the entire history of the field. Tools called compilers could transform a high order language into machine language. The first such language was Fortran, and it remains (after various transmogrifications) in use today. And, following quickly on its heels came COBOL, also remaining in use today. These languages were application-domain focused; Fortran spoke the language of scientists and engineers, and COBOL spoke that of business analysts.

Operating systems, as we know to this day, are tools that allow programmers to forget the mundane hardware-focused aspects of writing applications software, and concentrate on the application problem to be solved. In a sense, operating systems were a unified collection of hardware-specific modules, providing the services offered by the computer hardware in question. We were so grateful for the creation of the operating system back in those days, that it would be hard to foresee a future (today's) in which operating systems would be a source of controversy and even choosing up sides!

The 1950s rolled into the 1960s, and those creative leaps became ever more solidly embedded in the software field. New high order languages emerged. Newer and better operating systems came along. The rate of these changes was amazingly rapid, but they were evolutionary, not revolutionary. Evolution involved creating programming languages that were domain-independent (merging Fortran and COBOL into PL/1, for example) and even creating computer hardware that also straddled domains (most early computers had been either scientific or business oriented). New operating systems, of course, supported that more diverse hardware.

It was late in the 1960s that the academic computing disciplines came into being. First came Computer Science, and shortly thereafter Information Systems (Software Engineering didn't come along as such until more than a decade later). I suspect that most readers will be surprised by how late in the evolution of the software field these disciplines came along. (Note that 15 years had passed since J. Lyons did its thing). There was a lot of software being written before the ivy-covered halls began to ponder about how best to do it!

At about this same time, some of the most profound applications systems were being developed. We tried (and largely failed) to build complicated and integrated Management Information Systems. (Commercial vendors like SAP and PeopleSoft began working on similar systems at about the same time, and over a decade later because famously and fabulously successful at it). Reservations systems for airlines were put on the air successfully. The operating system for IBM's 360 was one of the largest applications of all time, and did what it was supposed to do. Huge and astonishingly complex space and weather predicting systems were developed. We had thought, back in the 1950s and 1960s, that the applications we built then were complex and impressive. Little did we know what was to come!

As applications became larger and more complex, systems and tools and concepts to attack that complexity became the focus of the field. First, in the 1970s, came structured programming. It consisted of a collection of methodological dos and don'ts about how to create software in a "structured" way. There were two amazing things about structured programming. The first was that it was hyped as being a breakthrough in our ability to build software, and it was accepted and used by almost all programmers in almost all practitioner organizations. The second is that no research was ever performed to demonstrate that the claimed and hyped value existed. Studies a decade later examined the evaluative literature on structured programming and found "equivocal" results that by no means supported the original hyped claims. It is important to note that, although the hype was clearly in excess, most people agree today that the structured approaches were beneficial, and in fact most of today's programs are in some sense "structured."

The field was by no means finished with hyped approaches. Tools and languages were envisioned as techniques for "automating" the field of software, such that anyone—not just professional programmers—could do that job. CASE (computer-aided-software-engineering) and 4GL (Fourth Generation Languages) were the tools that would make that possible in the 1980s. Never mind that many CASE tools were purchased, then put aside and ignored (the standing joke of the time was that they became "shelfware"). Never mind that practitioners and academics totally differed on what 4GLs were (to practitioners, they were languages that generated reports from data bases; to academics, they were non-procedural languages wherein the programmer specified what was to be done, but not the order in which to do it). It was no coincidence that about this time Fred Brooks published his historically important "No Silver Bullet" article, in which he took the position that most breakthroughs in the software field had already happened, and that there quite likely wouldn't be anything as exciting in the future as the languages and operating systems of the 6os had been.

And what happened to CASE and 4GL? My suspicion is that we still use them to this day, but the terms themselves have fallen into such disregard that we rarely see them. And certainly, the hyped benefits were never achieved.

Structured programming was not the end of the notion of methodology as breakthrough. Object-oriented (OO) approaches became all the rage, and the same kinds of benefits were claimed for them that were claimed for the structured approaches. It is difficult to be objective today about OO, since there has been no next big thing to replace it as of this writing. But there are mixed claims about how much the OO approaches are used (some claim they are ubiquitous, but the studies I have seen show the penetration in computing organizations is less than 50%). And there are mixed claims about the OO benefits – it is supposed to be a novice-friendly approach, but studies have shown that novices do better with functionally-focused rather than object-focused approaches. It is supposed to facilitate reuse (remember the discussion of modular programming earlier?), and studies have shown that for some application domains fully 70% of the code can be reused instead of written afresh (but similar studies have shown nearly the same benefits from non-OO approaches). It is also supposed to allow the creation of software in solution objects with direct correlation to the objects in the problem to be solved, but the OO field has now embraced "use cases," a decidedly functionally-focused approach to define system requirements. Once again, as the hype of OO dies away, we are beginning to see clearly that it is a good but not best approach to building software.

What remains in the department of creative milestones in software history? Today's contributions—the Agile approaches, and Open Source software. There are those in either/both of these camps who take the position that these are, indeed, magnificent creative milestones in the world of software development.

And there are others who see Agile as appropriate to only small applications of a limited number of kinds, and Open Source as an emotional blip appreciated more by its fanatical supporters than by the software world in general.

12.3
creativity vs.
routinization

There is no doubt that all those creative milestones in software engineering history described in the previous section of this book were really creative. But there is an interesting question that must be addressed – exactly whose creativity are we talking about?

Most of this book is about creativity in software engineering. I am most concerned with all the issues surrounding helping those who build software do a better—and more creative—job. But were all those milestones really supportive of that?

This is not only an important and interesting question, but it is one that had—a few decades ago—quite a bit of political stigma attached to it. But before I explain about the stigma attached to these milestones, let me address the question itself.

My first answer to the question would be "Of course, these milestones were all creativity enhancers for software engineers," and I suspect that might be your automatic answer as well. After all, didn't high order languages and various methodologies and software tools add monumentally to our ability to do our jobs?

On deeper thought you might begin to feel some doubt, as I did. Yes, software engineers were helped big time by all these advancements. But did they help our creativity?

Before I deal with that question, I need to say where the primary creative act occurred. The obvious creativity in these milestones occurred in the minds of those who invented the milestones themselves. Think of the first person who invented a high order language (and, of course, its necessary tool supplement, the compiler). Conceiving of HOL+compiler required seeing the "computer" in a whole new light, the light of symbol manipulator. In fact, it was about this time that the term "computer" became rather obsolete for our field, since machine usage was no longer limited to doing arithmetic on numbers, but was extended to doing complex logical manipulation of non-numeric symbols. HOL+compiler was a breakthrough—a silver bullet—on an astonishing number of levels.

But, once again, was it an act that enhanced the creative abilities of software engineers? My answer, after some deeper thought, remains "yes." Given the ease with which a program can be written in an HOL as opposed to assembly language, the programmer was freed from machine-specific details and allowed to apply his mind exclusively to the problem being solved. And if that isn't a creativity-enhancer, I don't know what is. Granted, the kind of creativity we are talking about here is different from that of the original creator of the concept.

Now, those original silver bullets were almost all clearly software engineering creativity enhancers, I would assert, if we use the same logic I used for HOL+compiler. Operating systems allowed the software engineer to concentrate on the problem instead of the machine's architecture. Modular programming allowed the software engineer to work with encapsulated ideas, rather then ideas that spread freely (and sometimes randomly) across the problem/solution space.

It's when we get to the subject of methodologies that the creativity argument begins to unravel. Is it more creative to work within a methodology like the structured approaches, or object-orientation, or are those methodologies simply a framework within which the programmer is constrained from doing things wrong, rather than helped toward being more creative? It's possible to argue either side of that argument, I would assert, but to be honest my heart is less in arguing the "pro" side of this one than it was in arguing the "pro" side of HOL+compiler. What management had in mind in supporting the use of methodologies, both then and now—I would assert—is imposing more control on the programming process. And, put that way, methodologies are not really about creativity at all.

That sets the stage for that discussion of political stigma I promised you earlier. There came a time, back in the late 1970s, when that whole issue of the benefits of software engineering milestones became the subject of some fairly radicalized discussions. Two authors with political leftist leanings took the position that all those software engineering milestones we presented above were largely nothing more than a management ploy, a plot not designed to make their workers more creative but rather to "deskill" them! Why would managers want to deskill their workers? In order to make it easier to control their performance, and thus to control the products they produced.

The two authors who strode forward on the computing scene at this time to mix the notion of political system and the notion of computing system were:

- Philip Kraft [Kraft 1977], who was a sociologist who viewed computing from a largely labor-management point of view ("Quite frankly," he says in the cited book, "I have become a partisan on the side of the programmer")
- Joan Greenbaum [Greenbaum 1979], a one-time programmer who explored a radical view of social systems and fairly frequently, in her cited book, quoted Karl Marx to make her point

And the idea they presented in their two books was that all those milestones we mentioned above, especially the methodology ones, were intended to "routinize" the work of programmers, to "de-skill" them.

How did their argument go?

First, both authors based their books on research that involved interviewing programmers and their managers from the point of view of what was happening in the software world. Kraft saw, emerging from those interviews, a number of technical trends of the time that he interpreted to be meant specifically by management to lead to deskilling: structured programming, modularization and "canned programs," and chief programmer teams (CPTs, an organizational approach likened by some to the chief surgeon approach to managing a surgical team). In each case, Kraft felt that these concepts, instead of leading to increased productivity (which nearly everyone in the field saw them producing), would lead to more management control of the programming process (structured programming by limiting the number of logic structures programmers could use, for example, modularity by maximizing the amount of pre-built code that could be used instead of new programming, and CPT because he saw it as "the most structured, hierarchialized, and status-bound [organizational approach] of any in the industrial world").

It is interesting to note that Kraft also saw the locked computer room (programmers of that era were not allowed to run computers; professional operators did) as yet another attempt by management to deskill, in this case by separating "head" and "hand" work.

Given today's world of computers everywhere, if the closed computer room was really an attempt by management to exert further control, it was certainly an abysmal failure!

Kraft admitted, in passing, that the creators of these productivity enhancement approaches did not intend them to be deskilling, but he did not let that slow down his concern.

Greenbaum's (later) book certainly picked up on Kraft's view of structured programming, but apparently ducked his other concerns like modularity and the CPT. However, she was equally convinced that the so-called productivity improvements were really management plots to exert more control over their programmers, "in the name of efficiency" as her book title put it.

Not only did Kraft and Greenbaum see a management plot to deskill, they were surprised to find that, although programmers grumbled about management's efforts, they made no attempt to resist or oppose them. Kraft said, for example, that he was "astounded by how routinely ... programmers accepted their manager's point of view, even though it came nowhere close to accurately describing the programmer's real situation."

Both authors noted the trend away from fun in the programming process (a topic we addressed earlier in this book!), toward a much more management-controlled form of work, a trend which – they said—emerged as a pattern from their interviews with programmers. Greenbaum noted that "back in the sixties, the people came from rebel stock: they were bright, creative ... pioneers. Today they are a new breed, technically knowledgeable but more plodding." Kraft said much the same thing—"Barely a generation after its inception, programming is no longer the complex work of creative ... people. Instead, divided and routinized, it has become mass production work." (Note that a concern for creativity keeps showing up here. Certainly, Kraft and Greenbaum saw a need for creativity in software work).

With the wonderful benefit of hindsight, of course, we can now see that most of what Kraft and Greenbaum foresaw would turn out to be untrue. (Some of us saw it at the time, but to say so would be bragging!)

- That "centerpiece of management efforts to deskill programmers," structured programming, has largely disappeared at least conceptually from the landscape, to be replaced by object-oriented programming, which no one is claiming to be deskilling

- "Almost certainly, the process of work fragmentation and programmer deskilling will continue and intensify" is almost laughably wrong in today's world of ever more complex software systems
- "Maintenance in particular can be more quickly defined and controlled by bureaucratic forms of management" was wrong then and, in a world where maintenance remains untamed, continues to be wrong now!

In spite of all that, it must be acknowledged that Kraft and Greenbaum raised some interesting and important concerns, way back all those nearly 30-something years ago. Any attempts to deskill programmers would certainly be counterproductive (and counter-creative) to the world of software as we know it (although I think none of us would put it beyond the reach of managers to consider such a ploy). But their fundamental notion, that all those creative advancements to the field of software engineering were really de-skilling anti-creativity acts instead, can be disposed of fairly rapidly, simply by looking at how complex the task of building software remains today.

The political stigma Kraft and Greenbaum raised is, however, worth remembering. If management ever does plot to deskill the programming process, creative technologists everywhere need to be ready to respond.

references

Greenbaum 1979—*In the Name of Efficiency,* Temple University Press 1979; Joan M. Greenbaum.

Kraft 1977—*Programmers and Managers,* Springer-Verlag 1977; Philip Kraft.

A Brief Look at creativity in other fields

Introduction to
Part III

"Students of the creative process have long distinguished
between two kinds of thinking: analysis and synthesis.
Sometimes the Latin word cognito, meaning 'I think' in
the sense of analyzing or taking apart, is contrasted with
intelligo, meaning 'I understand' in the sense of gaining
insight into the nature of something ... We can look at
the world and see how things differ (make distinctions)
or how they are the same (make analogies). The first
approach usually results in the creation of new categories,
the second usually involves shifting contexts."

—*Ellen J. Langer*
Mindfulness, Addison-Wesley 1989
(© 1989 by Ellen J. Langer, Ph.D. Reprinted by permission
of Addison-Wesley Publishing Company, Inc.)

There is something fascinating about the field of software. It
consumes our energies, our talents, our interests. We can
make a career out of doing nothing but software-related things,
and be quite happy in the doing.

But people who focus their attention only in one direction begin
to realize, after a while, that their horizons have become narrow

and their judgments impaired. Do those of us who focus too long and too hard on software suffer from that malady?

I think the answer is yes. In this, Part III of the book, we will take a brief tour of the role of creativity in other fields. Some interesting lessons can be learned in doing so.

One field that particularly deserves our attention is the ages-old field of problem-solving. There is a strange history to this field. Although problem-solving is, of course, as old as the human race and has been written about sporadically through the centuries, it took the advent of computers to spur renewed interest. In the early 1960s some remarkable new work in problem-solving took place.

There are three particularly interesting findings from that new spurt of interest in problem-solving:

1. The thing we call the software life cycle is really a universal problem-solving approach (this theme is elaborated in Chapter 17, to follow).
2. As problems increase in complexity, heuristic methods become more and more important, and formal approaches begin to break down (this theme was elaborated in Part I).
3. General problem-solving approaches, which have led to so much success in the field of computing to date, are characterized as "weak" approaches to problem-solving, whereas special-purpose approaches are characterized as "strong" (contrast the role of an adjustable wrench vs. specific-sized wrenches in loosening a nut, for example).

Taken both individually and as a whole, these three findings suggest some dramatically different approaches to both software practice and software research in the future. One might imagine a future, for example, that looked at variations within the life cycle rather than trying to scrap it entirely, as some in computing suggest; focusing away from formal approaches and toward heuristic ones, which is substantially at odds with much conventional wisdom in computing today; and moving from generalized, cure-all software solution approaches toward application-focused ones: application-specific methodologies, tools, languages, and perhaps even computers, for example.

What's the point here? That looking beyond our own field can lead us to a place where our own field is seen in a much clearer perspective. That in so doing, we may spot some fundamental problems with the contemporary directions of our field. That is the purpose of this Part of the book.

In the first two chapters to follow, we look at creativity as both an organizational and individual trait. (In the world of this millennium, it is easy to imagine that both individual brilliance and organizational innovation will be required to address the massively increasing problems we in our field tackle.)

Next, we look at the issue of using the computer to enhance the creativity of people in other fields (this is the ultimate form of looking outward!). The results of experiments in this area to date, we see, are surprising—and disappointing.

Perhaps some of that disappointment is related to some fundamental paradoxes in the field of creativity. Those paradoxes are defined and discussed in the next chapter.

Finally, to add perspective to this Part of the book that is already focusing on perspective, we do a reprise of the subject matter of this book from the point of view of how it all fits in with the experiences of other disciplines. One author tells us about "the classical contradiction between control and creativity."

"'Twas always thus," we say in Chapter 17.

The fundamental underlying concept of this book—that software must use a combination of control-oriented and creativity-enhancing approaches—is not a new idea at all! And that's probably the strongest lesson to be derived from a brief look at creativity in other fields.

chapter 13
organizational creativity

"The new millennium needs bold, creative men and women who can turn their dreams into reality."
—*Dr. Kirpal Singh,* Professor, Singapore Management University, in a testimonial for Creativity Workshops.

"A lot of times when we have a problem, instead of calling a meeting, we'll just say what the problem is—maybe on an email—and then just let everyone come to their own conclusions and think about it at different times."
—*Laurie Ann Goldman,* CEO, SPANX, Inc., in "The Creative Edge," *Atlanta Business Chronicle,* September 16, 2005

The subject of creativity has been around for a long time. That should mean that here is a topic that can lean heavily on the findings of other researchers in other disciplines, right?

The surprising answer to that question is a qualified no. According to a comprehensive survey of creativity issues in the broader workplace (not just software) there has been a "limited amount of research on creativity in organizations," but "decades of research on organizational innovation" [Woodman, Sawyer, and Griffin 1993]. The paper elaborates on that theme: "researchers still know surprisingly little about how the creative process works;" and "from the applied side, we also know little about how organizations can successfully promote and manage individual and organizational creativity."

Part of the problem, the authors say, is that "organizational researchers have done a relatively poor job" of "disaggregat[ing] the construct of creativity from the broader construct of innovation." How do they distinguish between creativity and innovation? "We frame the definition of organizational creativity as a subset of the broader domain of innovation. Innovation is then characterized to be a subset of an even broader context of organizational change ... even though creativity may produce the new product, service, idea or process that is implemented through innovation ... innovation can also include the adaptation of preexisting products or processes ... " In other words, creativity conceives novelty, and innovation puts creative and/or modified ideas into usage.

But let's step back a little and look at the picture being painted in [Woodman, Sawyer, and Griffin 1993]. The subject that interested them, and forms the basis for their paper, is something they call "organizational creativity." Organizational creativity comes about, they say, through interactions involving individual creativity and group creativity. "Organizational creativity is a function of the creative outputs of its component groups and contextual influences (organizational culture, reward systems, resource constraints, the larger environment outside the system, and so on) ... Group creativity is a function of individual creative behavior inputs, the interactions of the individuals involved, group characteristics, group processes, and contextual influences." In other words, although individual creativity plays an escalating and important role in organizational creativity, there are other factors that also play a role.

Since individual creativity is a key building block, the authors look at it a little more deeply. They see it as consisting of both personality traits and cognitive factors. To be specific, these are the personality traits they identify:

- High valuation of esthetic qualities in experience
- Broad interests
- Attraction to complexity
- High energy
- Independence of judgment
- Autonomy
- Intuition
- Self-confidence
- Ability to resolve apparently conflicting traits in one's self-concept
- A firm sense of self as creative
- Persistence
- Curiosity
- Intellectual honesty
- Cognitive factors
- Associative fluency
- Fluency of expression
- Figural fluency
- Ideational fluency
- Speech fluency
- Word fluency
- Practical ideation fluency
- Originality

That apparent laundry list of creative traits emerges from an interesting history of exploring creativity. "Much of the early research on creativity," the authors say, "was characterized by catalogs of biographical and historical information on eminent creators." However, analyzing that information didn't bear much fruit: "Attempts at empirically keying these measures resulted in factorial complexity that makes theoretical interpretation ... virtually impossible." To overcome that problem, as well as to fill in the apparent missing gaps in a biographical approach, other researchers began including the interaction of personality data with the biographical data. According to the authors, some of those researchers have "demonstrated that personality data interact with biographical data to predict creativity."

The main contribution of the paper, in addition to supplying a strong foundation of references to the earlier creativity literature, is to postulate a set of beliefs about creativity in the form of hypotheses. The paper, unfortunately, does not go on to test the hypotheses, leaving that as an exercise for future researchers! Here are the hypotheses.

About individual creative performance:

> 1a: It will be increased by group norms that support open sharing of information.
>
> 1b: It will be decreased by group norms that create high conformity expectations.
>
> 1c: It will be increased by organizational cultures that support risk-taking behaviors.
>
> 1d: It will be decreased by reward systems that rigorously evaluate creative accomplishment and link these outcomes tightly to extrinsic rewards.

About group creative performance:

> 2a: It will be increased by group diversity.
>
> 2b: It will be decreased by autocratic styles of leadership.
>
> 2c: It will have a curvilinear relationship to group cohesiveness.
>
> 2d: It will be increased by the use of highly participative structures and cultures.

About organizational creative performance:

> 3a: It will be increased by the availability of slack resources.
>
> 3b: It will be decreased by restrictions on information flows and communication channels within the system.

3c: It will be increased by the use of organic organizational
designs (e.g., matrix, network, collaborative groups).
3d: It will be decreased by restrictions on information
exchanges within the environment.

Many of the hypotheses, although unevaluated within the paper,
emerge from the writings of previous creativity scholars. For
example, the authors point out that "motivational interventions
such as evaluations and reward systems may adversely affect
intrinsic motivation toward a creative task because they redirect
attention away from the heuristic aspects of the creative task and
toward the technical or rule-based aspects of tasks performance."
Note that hypothesis 1d directly evolves from this finding.

Note also the apparent underlying assumption on the
researchers' part that creativity is harmed by "technical or rule-
bound aspects" and helped by "heuristic aspects." This provides
some justification for the positions taken in other essays in
this book that formal, methodological, disciplined approaches
to building software may indeed get in the way of the creative
processes also needed.

Other findings cited by the authors that tend to support the
hypotheses include these:

"The number of formal supervisory levels and the number
of R&D employees were negatively correlated with innovation [not creativity], whereas the [small] size of the
research project teams ... was positively correlated ..."

"We expect creativity to be enhanced by adaptive, flexible
organizational structures ..."

"A reasonable conjecture is that when functional managers
control rewards, engineers fear that nonroutine behavior
will be evaluated negatively by those managers. However,

when project managers control rewards, the overall outcome is evaluated regardless of the means used to accomplish the task."

Interestingly, and harking back to an earlier Part of this book, this suggests that too much emphasis on process can get in the way of creativity, and that a product focus—the goal, after all, of the project manager—is more likely to allow employees the freedom to be creative.

What do the authors of the paper see as their bottom line? "To understand creativity in a social context necessitates an exploration of creative processes, creative products, creative persons, and creative situations. A useful theory of organizational creativity must provide a framework of sufficient complexity and richness to integrate these four components."

That sets the stage for future research very nicely. But a great deal of it still needs to be done.

Reference

Woodman, Sawyer and Griffin 1993—"Toward a Theory of Organizational Creativity," *Academy of Management Review*, Vol. 18, No. 2 1993, Richard W. Woodman, John E. Sawyer, and Ricky W. Griffin.

chapter 14
The creative person

"Rationalists, wearing square hats, think, in square rooms
Looking at the floor, looking at the ceiling.
They confine themselves to right-angled triangles.
If they tried rhomboids, cones, waving lines, ellipses—
   As, for example, the ellipse of the half-moon—
Rationalists would wear sombreros."

   —*Wallace Stevens*, in "Six Significant Landscapes"

What constitutes a creative person?
   That turns out to be a hard question. It's hard partly because there are a lot of different studies that give a lot of different answers, but it's also hard because there is enormous debate about whether there is, in fact, such a person.

The latter issue—the debate about whether there is such a thing as a creative person—centers on the issue of whether creativity can be learned. The answer to that question is, of course, extremely important. Given that we have already seen that some portion of software's tasks demand creativity, the question boils down to this: "Must we hire people who are inherently creative to build software, or can we train creativity into those we already have?"

   If only a few are creative, that is an important but also depressing answer. First of all, that answer enormously compli-

cates the task of hiring software specialists, since the role of
creativity in the skill mix of new employees suddenly becomes
critical. It is also a depressing answer because it means that only a
chosen few can perform those software tasks that are creative.

Fortunately, creativity experts largely believe that creativity
can be learned. That is especially good news to people who offer
courses in improving creativity, since of course such an effort
would be pointless if creativity is one of those things you either
have or don't have. But it is also good news to all of us, because
it means that we don't have to worry about whether there is a
creativity barrier in our lives that we are either able to overcome or
not.

Be all of that as it may, let us pursue a related issue at this point.
Suppose that some people are dramatically more creative than
others. This does not force us to assume that the others cannot be
creative, only that there are people who are really good at it. What
are the characteristics of these creative people?

There are lots of interesting studies of that question. Here are
a couple of sets of answers from some particularly interesting
sources.

"One trait I quickly noticed," according to David Johnson
[Johnson 1990], writing in an unusual publication called Midnight
Engineering (it's a journal for people considering starting their
own technical business), "was their intense concentration on their
work. At times they seemed to be in another world, taking little
or no interest in the activities around them. Although I would not
call them anti-social, they did prefer to work with their computers
or test equipment than with other people."

Johnson went on, "When they were not concentrating on a
problem they were very easy to get along with and they had a
keen sense of humor. However, I did notice them to be much less
tolerant of disturbances. When working on an especially difficult
problem, loud music, clerical work, group meetings and report
writing were all viewed as interruptions or distractions …

"When they did allow themselves a break it was to read. They seemed to have an unquenchable thirst for knowledge ... It didn't seem to matter what the subject was, as long as it was interesting ... Perhaps this general interest is why few of the individuals I knew had advanced college degrees and why many crossed over from one technical area to another ...

"The generalist attitude of many creative people I knew was also displayed in their problem solving techniques. I noticed that they did not rely heavily on detailed mathematical tools when solving problems. If calculations were needed only ball-park figures were used ... They relied much more on trial and error methods. For them it was faster to wire up a circuit and test their design than wait for a paper
study ..."

Johnson's informal analysis of creative people gives us a lot of practical, deeply felt insight. But are there more rigorous, scientific studies of the same issues?

As you might expect, there are. In an interesting series of studies, [Barron 1958] offers us an analysis of "The Psychology of Imagination."

The bottom line of Barron's studies is this: "Creative individuals are more at home with complexity and apparent disorder than other people are." How did that manifest itself in his studies? Here is a particularly interesting answer:

"When confronted ... with the Rorschach inkblot test, creative individuals insist to a most uncommon degree upon giving an interpretation which takes account of all details in one comprehensive, synthesizing image. Since some of these blots are quite messy, this disposition to synthesize points up the challenge of disorder. It also illustrates the creative response to disorder, which is to find an elegant new order more satisfying than any that could be evoked by a simpler configuration."

Barron also found that creative people resisted giving in to group consensus. In a series of contrived experiments, he set up a situation in which the majority under test gave an agreed-upon false answer, and the real test subjects, knowing what the majority had chosen, had to make their own choice. Only about 25% of the real subjects were able to resist the erroneous consensus. Barron tested those subjects further, and found they expressed their independence in such statements as:

"I like to fool around with new ideas, even if they turn out later to be a total waste of time."

"Some of my friends think that my ideas are impractical, if not a bit wild."

"The unfinished and the imperfect often have greater appeal for me than the completed and polished."

As a result of these and other tests, Barron came to these conclusions about creative people:

"They are especially observant, and they value accurate observation."

"They often express part-truths, but this they do vividly; the part they express is the generally unrecognized ... and unobserved."

"They see things as others do, but also as others do not."

"They are thus independent in their cognition, and they also value clearer cognition. They will suffer great personal pain to testify correctly."

"They are motivated ... both for reasons of self-preservation and in the interest of human culture and its future."

"They are born with greater brain capacity; they have more ability to hold many ideas at once, and to compare more ideas with one another—hence to make a richer synthesis."

"They are by constitution more vigorous and have available to them an exceptional fund of psychic and physical energy."

"They usually lead more complex lives, seeking tension ... [and] the pleasure they obtain upon its discharge."

"They have more contact than most people do with the life of the unconscious—with fantasy, reverie, the world of imagination."

"They have exceptionally broad and flexible awareness of themselves."

"The creative person is both more primitive and more cultured, more destructive and more constructive, crazier and saner, than the average person."

Now let me ask you an odd question. As you read those statements, did you do a little self-analysis, measuring your own creative instincts? I know that I did. And I suspect that all of us feel within ourselves some sense of the creative, and thus some kinship with that elusive "creative person." In other words, we may or may not view ourselves as creative people, but we know that we can be creative when the need arises. That's a nice feeling, of course, but also an important one. We have met the creative person, and he (or she) is us.

References

Barron 1958—"The Psychology of Imagination," *Scientific American*, Sept. 1958; Frank Barron.

Johnson 1990—"The Creative Person," *Midnight Engineering*, January/February 1990; David Johnson.

chapter 15
computer support
for creativity

"Software environments can both enhance [and] ... inhibit
desired outcomes."

—Joyce J. Elam and Melissa Mead
"Can Software Influence Creativity?"

"Solutions developed with the aid of the software were
judged less creative."

—Douglas E. Durand and Susie H. VanHuss
"Creativity Software and DSS: Cautionary Findings"

Most of this book is inward-focused. That is, it is about the
role of creativity in building software; the inward focus is
on the field of software itself.

However, this Chapter is outward-focused. It is about the role
of computers and software in helping others to be creative. It is
included because there is quite an active community within the
computing and software field, looking at creativity issues outside
the field.

For example, in the spring of 1993 an international symposium
was held in England with the theme "Creativity and Cognition."
The title itself does not express what was unusual about this
conference, but the subtitle does:

"Artists, musicians, designers, cognitive scientists and computer scientists present ideas on creativity and cognition that cross the boundaries of art and science."

This was a truly interdisciplinary conference, where experts from both "soft" and "hard" fields met to share ideas. A book based on the symposium was published by MIT Press in early 1994.

Themes of the conference were:

- Concepts, processes, and computational models
- Art and science: intersections and boundaries
- Computer technology: methods and tools
- Reflections on art practice; studies in design practice

The interaction of the different disciplines came through nicely in the titles of some of the papers presented: "Towards Artificial Creativity," "Using the Computer to Augment Creativity: Computer Choreography," "Culture, Knowledge and Creativity: Beyond Computable Numbers," and "Tamed Equations." The image of Computer Choreography through Tamed Equations is especially wonderful!

There is a fundamental concern beneath all of this disciplinary interaction, however: Does the use of a computer really enhance the creative efforts of those in other disciplines? It is easy to imagine that the answer ought to be yes, especially from the point of view of us computer folk who are used to the many and diverse wonders that computers can work. But is there any hard evidence to support that intuition?

Two studies have addressed this issue. Interestingly, these studies come not from the world of the arts, where we might expect the most interest in creativity, but from the world of business. In [Elam 1990] and [Durand 1992] we find studies of the value of creativity-enhancing software packages in the decision-support application domain.

Traditionally, decision-support systems (DSS) are focused on a particular problem, and on the structuring of solution approaches through a database and a model base specific to that problem. Notice that the traditional DSS is, in some ways, the exact opposite of what a creativity-enhancing DSS might be, since it is specific-problem-focused and provides a structured solution approach, whereas a creative DSS might be expected to be applied to a number of different problems, and facilitate different, free-wheeling, creativity-enhancing skills.

The first study

In the first referenced study [Elam 1990], the authors found a commercially available creativity-enhancing DSS and set up an experiment in its value. The software chosen (ods/CONSULTANT, by Organization Development Software) had not yet been announced in the marketplace at the time of the study, but it seemed to the authors that what it offered was closer to their study goals than any other available package. (For a more complete discussion of available creativity-enhancing software packages, see [Thierauf 1993]). The tool offered facilities for encouraging idea generation, facilitating brainstorming, provoking questions, and combining idea fragments, as well as quantitative support for prioritizing/grading ideas, identifying interdependencies among ideas, and allowing for categorizing ideas along user-selected dimensions.

The study involved three groups, assigned a common set of problems but using three different approaches to solving them:

1. No computer support
2. ods/CONSULTANT support using the following model (called Version 1):
   - Describe problem
   - Gather candidate facts
   - Assess relevance and validity
   - Organize facts

- Develop explanations
- Identify solutions

3. ods/CONSULTANT support using the following model (called Version 2):

- Gather candidate facts
- Determine objectives
- Assess relevance and validity
- Identify obstacles
- Inventory resources
- Generate ideas
- Edit and translate ideas
- Make decisions
- Test decisions

What was the fundamental difference between the two versions? The authors saw Version 1 as focusing on underlying causes, moving from causes to explanations and then solutions. Version 2, by contrast, focused on practical solutions at every step. The authors summarized the two by saying, "Version 1 looks backwards for causes and depth of understanding while Version 2 looks ahead for practical solutions."

The subjects of the study were practicing professionals with similar backgrounds from a Big Eight accounting firm. The tasks assigned included a business problem and a public policy problem. The results of the problem solution were judged for their creativity by a panel of expert judges who were asked to use their own subjective definition of creativity. The expectation was that the judges would evaluate results on the novelty and appropriateness of the problem solution. Judges were people like corporate presidents, management consultants, college professors, and directors of national funding agencies.

What were the results? They were quite surprising and, in fact, somewhat unsettling. Using a rating scheme in which lower numbers indicated greater creativity, the results were:

- Version 1: 8.0
- No Software: 12.7
- Version 2: 16.8

That is, there was considerable difference between the two software versions (this difference was the only one the authors considered statistically significant), and the creativity of those who used no software aids at all fell between the two software-supported versions. The authors called the results "intriguing," noted that "we expected both software treatments would result in more creative responses than no software," and summarized: "The difference in the results for the two software treatments is an important one for DSS designers ... software environments can both enhance [and] ... inhibit desired outcomes."

The authors also obtained user perceptions of the two versions of the software tool. Version 1 was seen as more fun to use and more helpful than Version 2, but more difficult to use.

And the authors, who did not consider time taken by the subjects in evaluating creativity, noted that the Version 1 users took more time than the others.

The authors do not say so, but the implication seems to be that creative solutions may take more time than less creative ones, but generate more fun during the doing.

The second study

In the second referenced study [Durand 1992], a similar experiment was conducted. The area in which creativity was sought was in the decision-support domain, and a commercially available software package—in this case, Idea Generator—was employed. (The package is said to increase the ability of its user to brainstorm, generate alternatives, defer judgment about alternatives until a sufficient number are available, and select among the alternatives.)

Hoping to improve on some of the limitations of the first study, the researchers chose 88 subjects (MBA students with about two years of work experience), pre-measured the subjects for innate creativity, assigned them two short case studies to perform, and used independent judges to evaluate the results on a comprehensive set of criteria, only a few of which were related to creativity. (Neither the judges nor the subjects knew the experimental subject was creativity.)

Subjects worked the case studies either using the software or with no software support.

And what were the results of this second study? For 28 measurement techniques, only five of which were related to creativity, the software-supported subjects scored more poorly in every single category. Let's say that again: Software not only did not help induce creativity (or any of the other possible improvements in the assignment), it actually hurt.

What possible explanation can there be for such a surprising finding? Did the subjects fail to use the software properly? No, the researchers gathered information that said the subjects using the software accomplished the kinds of things the software was designed to support (a high quantity of ideas, fleshed out in detail and depth).

Was there some sort of bias caused by people with inherent high or low creativity? No, the software diminished the performance of both!

What then? The authors admit to being "puzzled," and call the findings "clear and unexpected." In their discussion section, they conclude that "solutions developed with the aid of the software were judged less creative." And they provide, as perhaps the only possible conclusion, "creativity inducing software appears to need further development before it can contribute meaningfully to improving Decision Support Systems."

We have seen, throughout much of this book, that creativity is an elusive thing to define, discuss, and measure. Even when we succeed in defining, discussing, and measuring, if we test for creativity we get considerable variance in our responses. (See the Chapter in Part I on creative vs. intellectual and clerical tasks, for example.)

The findings of these studies simply echo that theme. We can still hypothesize, for example, that computers can be used to enhance creativity; but we must quickly add that we don't understand very much about how to do that, and that badly done computer-enhanced creativity can have a negative, not positive, impact on our goals.

That's not a very satisfying finding. However, it does appear to be an accurate assessment of the state of the art in computer-aided creativity.

References

Durand 1992—"Creativity Software and DSS: Cautionary Findings," *Information and Management 23* 1992; Douglas E. Durand and Susie H. VanHuss.

Elam 1990—"Can Software Influence Creativity?" *Information Systems Research,* March 1990; Joyce J. Elam and Melissa Mead.

Thierauf 1993—*Creative Computer Software for Strategic Thinking and Decision Making: A Guide for Senior Management and MIS Professionals,* Quarum Books 1993; Robert J. Thierauf.

chapter 16
creativity paradoxes

"The rise of planning departments and plans tends to circumscribe the discretion of the man on the firing line. Thus, it usually is true that with more extensive planning a large group of employees have less freedom in the exercise of their own judgment. Conformity, rather than originality, is expected of them. This restriction on initiative tends to snuff our the creative spark that is so essential in a successful enterprise, and it also has a bad effect on morale."

—William H. Newman,
*Administrative Action: The Techniques of
Organization and Management*, Prentice-Hall 1951

Creativity, we have already seen, is a difficult subject to pin down. It has been defined perhaps a million times, and its definitions differ depending on the definitionist. Its effects have been described over and over again, and yet it is hard to say precisely when an effect is creative and when it is not. Can creativity be learned? Many say it can, some say it can't. There seems to be something magical about this elusive notion of creativity.

Because of all of the above, it probably should not surprise us that there are significant paradoxes involved in creativity. At least two can be found in the literature:

creativity paradox number 1: The more a creative person knows about the subject of focus, the less the need for creativity.

creativity paradox number 2: In order to think originally, we must familiarize ourselves with the ideas of others.

And, fascinatingly enough, the juxtaposition of those two paradoxes creates a third:

creativity paradox number 3: Creativity paradoxes 1 and 2 do not agree with each other. Let's elaborate on each of those paradoxes in turn.

The more a creative person knows about the subject of focus, the less the need for creativity.

Suppose you are presented with an extremely complicated problem to solve, but also suppose that you have solved similar problems many times before. Your approach to solving this current problem, naturally, is to examine your successful past solutions and begin to find one or more to modify to match the new problem.

However, in the act of reusing past solutions, you are short cutting some of the facets necessary to allow an act to be labeled creative. If we accept the [Newell 1962] definition of creativity used earlier in this book, creativity must involve novelty or value, use unconventional thinking, be a product of high motivation and persistence, and deal with vague and ill-defined problems. Your reused solution certainly has value, but its reuse has stripped it of the notion of novelty; yesterday's unconventional thinking is rapidly becoming today's conventional thought; high motivation and persistence are certainly less needed now; and although the initial problem may have seemed vague and ill-defined, famil-

iarity is beginning to breed a sense of understanding and definition.

Perhaps it was said best in [Sasso 1989]. "What part does
creativity play in the design process?" the authors ask. "From
our perspective, it does not fit neatly in at a particular point in
a certain process. Rather, we see creativity as permeating each
of [its] ... activities ... The extent to which this occurs is largely
determined by the interaction of the designer's experiences and
the design space—if his experience includes an overall solution
obviously adaptable to the current design space, very little
creativity will be needed. If, on the other hand, the design situation is entirely foreign to the designer, practically every aspect of
the design process will require creative thinking."

How ironic! In a problem-solving situation, the potential is there
for the most creative solutions to be provided by those who understand the problem least. Isn't that fairly unsatisfying? In fact, can
that make any sense at all?

In order to think originally, we must familiarize ourselves with
the work of others.

This thought, too, represents a paradox. Doesn't the very act of
familiarizing ourselves with the work of others detract from the
originality of what we produce?

Those who have identified this paradox see it emerging from
what they have called the "four phases of creativity": preparation, incubation, illumination, and verification. Creative thought,
according to this "life-cycle" view of creativity, cannot occur in a
vacuum. It must be stimulated (preparation and incubation) before
it can bring forth fruit (illumination). And it is during this stimulation, when the problem-solver is exploring the subject area of the
problem, that stimuli are ingested that can later drive the creative
force. For example, [Henle 1962] (as quoted in [Couger 1990]) says:

"It seems that creative ideas do not occur to us unless we spend
a great deal of time and energy engaged in just the activity that
makes their emergence most difficult ... It may be that immer-

sion in our subject matter is a condition of creative thinking not only because it gives us the material with which to think but also because it acquaints us with the difficulties of the problem."

Not all creative ideas, of course, emerge from a four-phase process. The notion of the "aha," or serindipitous solution, is well-known. Yet even with situations where solutions appear to fall out of the blue, a little thought usually suggests that some part of the brain has been ingesting input and mulling over the problem, even without a formal identification of those activities.

This paradox, unlike the first, is more satisfying. It seems to match our western ethic, that those who work at a problem are more likely to solve it satisfactorily than those who do not.

And that brings us to the third paradox:

Creativity paradoxes 1 and 2 do not agree with each other.

How can it be true that we must immerse ourselves in a subject area in order to be creative, and yet to the extent that we draw from our mind past solutions we are not?

Perhaps a resolution to this dilemma can proceed something like this:

• Paradox 1 presents us with the situation in which the problem-solver has already immersed himself (or herself) in the problem, and (at some point in the past) come up with a solution. The act of creating that solution is what moved the problem-solver past the stages of novelty, unconventional thinking, and the need for persistence, and moved the problem toward being one that is well-defined.

• Paradox 2, on the other hand, presents us with the situation in which the problem-solver is at an earlier stage in the creative process for this problem. Preparation and incubation must precede illumination. No readymade past solution is available.

Thus, the differences seems to be one of degree. A little exposure to the problem at issue is vital to the instantiation of creativity, but a lot moves us past the need (and, of course, into a different phase of that creativity life cycle).

Seen in this way, the third paradox, although interesting as a semantic exercise, is probably less significant than the first two. And that's probably just as well. There are enough difficulties with understanding the nature of creativity without the need to deal with conflicting paradoxes!

References

Couger 1990—"Ensuring Creative Approaches in Information System Design," *Managerial and Decision Economics,* Vol. 11, pp. 281–295, 1990. J. Daniel Couger.

Henle 1962—"The Birth and Death of Ideas," in *Contemporary Approaches to Creative Thinking, Atherton Press,* p. 43, 1962; M. Henle.

Newell 1962—"The Processes of Creative Thinking," in *Contemporary Approaches to Creative Thinking, Atherton Press,* 1962; A. Newell, J. Shaw and H. Simon.

Sasso 1989—William C. Sasso and Monte McVay. "The Constraints and Assumptions Interpretation of Systems Design: A Descriptive Process Model," submitted to the *Journal of Systems and Software* in late 1989 but never published.

chapter 17
'Twas Always Thus

"The Romantic philosophers were not interested in taking
the universe apart like a machine, in analyzing it into its
smallest atoms. No, they wanted to contemplate, understand, interpret, feel and see through the world to its
hidden meaning, like you do with a poem or painting."
>   —Bo Dalhbom and Lars Mathiassen,
>   Struggling with Quality, The Philosophy of
>   Developing Computer Systems, Academic Press 1992

We in software like to believe that the problems we encounter
are fresh and new, just like our profession.

That is a tempting belief. It is fun to employ this marvelous new
technology to solve problems, and it would be fun to think that the
problems we are solving are just as new.

Some of them are, of course. Space exploration and automated
flight control were areas of speculation before the computing era,
but they were not real problems capable of being solved in any
meaningful way.

However, most problems that we solve are not new. Information
systems and financial systems and manufacturing systems
were possible and existed long before computers. They may be

enormously more efficient and effective now, but the problems themselves are not new.

Many attempts have been made, in the field of computing, to capitalize on this past history. People examine ideas from the rich past of other disciplines to try to identify those ideas that could be useful in the new era of computing and that, of course, is a worthy endeavor.

But along the way, something odd has happened. We have tried to borrow ideas from the solution domain of other disciplines, but we have ignored what we have learned about the problem domain.

What do I mean by that?

With the advent of the field of software engineering, many attempts have been made to use analogy as a vehicle for identifying traditional engineering approaches that might be useful in software. We have examined manufacture by parts, for example, and statistical quality control. These kinds of approaches have been problematic in software, however. There are some fundamental differences about software that make these kinds of solution analogies difficult to employ. The uniqueness and weightlessness and spacelessness and near-zero manufacturing cost of software products mean that many ideas simply do not transfer well into its world.

Perhaps, however, we have been looking at the wrong side of the analogy picture. The topics we mentioned above were about solution approaches. What could we learn if we focused, instead, on past understandings of addressing the problem itself? The field of problem-solving, although eons old, is not as rich in concepts as we might like, but it still offers some worthwhile analogies to the software problem-solver.

The Life cycle as universal problem-solving Algorithm

Take the idea of the software life cycle as an example. Although notions of the life cycle differ, most would agree that the life cycle consists of something like this:

1. Identify a problem.
2. Define the requirements of the problem.
3. Design a solution to the problem.
4. Implement the design.
5. Test the implementation.
6. Use the implemented product.

To those of us in software who are used to reading, and sometimes arguing, about the life cycle, the discussion above probably seems simplistic and rather boring. But let's take another look at this life cycle from the more traditional point of view of problem-solving.

Those steps above are, essentially, a universal problem-solving algorithm. None of them is intrinsically software-specific. If you look at the traditional great books on applications of problem-solving, like Polya on mathematics or Alexander on architecture, you will find something resembling this same life cycle as a part of what they present. And that's not all. Writers use this same approach. Artists use the approach. I have even been told that, at a meeting of a business and professional women's club, something akin to this life cycle was presented as the proper approach to starting a business!

If we in software could only see the life cycle as an analogy borrowed from the problem-solving past, we could save ourselves a lot of arguments about whether the life cycle is appropriate or not. Of course it is appropriate—we in software are not about to rewrite the history of problem-solving. What we have sometimes failed to see, in our often-endless arguments about the appropriateness of the life cycle, is that the basic framework of the life cycle can be bent to include a lot of variations. Spiral life cycles and proto-typing, for example, are simply variations on the basic life-cycle theme. The fact that iterations occur within the life-cycle stages should not be a problem to any but the most pedantic of life-cycle believers.

The life cycle as a universal problem-solving algorithm is only one benefit we can achieve by focusing on the problem domain instead of on the specifics of solution domains. The real purpose of this chapter of the book is to focus on another.

The underlying message of this book has been that there are two approaches to building software. One is management-driven, control-oriented, formal, and disciplined. The other is skill-driven, creativity-focused, informal, and freewheeling. Which of the approaches we choose can have a profound effect on both the process of building software and its product. The suspicion with which we began the book, reinforced in various ways throughout, has been that the appropriate construction approach to software must somehow include a blending of these two approaches. The theme of the book has been to emphasize the importance of the second approach, primarily because the forces that bear on the world of software have concentrated almost exclusively on the first, and some important things have been lost along the way.

But wait. The message of this chapter has been that an examination of the historic notions of problem-solving can be useful. Is that true of this dichotomy of approaches, as well? Do we find anything about the Roman vs. Greek, management-driven vs. technologist-driven, dilemma in older information sources?

Mechanistic vs. Romantic; Hard vs. soft; Rational vs. empirical

The answer is, as you might expect, yes. In fact, this dichotomy is ages old. Perhaps the best description of the history of this difference is given in [Dahlbom 1992].

Dahlbom identifies these same two very different approaches as the Mechanistic approach, characterized by a focus on representation, formalization, program, order, and control, and a Romantic approach, characterized by individual artistic expression, genius, and creativity. "The Romantic reaction to the Mechanistic world view," Dahlbom says, "made much of the difference between

organisms and machines, wanting to defend nature and everything natural against the machines and everything artificial."

Dahlbom goes on: "The Romantic philosophers were not interested in taking the universe apart like a machine, in analyzing it
into its smallest atoms. No, they wanted to contemplate, understand, interpret, feel and see through the world to its hidden
meaning, like you do with a poem or painting."

Dahlbom labeled this dichotomy as "the classical contradiction
between control and creativity." He then evolved this dichotomy
into a discussion that he (and many other authors) characterize as
"hard" and "soft" approaches. Here, the two words have meanings
that differ somewhat from what our intuition might suggest. Hard
means objective, algorithmic, consisting of facts, with the world
being representable in an exact and true way. Its history rests in
the Mechanistic. Soft means fuzzy, consisting of ideas, subject
to interpretation, emphasizing cultural differences. Its history
rests in the Romantic. Hard subjects are easily taught—they can
be memorized, they can be tested via multiple-choice or true/false
approaches. Soft subjects are difficult to teach—memorization is
not possible; testing must be by discussion or essay.

Educational institutions, especially in the United States, tend
to focus on hard subjects. There is even an expression about
academe: "hard drives out soft." (That is, those who espouse hard
subjects tend to reject those who espouse soft ones. Tenure battles,
for example, are all too often fought along these lines.) There is
something satisfying (and easy!) about teaching and testing a
collection of facts. There is something unsettling (and difficult!)
about teaching a collection of ideas, where today's ideas may be
significantly different from those of yesterday or tomorrow.

Students tend to be more comfortable with hard subjects. We
are taught, starting in the lowest grades, that a learning experience consists of accumulating facts. If the student does not make
the transition, as he or she moves up the learning ladder, that
the mature person must add idea-based concepts to a fact-based

mindset, the student is very uncomfortable in a class where what is learned is soft. Not only is this true for the traditional soft subjects, like philosophy and sociology, but it is true in software-related pedagogy as well. Management topics, for example, are inevitably soft. Software engineering, in the sense that there is no fixed formula that is best for all problems, is soft. (Some computer scientists try to convert it into a hard subject by teaching formal ways of building software, but the bias of this author is that it is at best premature to teach formal approaches exclusively, since these approaches have yet to be shown to be a demonstrated improvement over informal ones through evaluative research. Further, this seems about as imaginative as teaching history as a collection of dates, a sure way to spoil the subject of history!)

The notion of mechanistic vs. romantic, now evolved into hard vs. soft, takes one more turn of the evolutionary wheel in Dahlbom's book. He makes a distinction between "rationalism" (the theory that reason is the foundation of certainty in knowledge) and "empiricism" (the doctrine that knowledge is obtainable by direct experience through the physical senses). He then elaborates that distinction into one between systems construction, which he says "belongs to the rationalist tradition," and problem/solving, which is "an expression of more empiricist ideas." "The main concern in the systems construction approach is complexity," he says, "whereas the main concern in the problem-solving approach is uncertainty. This suggests the following principle: In situations where the complexity of the problem is high and the uncertainty is low we should choose a systems construction approach and in situations with high uncertainty and low complexity we should prefer a problem solving approach."

Be that as it may, Dahlbom does offer one interesting gleam of hope in this spectrum of dichotomies. "The fierce antagonism between rationalists and empiricists has mellowed over the years," he says. "In this century science has arrived at a somewhat loose, but healthy, combination of the two methods. The kind of inductivism stressing the need for unbiased observation has been abandoned as impossible in favor of theoretically based hypothesis testing. You use induction to infer the empirical implications of your theories and you then test these implications by collecting data, using induction to order the data. It is [just] such a healthy mixture of deduction and induction that we would like to see in the problem solving approach."

What does all of this mean? That the dichotomy between Roman and Greek, management and technology, mechanistic and romantic, hard and soft, rational and empirical, or whatever one chooses to call it (or them)—that this dichotomy is not unique to software, and it dates back to antiquity. Remember that Dahlbom called it "the classical contradiction between control and creativity."

'Twas always thus. It is unlikely that we in software, like our brethren in much older disciplines, are going to solve the problem, to blend the dichotomies, to end the contradiction, in our lifetime. But perhaps, using the vision of Dahlbom, the "fierce antagonism" can, as it has in those older fields, "mellow over the years." One of my hopes is that this book, exhibiting much sympathy for the creativity required in software but at the same time acknowledging the need for discipline and formality as well, will help move us toward the "mellowing" that we in software need so badly.

reference

Dahlbom 1992—*Struggling with Quality, The Philosophy of Developing Computer Systems*, pp. 16–17, 52–55, 94–95, 142–143, Academic Press 1992; Bo Dahlbom and Lars Mathiassen.

part iv
summary and conclusions

contents of part iv

introduction to part IV

"Learning takes place when we are receptive to information that does not fit and creates conflict with our models.
Complacency thrives on harmony."

—*Moshe F. Rubinstein,*
Tools for Thinking and Problem-Solving,
Prentice-Hall 1986

A reviewer of one of my earlier books provided a piece
of important insight. After getting to the end of that
manuscript, his reaction was, "Remind me now, where was the
beef?" There are a lot of different ideas in a collection like this, and
it's kind of nice for the author to do a tatting up at the end.

I followed that reviewer's advice for that previous book, and I
was pleased with the summary section that ended the book. It
provided not just the reader, but myself as well, with a clearer
picture of just where the book had taken us.

Because of that, I set about to do the same for this book. The two
chapters in Part IV are the result of that effort.

chapter 18

A synergistic conclusion

"It is ideas, as much as money, power, or sex, that make the world go 'round."

—*John Forbes Nash, Jr.*, mathematician and economics Nobel laureate, in his biography *A Beautiful Mind* by Sylvia Nasa

As I struggled to wrap a gestalt over the varied facets of software creativity this book addresses, I was surprised at what began to happen. I began to get the feeling of synergy; the gestalt began to become more than just the sum of the individual parts of the book.

As I reprised the material, several themes played in my mind. There was the theme of Jeff Offutt, closing the door of his laboratory and discarding all the formal methods he had just finished teaching his students, resorting to ad hoc and—yes—creative solutions instead.

There was the theme of David Parnas, acknowledging that true top-down design was simply not possible, advocating instead that we "fake it" in our final documentation efforts.

There was the theme of Bill Curtis, expecting to find balanced and controlled evolution in design activities, finally coming to the conclusion that design is instead an opportunistic process.

There was the theme of Douglas King, quoting Herb Simon as saying that solving well-understood problems via formal approaches is very different from solving ill-understood problems, using weakly structured, heuristic approaches.

There was the theme of Bruce Blum, who told us that software process optimized for fun was only good when the tasks were small and the motivation for quality was based on an individual's insight, and that software process optimized for phased compliance is only valid when there are firm and stable requirements.

There is a common theme running through all these separate ones, I began to see. And that common theme, as I thought about it some more, began to take this form:

We in the academic world of computing have been trying to treat the construction of software as a monolithic entity. We define and advocate one-size-fits-all methods, languages, computers, and tools. We expect each new methodology to solve all problem types. We construct a process evaluation model and expect to apply it to all software projects.

I believe the message of all those themes is that our one-size-fits-all approach is wrong. No, it is worse than that. It is WRONG! It is important that we in computing begin to address software projects with the nature of the project itself as one of the determiners of how we go about running the project, how we go about solving the problem.

This was not an entirely new thought to me. I had already done some research work in the application-domain dependence of solution approaches, and realized that—far more than we yet understand—different domains require different solution approaches. But that was another neat and tidy compartment in my mind, the subject of another set of essays and research papers, and I had not yet seen that there was a relevance to this software creativity material.

I had also done some work on the size and criticality aspects of software projects. My Prentice-Hall book Building Quality

Software, for example, contains as appendices recommendations for quality solution approaches that are dependent on the size and criticality of the project in question.

However, what seemed to be emerging from these themes on creativity was a whole new dimension, the dimension of "Innovativeness of the Problem to Be Solved." Thoughtful writer after thoughtful writer had said, each in his own way, "formal approaches lose their effectiveness as we move in the direction of more innovative problems," and "disciplined approaches must at least be blended with creative ones for problems that tax the mind."

I began to struggle with the notion of a way to represent software projects, based on some essential criteria. It was clear, for example, that project size played an important role in the techniques to be used in the solution. It was equally clear that project criticality played the same kind of role. The new thought emerging here was that Innovativeness of the Problem also played the same sort of role. There were a lot of different dimensions, in short, that should have an effect on the methods we use to solve problems in software.

Remember, this struggle was happening at the same time that the Software Engineering Institute was advocating a Capability Maturity Model, and a five-level management maturity rating scheme, that was being applied across the board to all software projects. It was happening at the same time that each new formal method and methodology that came along from both computer science researchers and vendor salespeople was being advocated for all projects.

I expect, in years to come, that people will see the hard-won insight I am describing here as something that should have been obvious all along. But in the era in which I extract these notions from the threads of my contributors, this was radical thinking indeed.

424

What am I trying to say here? That each new approach to building software must be evaluated as to its appropriateness along several project characteristic dimensions:

- The nature and need of the application domain
- The size of the project
- The criticality of the solution
- The innovativeness of the problem

There may be other appropriate dimensions; this is still evolving thinking. For example, other candidates might be the knowledge/style of project managers, or the quality/capability of the technical project members.

It is interesting to note, in fact, that these candidates emerge from an organization/focused, as opposed to a project-focused, view of approach selection. For a fascinating look at an elaboration of that concept, see [Constantine 1993], which offers these organizational paradigms for different kinds of projects:

- Closed (the traditional hierarchic organization—Constantine says this approach is best for "routine, tactical projects")
- Random (based on innovative independent initiative—Constantine says this is best for projects requiring "creative breakthrough")
- Open (adaptive and collaborative—best for "complex problem-solving")
- Synchronous (efficient, harmonious alignment—best for "repetitive, critical performance")

[Hyman 1993] is a nice case study of the applications of some of these concepts.

But let's stay with the previously mentioned project-first set of project approaches for the moment.

Let's apply the various issues of Part I of this book against each of these dimensions.

discipline: Strong discipline is needed for super-large and/or critical projects. For other projects, it decreases in importance.

formal methods: Formality is appropriate for small projects (perhaps large ones, after appropriate research is done); we do not yet know if it is important for critical projects, although many advocates believe it is essential; and (most important) it is only useful for projects where the problem is not very innovative. Heuristic approaches seem to be more effective for complex projects. (Rettig and Simons, for example, take the position that an "iterative strategy," involving divide-and-concur approaches, a spiral life cycle, object technology, rapid prototyping, and incremental testing, are best when the problem is complex [Rettig and Simons 1993].)

optimizing solutions: Optimization may only be possible for small projects. It is relatively independent of project criticality (we would like to obtain optimal solutions for critical projects, but that does not make it possible) or problem innovativeness.

quantitative reasoning: In spite of the desirability of quantitative approaches, it is probably true that they are only applicable to relatively small and not very innovative projects.

process: Process probably should move hand-in-hand with discipline. That is, the more the need for discipline, the more the need to define the process on which discipline will be applied. See the discussion of discipline above.

Intellectual, creative tasks: The need for intellectual and creative approaches increases with project size, solution criticality, and especially the innovativeness of the problem.

fun: The role of fun is probably the inverse of the role of discipline. That is, it happens most on small projects that are non-critical but represent at least somewhat innovative problems.

Now, there's a problem here. It took a lot of words to say all those things. And those words will tend to obscure the simplicity of the underlying idea. I tried to draw a graphic that would simply and cleanly represent these several dimensions playing across these creativity issues, but it quickly got out of hand. So, before I move on here, let me underscore the underlying idea one more time:

The one-size-fits-all approach to software problems and solutions prevents us from seeing some important truths. Those important truths help us see when certain solution approaches will work well and when they will not. Such highly touted approaches as disciplined methods, formal methods, and defined processes, which have been advocated for all projects no matter their nature, are fairly limited in applicability to a certain subset of all problems. It is important to begin a discussion about when each such approach is appropriate (and, perhaps more important, when it is not). This section suggests a first cut at that discussion.

In the field of human relations, and especially its subset interested in civil rights, it is popular to talk about "celebrating the differences" among human beings. What that means is that, although we humans differ in race and sex and religious preference and certain other key parameters, those differences are things to be explored and appreciated, not feared and avoided. It is time for the field of computing to celebrate its differences. And the dimensions we discuss above—application domain, project size, criticality of solution, and innovativeness of the problem—define the types of differences that the field of computing and software ought to be beginning to understand—and celebrate.

References

Constantine 1993—"Work Organization: Paradigms for Project Management and Organization," *Communications of the ACM*, October 1993; Larry L. Constantine.

Hyman 1993—"Creative Chaos in High-Performance Teams: An Experience Report," *Communication of the ACM*, October 1993; Risa B. Hyman.

Rettig and Simons 1993—"A Project Planning and Development Process for Small Teams," *Communications of the ACM*, October 1993; Marc Rettig and Gary Simons.

chapter 19
other conclusions

"Great scientists tolerate ambiguity very well. They believe
the theory enough to go ahead; they doubt it enough
to notice the errors and faults so they can ... create [its]
replacement. If you believe too much you'll never notice
the flaws; if you doubt too much you won't get started. It
requires a lovely balance."
> —*Richard Hamming,* in "You and Your Research,"
> a transcription of his Bell Communications
> Research Colloquium Seminar, March 7, 1986

That celebration of differences through the varying dimensions
of the software project is, I think, the most important thought
I would like you to take away from the reading of this book; but
there are some others.

First of all, the creation of this book, as you recall, represented
a personal odyssey for me, as I moved from a view of software as
creative art to a more balanced view of software as disciplined and
creative art. Perhaps you have had some sort of odyssey of your own
as you have read what I have written.

Underlying that odyssey, I would like to believe, are some other
interesting thoughts.

There are major cultural differences in the ways we approach the construction of software. Whether those differences are called agile vs. structured, open vs. proprietary, Greek vs. Roman, technology-driven vs. management-driven, or assembly line vs. craftsmen; or whether they take the much older form of mechanistic vs. romantic or rational vs. empirical, those differences become very real when we consider their implications for how we build software.

There is little data to show that one such culture is better than the others. However, there are a few findings, scattered along the fringes of the chasm between them, which suggest that on some occasions each side might be right.

Perhaps the most interesting data in the book results from a couple of experiments into the nature of software tasks. Breaking those tasks down into their creative, intellectual, and clerical natures, one experiment demonstrates a consistent finding that roughly 80% of software's tasks are intellectual, and only 20% clerical. Regarding the degree of creativity in the tasks, the other experiment is less conclusive. Expert judgments vary, some saying that only 6% of software's tasks are creative, with others putting the figure as high as 29% (the average is 16%). Whatever else the findings mean, certainly they show—in a quantitative way—that software's tasks are a considerable intellectual challenge.

For which tasks is creativity needed? Although there is disagreement here, it seems fairly clear that it includes at least these activities:

- Translating business needs into problems for creative solution (strategic planning and competitive advantage tasks come in here)
- Resolving problem statements defined by multiple and conflicting enterprise organizations
- Designing solutions to complex and new problems

- Establishing a necessary and sufficient set of test conditions and cases
- Making a major enhancement to a software system where the enhancement is outside the design envelope of the original system

Given that creativity must be part of producing software solutions, what does that mean in terms of staffing? We have seen throughout the book support for the notion that all of us have the capability to be creative. We also saw, through the studies of the late Dan Couger, that the cost of training approaches to enhance that inherent creativity need be no higher than 0.5% of project costs; we further saw that there are a lot of well-known techniques for enhancing creativity; and finally, we saw that those techniques can raise individual creativity by a perceived 23%, and the creativity of the organization in which those individuals function by 27% (according to one informal study).

Interestingly enough, we also learned that software tools for enhancing the creativity of non-software people have mixed, if not negative, success. It looks like we can make more progress, at this point, focusing creativity on software tasks, rather than focusing software on creative tasks.

There is one more set of ideas that I, at least, will retain from my odyssey in the creation of this book. They are the pithy quotes I obtained related to the role of creativity in software. Here are some of my favorites:

> On quantitative approaches: "If you torture the numbers long enough, they will tell you anything you want to know."

> On "you can't manage what you can't measure": "We do it all the time."

On the role of discipline and process: "We follow all the rules, and fail."

On the war between theory and practice: "Weak theory gets laughed out of the halls of practice," and "Stuck practice does not upgrade to match the legitimate findings of theory," and "When theory and practice battle, it's a sure sign that something is wrong."

On researchers who believe they are entitled to government support but produce work that no one ever references: "They are welfare queens in white coats."

On generic vs. ad hoc approaches: "Generic approaches are 'weak' in the sense that they solve no problem really well; ad hoc approaches are 'strong' in that they focus on the problem at hand."

On the conflict between creativity and discipline: "They are an 'odd couple' in that both are necessary."

That last pithy quote brings us full circle. Should software approaches be formal and disciplined or freewheeling and creative? In the final analysis, the message of this book is clear. The answer is simply:

"Yes!"

Index

About the Author:
Robert L. Glass

obert L. Glass (Bob) has meandered the halls of computing for over 50 years now, starting with a three-year gig in the aerospace industry (at North American Aviation) in 1954–1957, which makes him one of the true pioneers of the software field.

That stay at North American extended into several other aerospace appearances (at Aerojet-General Corp., 1957–1965) and the Boeing Company, 1965–1970 and 1972–1982). His role was largely that of building software tools used by applications specialists. It was an exciting time to be part of the aerospace business - those were the heady days of Space Exploration, after all - but it was an even headier time to be part of the Computing Field. Progress in both fields was rapid, and the vistas were extraterrestrial!

The primary lesson he learned during those aerospace years was that he loved the technology of software, but hated being a manager. He carefully cultivated the role of technical specialist, which had two major impacts on his career—(a) his technical knowledge remained fresh and useful, but (b) his knowledge of management—and his earning power (!)—were diminished commensurately.

451

When his upwards mobility had reached the inevitable techno-logical Glass ceiling (tee-hee!), Glass took a lateral transition into academe. He taught in the Software Engineering graduate program at Seattle University (1982-1987) and spent a year at the (all-too-academic!) Software Engineering Institute (1987-1988). (He had earlier spent a couple of years (1970-1972) working on a tools-focused research grant at the University of Washington).

The primary lesson he learned during those academic years was that he loved having his Head in the academic side of software engineering, but his Heart remained in its practice. You can take the man out of industry, apparently, but you can't take the industry out of the man. With that new-found wisdom, he began to search for ways to bridge what he had long felt was the "Communication Chasm" between academic computing and its practice.

He found several ways of doing that. Many of his books (over 25) and professional papers (over 90) focus on trying to evaluate academic computing findings and on transitioning those with practical value to industry. (This is decidedly a non-trivial task, and is largely responsible for the contrarian nature of his beliefs and his writings). His lectures and seminars on software engineering focus on both theoretical and best-of-practice findings that are useful to practitioners. His newsletter, The Software Practitioner, treads those same paths. So does the (more academic) Journal of Systems and Software, which he edited for many years for Elsevier (he is now its Editor Emeritus). And so do the columns he writes semi-regularly for such publications as Communications of the ACM ("The Practical Programmer") and IEEE Software ("The Loyal Opposition"). Although most of his work is serious and contrarian, a fair portion of it also contains (or even consists of!) computing humor.

With all of that in mind, what are his proudest moments in the computing field? The award, by Linkoping University of Sweden, of his honorary Ph.D. degree in 1995. His being named a Fellow of the ACM professional society in 1999, and an Honorary Professor at Griffith University in Australia in 2006.

On the personal level, he is the father of two biological and two adopted interracial children, and is married to Iris Vessey, an Information Systems academic.

contributors

TOM DeMarco, Atlantic Systems Guild

Guest Foreword

Tom DeMarco is a Principal of the Atlantic Systems Guild, and a
Fellow of the Cutter Consortium. He was the winner of the 1986
Warnier Prize for "lifetime contribution to the field of computing,"
and the 1999 Stevens Award for "contribution to the methods
of software development." He has a BSEE degree from Cornell
University, an M.S. from Columbia University and a diplome from
the University of Paris at the Sorbonne. He is a member of the ACM
and a Fellow of the IEEE. He makes his home in Camden, Maine.
Tom is the author of several books, including Peopleware, Waltzing
With Bears, The Deadline: A Novel About Project Management, and
Slack.

http://www.systemsguild.com/GuildSite/TDM/Tom _ DeMarco.html

Dwayne Philips

Author of "A Peculiar Project"

Dwayne Phillips has worked as a software and systems engineer
with the US government since 1980. He helps people manage
software projects and has found that simple metrics do help project

454

managers know where they are and where to shift resources in projects. He has written *The Software Project Manager's Handbook: Principles that Work at Work* and *It Sounded Good When We Started: A Project Manager's Guide to Working with People on Projects.* Dwayne has a Ph.D. in electrical and computer engineering from Louisiana State University.

http://home.att.net/~dwayne.phillips/

Giles Hoover, osprey Design

Exterior and Interior Book Design

Giles Hoover worked in small-business and corporate graphic design for nearly fifteen years before discovering book design. Renowned for breaking moving men with his book collection, he jumped into book design freelance—and hasn't looked back. His book design weblog, *Foreword,* is currently the #1 return in a Google search for "book design," and have been visited by more than 1.7 million times in the past year.

While his passion for books and book design continues unabated. Mr. Hoover has added "professional photographer" to his resumé, and, together with four ~~children~~ cats, is slowly refurbishing an old house in Macon, Georgia.

http://www.ospreydesign.com

About the Publisher

developer.* Books was founded by the producers of the award-winning DeveloperDotStar.com web site. Our focus is general-interest, non-technology-specific titles that appeal to practitioners, researchers, and managers. A developer.* book has a timeless quality, apart from the pace of change in the underlying technologies.

developer.*

The Independent Software Development Source

Articles * Essays * Books * Interviews

Blogs * Discussions * Ideas

developer.* (pronounced "developer dot star," as a play on wildcard characters) is an independent web site and book publishing company devoted to topics of interest to software development professionals of all types—programmers, software architects, QA engineers, database designers, researchers, professors, and everyone in between—even managers!

Come check us out on the web
www.developerdotstar.com

Tell your friends!

Subscribe to the RSS feeds!

Buy a book!

Support independent publishing!

developer.*

Honored with a Software Development Productivity Award
by *Software Development Magazine*

Printed in the United States
99135LV00007B/199/A